Thomas Eder, Thomas Raab, Michael Schwarz (eds.)

Oswald Wiener's Theory of Thought

Conversations and Essays on Fundamental Issues in Cognitive Science

DE GRUYTER

Contents

Preface

As a versatile and creative thinker, Oswald Wiener (1935–2021) developed from an artist into a researcher out of sheer necessity. Throughout his life, the academic reception of his psychology of thought has been troubled. This has various reasons, among which his doubly eccentric-seeming approach of combining explorative thinking with empirical science and, related to this, of linking computer science to introspection, is not the least.

In the 1960s, Wiener was an influential *writer* of the German-language literary postwar-avant-garde. He belonged to the first generation of intellectuals and artists who turned their partly disappointed artistic and political hopes to the new thinking of cybernetics having emerged since the 1940s. The philosophy of language and the linguistic turn increasingly did not seem to offer any promise. But the fear of looming social engineering enticed Wiener, as other thinkers originally oriented toward the humanities, to dwell in positivist, scientific, even behaviorist provocation. So in one of the conversations in this book, Wiener attributes his oscillation between the hope in and the fear of technology to a kind of "Stockholm syndrome." He was one of the first who, as a writer and computer scientist, embodied "the two cultures" of science and the humanities in one person.

Today, Oswald Wiener's reputation as a prescient critic of the effects of computer engineering not only on our sensibilities, but also on our behavior – on habits, customs, and our implicit ideologies – is internationally undisputed (cf. the English translations of some of his key texts in the magazine *October* 2001 and 2019). Yet, so far this has been recognized primarily in the fields of the arts and humanities.

The present volume aims to vigorously correct this by elaborating both the content and the significance of Wiener's theory of thought for cybernetics, artificial intelligence, theoretical and engineering computer science, psychology, cognitive science, philosophy, and esthetics. We believe that an adequate reception of this theory, which has grown over decades, and, even more, its assessment and systematic adoption as well as elaboration in these fields, is still pending. So far, it has only proven fertile in practice, namely in a considerable number of thinkers and artists who have been inspired by aspects, concepts, or even just the forward-looking spirit of Wiener's theory.

So this book was originally intended to be a guide to the development and, thereby, also to a better understanding of Oswald Wiener's theory of thought, as it still seems unusual for laypersons and cognitive scientists alike. Three conversations between the editors and Wiener elaborate on its central concepts, which are derived from an epistemology supported by theoretical computer science and from a psychology of thought based on introspection. The conversations are intended to make Wiener's ideas, especially as expounded in the 2015 reference book *Selbstbeobachtung* (Suhrkamp, Berlin; Engl.: *Introspection*), more accessible.

Two developments during the work on the book led us to modify this mediatory approach. First, Wiener was rather inclined to attempt a forward-looking text elaborating on his new ideas than to reappraise the historical development of his old ones. Second, to our great sadness, Oswald Wiener passed away on November 18, 2021, and the fragments in the estate show that he never ceased to work on the one central question: "What distinguishes human thought and feeling fundamentally from statistical stimulus-to-behavior computation?" Unfortunately, he wasn't able to elaborate these fragments to the point of publication. So what he left behind are countless thought and introspection protocols. These, just as the entire estate, are still waiting to be processed and published.

Thus, the three conversations with the editors only form the first part of the book. They each detail one of three arguable phases of development of Wiener's theory of thought. The first phase was still marked by the linguistic turn, albeit often repulsively. During the second phase (since the 1970s), Wiener attempted to consistently define historically disputed epistemological concepts with the help of the theory of automata. Finally, the last phase, from the end of the 1990s, was dedicated to the psychology of thought and introspection and encompassed extensive discussions within an informal research group.

The second, additional part of the book is now opened by Wiener's last major essay published during his lifetime entitled "Cybernetics and Ghosts." It represents a kind of recapitulation of his life's work and, as an appendix, also contains a short glossary with explanations of some central theoretical terms, which are also used in the other chapters of the book. It is supplemented by three essays by the editors, each of which expands on a detailed problem of the theory of thought. Michael Schwarz addresses the genesis of "cognitive symbols" as a grounding of thought in the awareness of a proxy object, thus representing an *essentially* different model than deep neural networks in computational neuroscience performing "object recognition." Thomas Eder tackles the problem of memorizing texts as a model case of structuring insight learning. Finally, Tom Raab sketches out a theory of memory based on Wiener's ideas seeking to consistently integrate psychoanalytic "metapsychology" into cognitive science.

We hope that at least the consistency of the use of technical terms characterizing both the conversations and the essays will give the book an introductory, albeit still demanding character. May it further contribute to the study of the work of one of the – as we are convinced – pioneers of a new theory of thought.

Our warmest thanks go to Ingrid Wiener, who always greatly supported our joint meetings and discussions, even when the group expanded. You made our endeavor possible in the first place!

The editors, January 2023

Literature, Language, Thought: The Beginnings

A Conversation between Oswald Wiener
and Thomas Eder

First contacts with music and writing in the 1950s

TE: The three conversations in this book are supposed to document your intellectual development from the late 1950s and early 1960s until today. This one deals with your early phase as a poet and as an artist. What made you as a young man want to become a musician and a poet? Did you only have intrinsically artistic goals – to create innovative poetry, for instance? Did you want to add to the historic development of poetry? Or did you also have external goals relating to what art and poetry should develop into?

OW: If I had an external goal, it was only a metaphysical one. At that time I was a quite naïve philosopher of mind. Unraveling the mystery of consciousness – this was our ultimate goal. To this end, we hoped to gain insights and clues via poetry. I understood the question of consciousness to be beyond the reach of science, and this made me a fierce adversary of science right from the start. I invested a lot of time convincing myself of the idea that science is nothing but bullshit and a huge disaster.

TE: To which the alternative would be art?

OW: I didn't formulate my goals that clearly. Rather, I had the vague feeling that any possible breakthrough would come through art. Somehow we had to penetrate this blurry wall, and we did not really wonder much about what would loom behind it.

TE: Could you really separate your goals as neatly as you later claimed, namely that your work followed two tendencies in parallel or maybe against each other – toward the goal of intensifying sensation and experience through art on the one hand, and toward the goal of better understanding the mechanisms of consciousness through art and poetry on the other?

OW: The latter rather came by itself, so that I didn't realize it at first. At one point it became clear, of course, that I myself belonged to those people, whom I attacked with my criticism of science. In the end, I too wanted to understand in the sense of what I today call *clear understanding*. I didn't seek emotional understanding, which simply didn't satisfy me. A true artist, I believe, would have been content with it. I was very receptive to moods and affects though. But they just weren't enough; I wanted to know more clearly what we could discover behind this wall we tried to break through. In the process, I acquired new knowledge without realizing it. I read a lot. So during this phase, I took notice of a few authors' names for the first time – Spinoza, for instance. During these years, the first half of the 1950s, the foundations of my thought were laid, not very solidly but at least sketchily. For me, the main conflict, as I once wrote, was this: "On the one hand, one could cancel out the effect [of making or receiving art] by comprehensively explaining the mechanisms involved; this knowledge made it possible to contrive and create effects at will, relativizing one's own heightened emotion and making the manipulator proof against manipulation. On the other hand, one must intensify the effect of art as far as humanly possible [...]. [T]his dichotomy led to wild oscillations between mentalist philosophy and behaviorism. Naïveté dictated the following compromise. In the 1950s I turned myself into a fanatical artist, because I regarded art as the supreme means of gaining knowledge. Art was *experimental*, because its varying effects on others, and above all on myself, could be observed and could thus give rise to hypotheses concerning the underlying mechanisms. [...] [I]t was possible to have both emotion and insight, and (this was the apotheosis of 'self-referentiality,' the ubiquitous slogan that had by then supplanted Hegel's notion of 'synthesis') emotion through insight. [...] It was not until the 1970s that I realized that [André] Breton's *program* (not his results) had anticipated one aspect of our work. If Surrealism is a 'pure psychic automatism, whereby one seeks to express, in writing or by any other means, the true process of thought,' then in a sense I was looking for the same thing. The 'true process of thought' had as far as possible to be documented. However, the art work was not the documentation. It was not about the process of 'expressing' anything – indeed, that process was the problematic thing – but about observing the impression made by the given text [...]. Art as understanding, understanding as art. The role of the art work in the art process is now just this: to be neutralized by an effort on the viewer's part. [...] The maker is thus superfluous and his intention, if any, non-authoritative."[1]

TE: Outsourcing texts to blueprints, algorithms, or mathematical principles could be viewed as a complementary or the backside of this kind of automatic text production, e.g., the "methodical inventionism" of Marc Adrian,[2] who applied formal principles to generate texts from a stock of words to be manipulated externally. There had been similar attempts within the Vienna Group as well.

OW: Yes, these came from me. In a simpler form, Gerhard Rühm had achieved this already with his permutations, and I with my constellations. So it was obvious to further mathematize and complicate these attempts, which showed itself in the guise of texts such as "bissen brot" by Gerhard Rühm and Konrad Bayer.[3] This is an effective poem, I think. Then I realized that one could do similar texts by applying the theory and method of Claude Elwood Shannon, who had combined words by their probability. Shannon generated letter sequences according to probabilities of letters in natural language. At first glance, these sequences looked like letter salads. But if you then added the next letter of the statistics, it already sounded a bit like English, and so on and so forth. Eventually, the sequences became more and more like English, although the more English they become, the more banal they also get, of course.

TE: Had you heard of the German computer scientist Theo Lutz's similar experiments on Konrad Zuse's Z22 computer at roughly the same time? Or of the so called "autopoems" Gerhard Stickel produced on an IBM 7090?

OW: No, I didn't know these.

TE: He came from the circle around Max Bense.

OW: Max Bense annoyed me because of both his clear commitment to behaviorism and his belief in cybernetic esthetics, which is basically an esthetics of probability. I assume that efforts like these also had deeper, hitherto misunderstood facets, and a critical intelligentsia should scrutinize them and then write a monograph beginning with Shannon via Abraham Moles and Max Bense to Helmar Frank, etc. For their effort continues to have an effect, albeit in a slightly disguised form. Yet, it is still unclear what this approach is able to achieve and what it is good for. Obviously, it is good for something but not for creativity, I believe. One can fake creativity with it, and one can also deceive oneself and take the fake for the real thing.

TE: Yes, reading such a product generated by means of probability may give you similar esthetic experiences as reading a text written by a person. Yet, this is a consequence of the *esthetic attitude* with which the reader approaches and unfolds the text, and not a consequence of the text surface as such or of properties of the generating process.

OW: Once we have a chess program like Deep Blue, chess ceases to be an intellectual challenge. It will certainly continue as a sport, but there will be no further thought about how humans play chess, I guess. Obviously, Deep Blue proves that surface processes suffice to bring somebody who knows how to play chess to attribute depth to the machine. Kasparov, for example, the world's best chess player at that time, who nevertheless lost to Deep Blue, believed that his own thought was deep, and he also attributed "depth" to some moves by the machine. He thus was convinced that the machine was literally thinking, even though he knew how it worked technically. Nonetheless, he was inclined to say: "Yes, the machine does exactly what I do." And yet it doesn't.

The stream of consciousness

TE: There is probably a similarity to automatic or algorithmic text and art production. What about the text *der vogel singt* by Konrad Bayer? Is it true that you did its mathematical blueprint?

OW: Yes. Bayer asked me to do it after he had sketched out what he wanted. But it is clear that the quasi mechanically created text was only a rough draft, to which Bayer then added the highlights. His basic idea was definitely a constellation in the astronomical sense. His vision of the machine was connected to Ramon Lull and Giordano

Bruno. It was about rotating spheres coming apart and together again in certain moments, so that, for example, three planets appear in a straight line. Assuming, for example, that there are seven spheres, you can construct a machine that starts with the initial state in which they are all in a certain order. Then the constellation seems to become disorderly until it reaches some extreme disorder, but in the end everything falls back into a simple form. Many people had this idea, not just in the astronomical domain. But the latter is the closest metaphor for it.

TE: Was Bayer's goal, or maybe your own goal in some passages of the *verbesserung* (cf. infra), to mimic the stream of consciousness by means of language?

OW: At least I claimed so, for instance, in the passage "für kornbluth," in which I described visual perceptions at the end of a drunken night.[4] But I already knew that the last chapter of James Joyce's *Ulysses*, for instance, was no realistic depiction in the sense of mimicking conscious or even unconscious processes. Only columnists are able to say that these sentences copy the "stream of consciousness." In fact, this final monologue by Joyce is totally artificial. At least my consciousness is very different to that in Molly Bloom's monologue.

TE: Unfortunately, it's not only columnists who claim that. It is also advocated doggedly in some debates in literary studies and cognitive science. Patrick Colm Hogan, a cognitive literary scholar, a few years ago claimed that Joyce consequently followed an arguably "critical psychological realism." The latter Hogan defines as "a form of realism that seeks to enhance the reader's understanding of human mental processes. 'Critical realism' is a form of realism that sets out to displace false beliefs that have been fostered by earlier works (e.g., by earlier novels)."[5] Joyce's novel, Hogan believes, precisely illustrates the paradox that emerges when you try to represent parallel processes of consciousness by a linear medium, such as language, with its necessarily temporal order. The serial processing of linguistic sensations is used to represent the parallel processing in consciousness.

OW: This claim is evident but nonetheless misleading, because it aims at the mere surface of language. I don't see how one could render conscious processes into a somehow plausible linguistic representation. I have tried it repeatedly but always failed. The only thing you can do by means of language is triggering a number of specific experiences in the reader. One starting point would be the "time slices" of William James. In his *Principles of Psychology,* he writes: "As we take, in fact, a general view of the wonderful stream of our consciousness, what strikes us first is this different pace of its parts. Like a bird's life, it seems to be made of an alternation of flights and perchings. The rhythm of language expresses this, where every thought is expressed in a sentence, and every sentence closed by a period. The resting-places are usually occupied by sensorial imaginations of some sort, whose peculiarity is that they can be held before the mind for an indefinite time, and contemplated without changing; the places of flight are filled with thoughts of relations, static or dynamic, that for the most part obtain between the matters contemplated in the periods of comparative rest. [...] *Let us call the resting-places the 'substantive parts', and the places of flight the 'transitive parts', of the stream of thought.*"[6]

Onto this description I project a concept, which I name time slices. James's "perchings" are in actual fact relatively slight orientation developments, insofar as the major part of orientation remains more or less the same or seems static. Maybe some things change but at the periphery and not in focus of consciousness. In contrast, James's "flights" of the metaphorical bird are larger changes of background orientation. From this perspective I recently tried to precisely imagine the path of a gnomon's shadow as described in Alain Robbe-Grillet's novel *La Jalousie.* In order to do so, I had to reconstruct this path mentally according to the situations described in the book. At first I found this very difficult. I keep watch especially for introspection tasks such as this, *because* they are too difficult for me at first. But I want to observe how my attempts at understanding proceed. In some respect, this is comparable to what Bühler already demanded in 1909, namely to find an "appropriate degree of task complexity that is favorable to the results of introspection."[7] Tasks of this appropriate degree of complexity are still pending for the subject area of "language comprehension."

TE: Perhaps this also has to do with Gertrude Stein, who you, the members of the Vienna Group, read so intensely? She wrote (in her introduction to *Last Operas and Plays*, p. XII): "the mind is at every stage a theater of simultaneous possibilities." Stein was, after all, a student and early collaborator of William James.

OW: In the mid-1950s, I adored Gertrude Stein's *Last Operas and Plays*, especially the libretto "Four Saints in Three Acts"[8] (written in 1927) – even today I think it's the best piece Stein ever wrote. This text triggered a kind of pre-understanding in me, which, I believed then, the author intended. Today I must confess that I am not so sure about her intention any more. This work is the most difficult that I know of her. For me, it had the effect of triggering totally vague waves of emotion and mood. I still get that feeling when I leaf through it. One of her tricks in this play is that the acts and scenes are central. The actors are the acts and the scenes themselves, although the title suggests that it is about four saints in a drama of three acts, which is totally misleading. For there are many saints in many acts/scenes that cannot be traced clearly; some passages appear repeatedly, as do stage directions such as "Repeat First Act" or "Enact end of an act." So the acts and scenes are jumbled and repeated; they do not follow the numerical order. Suddenly at one point, for example, it reads: "Scene X." But what is being said in the tenth scene? Answer: "Could Four Acts be three." These words are thus both notation and text. You can't trace that so easily. Today I think I would be able to interpret quite a lot in the piece, but back then I didn't understand anything at all. It just touched me in a peculiar way. It was so mysterious that I hoped something would suddenly come to light ... As a young man, I was always inclined to believe in intangible powers, which I deemed real nonetheless – something like the objective chance of the surrealists, which I didn't know then. Maybe this feeling was in the air once they had put that idea into the world; it certainly felt that way to me. I hoped, that by way of art I would be able to achieve things that could not be achieved otherwise. That's why I became a fanatical art lover and art enthusiast.

TE: But back to the desire for *clear understanding* that you spoke of earlier. Would you say that your friends in the Vienna Group shared it?

OW: At least they understood the questions that I posed myself, I think, and that these topics interested me in particular. We shouldn't forget that these were the first years of us going at least a bit public, as well as the first years when the so-called *linguistic turn* made itself felt. It was an international change of atmosphere leaning strongly toward the humanities, that means away from science. Naturally, we didn't identify it as an entire international wave yet. But our very existence itself was evidence that something was just changing. It is very strange how such things develop. It seems that something is in the air, which some people realize and others don't.

Thinking about August Stramm or Gertrude Stein, for instance, and not about everyday language I wondered why their texts made such a strong impression on me? But hell, how come? So I thought about language. But if I had been friends with visual artists, who I could have taken equally seriously as my poet friends, I could have easily asked myself: Why the effect of painting? Why of music? I did pose the question, why music appealed to me, but any answer seemed totally out of reach. But if anything gave my philosophy of mind a direction, it was the experience of music. As a young person, I was brought to musical ecstasy incredibly easily. In fact, music functioned like a narcotic for me. With language, ecstasy seemed much more difficult to attain. But then I started reading some philosophy of language – at first Friedrich Kainz from Vienna University, who had written a five-volume work entitled *Psychologie der Sprache* (Psychology of Language). The Vienna Group had nothing to do with academia at all, but at least the names of philosophers were familiar to us. At that time, Hubert Rohracher, who had published, among others, the book *Die Arbeitsweise des Gehirns und die psychischen Vorgänge* (Brain Function and Mental Processes), was still the head of the psychology department, and the Hegelian Erich Heintel was teaching at the philosophy department. So the first few things I read sufficed to prove to me that I wouldn't find my answers there. Not that there was a lack of interesting facts, but step by step and more or less on my own I got to know more radical people. And then came the Wittgenstein accident, which would cost me an entire decade.

The Wittgenstein accident

TE: Accident? In what sense? At first you were certainly enthralled, weren't you?

OW: A friend of ours had stolen a Wittgenstein book from a library. One day the thief showed up in a café and claimed to have found an extremely interesting book at the British Council in Vienna. This was the British equivalent of the American Information Center, and it had a library on the Freyung in the first district. For us, these two institutes, but more so the American one, were the decisive sources of information about the Anglo-Saxon world. It was normal to be very unscrupulous in such libraries and to steal things. The man showed me the book, and I borrowed it from him right away. It was the *Tractatus*.

TE: In German?

OW: No, the bilingual Routledge edition. I was enthralled. At first the book was hard to understand, but I sensed that this man had had insights, and that they were important. But I didn't understand what the insights were. The tone in which the *Tractatus* is written is very certain: "I say how it is! And it is incredible that hitherto nobody has seen it this way!" But *how* it really is, Wittgenstein does not say. He only pretends to know it. The copy here on the table I then ordered at the bookseller Gerold am Graben, who had begun to import foreign-language books. I had to wait six months to get it – until June 1956. It was a different edition but the same book – the same publisher, the same design. Well, so I started to grit my teeth with "Luigi."

TE: Didn't you soon hold lectures, which could count as the first instances of Wittgenstein scholarship in Austria outside academia?

OW: Yes, but this didn't happen before 1961, I believe. So I have been chewing on the *Tractatus* for five years – not only on the *Tractatus* but also on other works.

They affected me much like the works of Gertrude Stein. Both authors' works have the same drive, if I may say so maliciously. Today, I'd say that the drive is due to the fact, that each sentence of Wittgenstein makes you expect something very important to follow in the next sentence. But this pertains to the entire book, so as soon as you reach the last line, you close it and ask yourself: What was that? Well, it was an experience of drive similar to the reading experience of Gertrude Stein's texts.

At the beginning of my pursuit I expected more and something different. I expected instruction on what interested me, for instance. It's just like I wrote in my later, already critical essay on "Wittgenstein's influence on the Vienna Group."[9] In *Tractatus,* Wittgenstein seems to "believe in the possibility of studying the postulated isomorphic mapping of language parts on 'facts' [*Tatsachen*] and 'atomic facts' [*Sachverhalte*] of the 'world' without any reference to mental or physiological processes. The central role given to Language conceals the further radicalization of this behaviorist idea. [...] today we expect answers to the questions of 'understanding', of 'meaning,' 'form,' 'content,' etc., as well as of the nature of Language most likely from a unified science of the 'mental,' which will encompass some mutations of psychology and focus on the 'representing relations.' It will not search for Wittgenstein's 'form of representation' in the mechanisms of language but in the nervous system and other material devices. [...] today i believe that we can and we should study 'mental' and physiological representations without special reference to Language; i believe that language may play an important role in cognitive mechanisms, but not that it is a crucial part of them (at least if defined as the phenomenon investigated by linguists)."[10]

These were the crucial questions for me then as they still are now. What is consciousness? How does it function? Wittgenstein couldn't have been less interested in these questions, or rather he might have been interested in asking but absolutely not in answering them, as I'd say today. On the contrary, I believe that he later said that if we ask such questions, we realize how stupid we are *that* we ask them. We should not explain, e.g., the psychological (mental) causes which lead to this and that use of concepts, but should rather elucidate concepts such as "aspectual seeing" and their position within experiential concepts, for example. But *why* we are stupid to ask such questions, Witty did not say. Thus he immunized himself. Because if you say, to ask such questions is tantamount to being stupid, you are right in any case and from any point of view.

TE: Wittgenstein later tried to justify this by demonstrating the misuse of words/phrases. Didn't that have some influence on you at that time?

OW: A tremendous one even! Above all, my Wittgenstein reading cost me a lot of time without learning one single theorem that I could have kept and used as a treasure from time to time.

TE: Did your reading of Wittgenstein eventually influence the collaborations within the Vienna Group? In the essay quoted above, for instance, you wrote the following about its literary cabarets: "our experimental arrangements of randomly found words and language parts: we wanted to test how and why one could always understand these arrangements, and which factors specified this understanding. We introduced simple arithmetic and combinatorial methods in order to preferably exclude any unconscious meaning intentions, and boosted our interest in formal relations; complementarily, we developed a new standpoint concerning 'automatic' production, whereby our interest in the surrealists obtained a new facet [...]; our already existing relativistic tendency, equal validity of all possible interpretations, the inner meaninglessness of symbols – all these now became conscious and used for production."[11]

OW: An indirect influence was noticeable. Indirect insofar as we in the group agreed that anyone who thinks this is a problem doesn't know what the problem is. This motto had something liberating about it, because if we didn't get anywhere with a text, we could either say that it doesn't go any further here, or, better still, we could ask, why we should even continue with it when it doesn't make any sense. That helped me to get a more detached attitude, even to what I myself was doing, and to cope with the disappointment that my reading of Wittgenstein constantly inflicted on me without having to admit it.

TE: I do think that there was some influence of Wittgenstein's writings on the two literary cabarets of the Vienna Group in 1958/59, to whose conception you and Konrad Bayer contributed a lot of theory. In your retrospective 1967 essay "the literary cabaret of the vienna group", you wrote that you also wanted to demonstrate the "control of concrete situations by the use of language." That, at least, sounds like an application of the later Wittgenstein. Then you once described what you call the "new realism" of the "literary cabarets": Realism "understood as direct symbolic manipulation of innate or habitual modes of reaction; [we had] the concept of a direct artistic impact on the life of the reader/audience by demonstrating or concealing their mechanisms of understanding."[12] And to quote further: "it was amazing that most combinations of any words could be made to mean things they did not signify – the fascinating aptitude of the human mind for constructing metaphors and mental images, the obviousness of 'meaning' projected on the most outlandish symbol combinations, but also the adherence to hypotheses once found, [and thus] a certain hopelessness of understanding."[13]

---

literary cabarets

The two "literary cabarets" of the Vienna Group took place on December 6, 1958 in the theater hall of the artist association "alte welt" (on Windmühlgasse in Vienna's 6th district) and on April 15, 1959 in the trade union's "Porrhaus" (on Treitlgasse 3 in the 4th district). They were jointly planned and performed by Friedrich Achleitner, Konrad Bayer, Gerhard Rühm, and Oswald Wiener. H.C. Artmann had already resigned from the group by that time. Named in reference – and distinction – to both the Dadaist cabarets in Zurich (1916) and the cabarets of Helmut Qualtinger and Carl Merz in postwar Vienna, these intermedia evenings could today also count as "happenings" *avant la lettre*. There is one structural parallel to this actionist art form, which has been thus dubbed predominantly in the USA and Great Britain, insofar as their press release called the literary cabarets "simply a happening [schlichte begebenheit]." The German word "Begebenheit" means "happening," as it was first used by Allan Kaprow in 1959 for an action in the Reuben Gallery in New York. In retrospect, Oswald Wiener classified the acts of the two "cabarets" as "chansons and dramatic poetry, polemic numbers, and happenings" (Wiener 1997: 310).

From today's perspective, the crucial features of these two events are not so much the traditionally Dadaist content of many of the sketch-like acts nor the qualities of the mainly sarcastic chansons written and performed by the artists themselves and meant to liven up the programs. With respect to the art movements to come, specifically to Viennese Actionism, mainly two closely associated questions are of interest. Firstly, the group did not represent or play-act their actions but rather showed persons and situations in their real and direct presence. Secondly, they challenged the traditional role of the passive audience: It was "one of the basic ideas of the event [...] to exhibit ‚reality‘ and thus, consequently, to abandon it. Another idea was to consider the audience as a group of actors and ourselves as spectators" (Wiener 1997: 308f.).

The protagonists of the literary cabarets should neither "present the illusions of other people (like Stanislawki's actors) nor will they pretend to be other persons (like Brecht's players)" (Achleitner, Bayer, Rühm und Wiener, 1997: 356). All persons involved should rather remain themselves. As "performative processes" the cabarets did not depict, perform, or represent but produce and present actions (Fischer-Lichte 2004). To this end, the group members instrumentalized their co-participants and pitted them against their flaws ("the miserable clumsiness, the naïve attitude, the lack of histrionic or musical talent, the complete lack of understanding of our ideas, their ‚personal interpretation‘" [Wiener 1997: 314]). In order to exhibit and thereby abandon reality, the group had also considered plans "of transmitting the speaking-clock announcements by loudspeaker during the entire performance" (Wiener 1997: 320). At one time, the artists "placed a radio set in front of the curtain, tuning it to some station [...] and leaving the audience alone with it" (Wiener 1997: 312). The idea of spraying "phenol" during an "olfactory chanson" in order to directly affect the sense of smell only failed because "this liquid had not been obtained through sheer negligence" (Wiener 1997: 318). The role of language as a medium for conveying reality, for instance, was critically questioned through tautological real-time descriptions of events taking place on stage – so the emptying of a bottle and a glass of beer in the number "Friedrich Achleitner as a Beer Drinker." With an onstage "piano smashing" the theme of destruction emerged in the second cabaret. It became more virulent in the 1960s, finally playing a crucial role not least in Viennese Actionism.

The wish to unveil and disturb the illusionary mechanisms of the theatre by reversing the roles of actors and audience is put into effect most concisely in the opening act of the second cabaret: "the curtain rose, the ensemble was sitting on chairs in three rows, facing the audience and looking at it with great interest. the stage was dark, the auditorium lighted. we behaved like ordinary theatre-goers. one of us was late and tiptoed to his seat. we pointed a finger on individual spectators in the audience, gawking through our opera glasses, whispering. after some five minutes occasional bursts of laughter rose from the audience, which we interpreted as an important turn in the play we were watching; so we started to applaud just when the audience had started to do so as well, calling for the occasional encore. the atmosphere was great" (Wiener 1997: 316).

So the insistence on reflecting the context of the happening on stage replaced passive reception. The spectators were confronted with a role they themselves believed to fulfill. "Thus, into the real situation [= framing] its difference to the fictitious internal situation [= stage situation] is introduced (and vice versa)" (Backes 2001: 312). So a "collapse of framing" is enacted, and the implicit contract between recipient and producer of the artwork – *a willing suspension of disbelief* – is cancelled. According to this contract, the audience reacts to fictitious texts and scenes at the theater emotionally similar that in reality, yet without interfering in the latter.

Achleitner, Friedrich, Konrad Bayer, Gerhard Rühm, and Oswald Wiener, 1997 [1959]. literary cabaret. In: Weibel, Peter (ed.), *The Vienna Group: The Visual Works and the Actions, a Moment in Modernity 1954–1960.* Vienna, New York, 356.

Backes, Michael, 2001. *Experimentelle Semiotik in Literaturavantgarden. Über die Wiener Gruppe mit Bezug auf die Konkrete Poesie.* Munich.

Fischer-Lichte, Erika, 2004. *Ästhetik des Performativen.* Frankfurt am Main.

Wiener, Oswald, 1997 [1967]. the "literary cabaret" of the vienna group. In: Weibel, Peter (ed.), *The Vienna Group: The Visual Works and the Actions, a Moment in Modernity 1954–1960.* Vienna, New York, 308–320.

TE

OW: Yes, of course, but at that time we wouldn't be aware of it. We only later saw that we had developed a theory of the "control of concrete situations by the use of language," although theory is too strong a word. Regarding this, Konrad Bayer and I are guilty of "blasphemies against the Holy Spirit," because we made experiments with real people. We deliberately agreed to make someone else we both knew do something by manipulating him or her. Then we drew lots: one of us was given the task of getting him to do something, and the other had the task of keeping him from doing it. Konrad and I were fighting implicit battles with each other all the time, and they went very far. Once it was about a girl who was undecided about which of two men she should choose. One of us sponsored one of them and the other sponsored the other. We had promised each other to keep working on it for a year. We even agreed on the allowed means of manipulation. So, for example, we were not allowed to praise our own protégé and belittle the other in direct conversation with the girl. That was taboo. But the more indirectly we manipulated, the more permissible and the more desirable it seemed to us. This reminds me of what I once paraphrased from Gustav Bychowski. I called it a "marauding dandyism" "that reinterprets the threat of an insight to be caused the inadequacy of the subject into and the unworthiness of the object."[14]

TE: This example stems from everyday life, when such an agreement on a manipulative competition might appear as an art form. But does that actually have to do with art forms? Can we separate it at all from art events such as the "literary cabarets"? How would you see the "literary cabarets" in relation to these life-world experiments?

OW: Our goal was to put an end to the very notion of artwork and instead view our own behavior as art. The "literary cabarets" constitute but one step on the way to this end. We wanted to free ourselves from previous forms of art presentation and to dissolve such narrow definitions like "language arts" or "visual arts." We were almost at the point of wanting to be an artist of everyday life – without an œuvre so to speak. The artist without an œuvre! Very early Artmann had attempted something quite similar with his "Eight Point Proclamation of the Poetic Act" of 1953. But to me his poetic act still seemed too romantic. Generally, my attitude towards Artmann wavered a lot between admiration and embarrassment. I was often embarrassed by his production, and then the pendulum swung back again. Yet, I hardly let him notice that. The periods when he embarrassed me also came later, when I didn't see him so often.

All in all, what I wanted to indicate is our attempt to change our whole life. And one of the ways to do that was to distance oneself from everything. In other words, we were unknowingly moving toward the ideology of the dandy.

Dandy

Wiener adapted the concept of "dandyism" to his theoretical interests at the latest in his essay "Eine Art Einzige" (An Ego of Her Own) in the pertinent anthology *Riten der Selbstauflösung,* which he co-edited in 1982 together with Verena von der Heyden-Rynsch for

Matthes and Seitz publishers (Wiener 1982). Both the concept and the social phenomenon developed from the mid-18th century to the beginning of the 19th century. But Wiener is neither interested in the affects nor in the fashionable demeanor of a specific social milieu. Instead, he dwells on a single trait of dandyism, which he allegedly adopts "for Baudelaire's sake:" "dandyism is a very particular form of resistance to the notion that the human can be explained down to the last aspects of his psychological life by mechanical principles. [...] in the *dandy*, this resistance takes the form of a lone warrior who will not consider more than occasional alliances. argumentative consensus, the consensus of philosophizing, is out of the question: formal agreement must in any event be endowed with subjective meaning; absent meaning, it is mechanical, contradicting the intention that may bring it about. [...] idiosyncratic in the forms of his society, the dandy is an exacting and sensitive observer of his inner and outer environments but a theorist only ad hoc (*maxims, apothegms, aphorisms*). he has understood that the emotions that seize him obey internal laws, which is to say, are forced upon him a priori. he discovers the mechanics of ever-larger parts of what he thought of as his freedom, including even the apparatus of despair. *where is i?*" (Wiener 2019: 69).

For a lecture at the Kunsthalle in Bern in 2017, Wiener amended: "Dandyism is a specific form of warding off the thought that I can be explained. What is necessary for success is to immediately recognize and interrupt regularities in one's own behavior. The dandy is on an inward spiral, he subtracts meaning from everything he has become aware of: that is not you. Or (in a dispute with Günther Anders [and his *Outdatedness of Human Beings*]) 'Promethean defiance,' wanting to remain a subject vis-à-vis objects that are better than me – 'I don't want to be made;' '... especially not by myself;' 'I don't want to play a role;' 'I don't want a mission;' 'I have no fate'" (Wiener 2017).

Wiener, Oswald, 1982. Eine Art Einzige. In: Heyden-Rynsch, Verena von der (ed.), *Riten der Selbstauflösung*. Munich, 34–78.

Wiener, Oswald, 2019. An Ego of Her Own, trans. Gerrit Jackson with Jakob
    Schillinger. *October*, 170 (Fall 2019), 69–94.
Wiener, Oswald, 2017. http://kunsthalle-bern.ch/veranstaltungen/2017-04-
    21-dandysme-in-der-globalisierung-vortrag-von-oswald-wiener/ (12
    Nov 2021).

TE

TE: But wasn't that already the content of your 1954 "cool manifesto" ["cooles manifest"], which was lost later?

OW: Yes, the "cool manifesto" was a very early attempt in the same direction. My first motive to write it was that I had come to know André Breton's *Manifestoes of Surrealism* and liked the word "manifesto" a lot. So I wanted to write one, too. Secondly my discussions, primarily with Konrad, had already progressed quite far, and we agreed that it's ultimately the recipient who renders something an artwork. Thus, everything becomes art as soon an artist sees and recognizes it as such. That was the basic idea. So the "cool manifesto" called for giving up art production. I had started to quote and make montages from existing poetry and from advertising, and Rühm and Achleitner also declared found texts to be works of art. I also connect this with the attempt to train the gaze to become an artist without having produced anything at all.

TE: But this could also mean a lyrical, rather uncool attitude towards the everyday and its objects, just like in Artmann's "Eight Point Proclamation of the Poetic Act." What then was cool in the "cool manifesto"?

OW: Yes, there are similarities between the two attitudes, but mine was much riskier. Konrad and I weren't harmless and didn't rule out connections to groups similar to the Red Army Fraction in Germany. At least I didn't, and neither did Konrad, I believe. We would have been strange terrorists, but the option to kill somebody was definitely there, if only to have tried it once.

TE: Did you both know Breton's dictum: "The simplest Surrealist act consists of dashing down the street, pistol in hand, and firing blindly, as fast as you can pull the trigger, into the crowd."

29

OW: Probably yes, but it didn't have anything to do with us, because this "firing blindly" would have sounded quite affected to me. My slogan in the "cool manifesto" was again paradoxical – stay cool in order to do away with affects. Carl Einstein had written the same thing decades earlier, but we didn't know it then.

TE: I find it remarkable that the "literary cabarets" coincided with, or even slightly predated, the happenings in New York.

OW: This was also something that was in the air internationally. It's one of those concurrences, which I have hinted to before.

TE: But weren't the "literary cabarets" more art-historically and theoretically motivated? Finally, you didn't only want to have an effect on the audience, you also wanted to connect your performance with epistemic claims, didn't you?

OW: For me it turned out to be more of an endpoint. The cabarets convinced me, that my artistic aspirations would never come true. I was searching for something I couldn't find in and through art. So I stopped doing art altogether and quit the Vienna Group, so to speak. I didn't declare my resignation though, but simply didn't meet the others any more and destroyed everything I had written so far. I realized that the texts, which I liked best, were still pretty much in Rühm's wake – and this view didn't please me at all. Various circumstances in my life prompted me to make the decision to stop doing art in favor of something completely different. I did not know exactly what that would be, but one option was to become a leader in real life, namely an important man in some industry.

TE: You mean your employment with Olivetti, where you became very successful as a sales manager?

OW: Yes, I joined the company right after the cabarets, because I hoped that Olivetti would achieve crucial innovations in the development of computers, and I could eventually contribute to it. But in contrast to IBM, Olivetti backed the wrong horse. So my engagement with them soon stalled too. In general, my life has been marked by many little shoves in the most different directions, which then lost momentum. These shoves were mostly connected to a change of residence. Olivetti sent me to Upper Styria where I lived in a farmhouse near the town of Judenburg. From there I ventured out professionally, because this was an industrial region then. I had no contact with my friends back in Vienna whatsoever, until Konrad started to send me letters. First, I received them from Vienna, then from Paris. He said what a pity it was that we were no longer in contact. And one day I traveled to Vienna to meet him in his apartment on Dannebergplatz, where he lived with his wife Traudl Bayer. Immediately, we became close friends again. But only the two of us.

die verbesserung von mitteleuropa, roman

OW: Being friends with Konrad Bayer, was one of the reasons why I started to write *die verbesserung von mitteleuropa, roman* (the improvement of central europe, a novel). I had the impression that both of us had emancipated ourselves from our 1950s attitude. So my incipient knowledge of computers and computer science, which was called cybernetics then, already informed the writing process. I had read quite a bit. This was the direction I headed towards, yet still in connection with the then fashionable philosophy of language. I hoped that cybernetics would somehow elucidate the problems of language. And this wasn't entirely wrong. More than anything, I felt a strong urge to liberate myself from everything that I had learned from the philosophy of language. That is why there are so many flat swipes at it in the *verbesserung*. Of course I knew that I was going way too far, throwing the baby out with the water. But I simply needed it for cathartic reasons. It *had* to be written down because Konrad didn't react when I was *saying* it to him. I had already said it dozens or hundreds of times. Now it had to be written down.

TE: Didn't you, from the very beginning of the writing process, have any doubts whether the philosophy of language and linguistics might fail to give you any new insight? Why didn't you switch to traditional science instead of writing the *verbesserung,* which so clearly had an artistic aspect to it?

OW: Well, it was exactly this traditional science that I rejected so fiercely! My opinion about science had stayed the same. I regarded it as a kind of bullshit mimicking the surface of things when fundamentally their depth would be important. Science knew nothing of these depths. On the other hand, I wanted to learn its tools because I wanted to know what I was talking about when I was denouncing it. Furthermore I was fascinated by the "drive" of writing the *verbesserung*, which I already discussed with regard to Wittgenstein, and I was still touched by experiencing and doing art. With this book I tried to somehow amalgamate art and science, at least in the sense I understood them then. At the beginning, the poetic elements were much stronger than the rational ones, but this gradually changed during the writing process.

TE: You once called the *verbesserung* an example of "suicide of a poetic artwork."

OW: Well, the *verbesserung* is a ceaseless manifestation of paradoxes. By "suicide of an artwork" I wanted to drastically emphasize that the author is permanently sawing at the branch he sits on. Each and every sentence is written, so that the author undermines – with respect to logic – his own principles. He is pulling away the carpet, which he stands on. "The suicide of a poetic artwork" aims at a language artwork, which despises and denounces language – what is more, in an artistic way. Basically this isn't possible. It contradicts itself.

TE: But your targets remained the philosophers of language, that is, Wittgenstein?

OW: Yes, of course! But practically, I targeted everybody whom I deemed an authority. As soon as a name came up, I took its bearer as a punching doll, no matter who it was – from Kant to the most obscure philosopher such as Ferdinand Canning Scott Schiller whom I was also reading then – a lesser pragmatist.

TE: Are there any affirmative references in the *verbesserung*? Perhaps, for instance, to the work of Noam Chomsky?

OW: If there are, I didn't intend to make any. I wanted to see the others'
defects only, but often I just couldn't find them. Then I would pretend
that I had found some.

At that time, I hadn't read Aragon's *Traité du style* yet. With this
book, Aragon tried something similar. At least in some passages he
really lets fly as unenthusiastically and unfairly as I did. If I had known
this book, my work would have taken another direction because I
wouldn't have wanted to take the same line. So I am happy that I hadn't
read it before. And then I almost stole from Proudhon. The epigraph
of the *verbesserung* is from the Gospel of John "ὅ γέγραφα, γέγραφα",
meaning "What I have written, I have written." In the introduction to
his book, Proudhon stated that he also could have taken this sentence
as a motto. So I thought: Well, I am happy that you didn't!

TE: As far as anarchism in the *verbesserung* is concerned, it reads on
page CXLVI: "let's put on record, that anarchy does not suffice; only
anomie could do. so far the conformity of anarchism is dismal."

OW: True enough! Anarchism based on science isn't anarchism at all, I
think. If anarchism, then it would have to be an anarchism of consciousness. The one and only conscious being that one believes to have
to identify with must control everything. Every rule would have to follow. There is no such thing as a social anarchism. Therefore, apart from
Konrad Bayer, one of the few authors I could accept was Max Stirner.
Brill publishers had begun to deal with anarchism by releasing the
book *Von Bakunin zu Lenin* by Peter Scheibert.[15] This work played an
important role in my early political education. The more individualis-
tic anarchism got, the more I liked it. That was clear. Stirner was most
impeccable. He wrote this one book, let it take effect – and then sat in
the dairy of his common-law spouse until the end of his life.

TE: Some sentences in the *verbesserung* seem to prefigure things you
wrote later and could thus be seen as early expressions of your theory
of thought: "that which affects you, your state, you attune to something, you understand in e flat major," for instance.[16] Is there a connection between sentences such as this and the notion of "attunement" in your theory today?

OW: Of course I have been preoccupied with this notion for a long time. Unfortunately, we haven't got very far with it until today. At the beginning I tried to view an attunement [which is felt as a kind of mood in introspection] as the antecedent of a concept. I believe that this idea was fortunate but it came before the *verbesserung*. I observed that putting me in a specific mood – by reading, say, Alain Robbe-Grillet's *La Jalousie* – I viewed things under this specific aspect only. Thus, the attunement to this text seems to represent a very generic concept. The things which have an effect on this attunement or which are, in turn, particularly salient or noticeable through it, are selected in the same way as the organism selects certain traits through a concept or, let's say more generally, through a theme.

TE: How do concept and attunement relate?

OW: I see gradual transitions between them. With respect to theory I think of a concept as an organization of structures, or a structure of structures, if I may say so. On the one hand, I view an attunement with the help of my concept of structure, and on the other hand, under the aspect of the notion of action readiness, which is by far not elaborated enough yet. Tentatively, a "concept" is an organization of readinesses. Much the same is true for "attunement," except that it is less structured than a full-fledged concept. The same holds true for concepts, which also exist at many developmental stages. My concept of a triangle as a geometric form is, or so I believe, quite precise, but my concept of "melancholia," for instance, is rather little structured but still more than my concept of "attunement." If you scrutinize something you don't really know yet, you always have to begin with a certain attunement, which, while recognizing the thing connected to it, is registered almost as a quale. Earlier in my life, I used the psychological concept of "screen," which was important to me for some time. My idea was so vague then that I rather should not have spoken of a concept. At the beginning there was only something which I wanted to label with this word but couldn't detail out. The only thing I had was a strong and recurrent attunement, and this already is the beginning of concept formation. When retrieving something you have already thought about before – let's call it a standpoint or a perspective – it doesn't matter that you don't experience it clearly. That's how I imagine an incipient concept. Its further fate is, of course, uncertain – either it develops fully or not. My concept of screen, if I may call it concept, did indeed develop and change over time. For some years I viewed it as the equivalent of a Turing machine; later the concept's material aspect vanished and it remained the border between two processes – between processes of type 1 and type 2, respectively.[17] So I was really able to experience its slow development from attunement to concept, as if something slowly emerges out of the fog. In the end, the concept may not be entirely clear but at least its shape, its outline is there. So I believe the transition is continuous.

TE: Now you are talking about concept formation in the individual. But concepts also have something objective or official, at least that's the consensus.

OW: But the objective and the official are two different things! Official is only the word denoting the concept and a specific way to talk about it, nothing else. The individual always depends on him- or herself, if he or she wants to apply the concept.

TE: That's how I see it too, but there are some approaches, albeit philosophical ones, emphasizing that the symbol reaches beyond the individual and its isolated mind. Think of Gottlob Frege, who, roughly speaking, aimed at distinguishing "sense" and "reference" of a concept from its individual "conceptions" (without, I think, satisfyingly defining these words). Others again, such as the pragmatists, want to proceed from social practice in language learning and use.

OW: This is legitimate as long as you remain within language alone. At least you have agreed on a specific sound pattern denoting the concept, if it even has one single name only. But many full-fledged concepts cannot be denoted by one single word.

TE: This leads to the question, to what extent thought is dependent on language and which role language plays for cognitive processes. Later in your life you seem to have reached a clear position on this question: Language is an encapsulated module only mnemonically supporting thought processes. At the time of the *verbesserung,* you weren't so clear on that. It's trivial to say that in the *verbesserung* you posited that there is communication by language because it is itself a verbal artwork. Did you have any hopes then, that language could be used to mediate content, even if only regarding the questions we just talked about?

ow: On the one hand, certainly! On the other hand, I hoped that language would implode or hang itself in the *verbesserung* – that it would commit suicide. I wanted to get rid of language. At that time I felt threatened by it. This was one of my paranoid traits at that time. I felt my thoughts were being constricted by language.

TE: What was your antidote?

ow: To quit writing. Or to develop other areas of interest – such as the bio-adaptor, solipsism, the technically feasible and sanctioned.

The "bio-adapter"

TE: Within the *verbesserung,* the sections on the "bio-adapter" (together with their theoretical underpinnings) count as the first sketches of a "bliss suit" or virtual reality (*avant la lettre*) in which man and machine fuse into a cyborg. Although you repeatedly undermine your own arguments in this sketch, I believe that they epitomize your stance, that the bio-adapter offers the "first debatable outlines of a complete resolution of all world problems."[18] Could you comment on the original idea?

ow: The sections on the "bio-adapter" are based on the concept of "functional equivalence."

Functional Equivalence

Based on metaphors taken from automata theory, functional equivalence refers, on the one hand, to the indistinguishability between the output or behavior of two different entities reacting on the same input or stimulus, e.g., of man and machine. On the other hand, an organism may react to two stimuli in the same way, thus making them functionally equivalent (see the example of the wooden board in this conversation). With a slightly different emphasis, namely pertaining to the relation of external objects and their models within an organism, Wiener stated: "A model of an object is a heterarchy of schemas and other structures realized in an organism that are able to generate a functional equivalent of this object with respect to these schemas as a set of internal symbols" (Wiener 2007: 169). But functional equivalence can also be interpreted as a behavior indistinguishable to an observer, although generated by two essentially different entities (man vs. machine, for instance): "May not machines carry out something which ought to be described as thinking but which is very different from what a man does? This objection is a very strong one, but at least we can say that if, nevertheless, a machine can be constructed to play the imitation game satisfactorily, we need not be troubled by this objection" (Turing 1950: 435).

Turing conceived of an imitation game (known as the Turing test) consisting of three players – a man (A), a woman (B), and a questioner (C). Today (2022), this setting based on sexual difference would have to be discussed separately and reformulated in view of wokeness, doing gender, and possibly Turing's own sexual orientation. "The players can neither see nor hear each other and thus communicate anonymously, e.g., by means of teletype or keyboard and screen. Their tasks are defined as follows: Player C (questioner): by asking A and B questions, C must try to find out who of the two is the woman and who is the man. Player A (man) must try to get the questioner to falsely identify him as the woman. Player B (woman) must try to get the questioner to correctly identify her as the woman. In the standardized test procedure devised to decide whether machines can think, a machine takes the role of a man and a male player takes the role of a woman [...]. Turing postulated that we should ascribe intelligence to a machine, if the machine is no worse at pretending to be a woman than the man. He predicted that in the year 2000, a questioner would mistake the machine for the man in three out of ten cases after a five-minute conversation, so that 'at the end of the century [...] general educated opinion will have altered so much that one will be able to speak of machines thinking without expecting to be contradicted'" (Stephan und Walter 2021: 168).

Among other objections to Turing's arguments concerning the imitation game the following objection is worth a discussion:

"Turing is merely aiming at a definition: '>thinking< is what passes Turing's test' [...] One may guess from occasional remarks that Turing himself preferred a behaviorist perspective in the narrowest sense. Psychology should restrict itself to publicly observable and instrumentally measurable behavior and, above all, avoid any reference to consciousness. This indeed points to his intention to define intelligence behaviorally, since the behaviorist dogmatic tried to save psychology from the 'mental' by merely censoring its vocabulary. But language restrictions by definition, of course, do not decide whether or not a theory is correct. Apparently, we did not have to wait until the year 2000 to be quite naturally served phrases like 'intelligent terminal,' 'thinking brake system,' 'compassionate zipper,' etc. in the sense of 'smart book.' On the other hand, language restrictions are unavoidable in this case. Even a complete formal description of thought acceptable for most people would encompass, among other things, language restrictions. The arbitrariness of behaviorists' terms results from the unscientific components of their dogma. By mere inference from sense data, like we do with physical systems, we simply cannot understand human behavior. We also get essential clues for a prospective theory from introspection, which can often be correlated intersubjectively. Behaviorism prevented scientific introspection by simply declaring it superfluous, even if behaviorist concepts, like any other, rely on semi-intentional, or unintentional, and, I think, intentional, albeit tacit introspection. Turing seems to define his notions by emphasizing the *functional equivalence* [emphasis TE] of the symbols on the terminal screen. Yet the matter must be decided on the basis of the adequacy or inadequacy of interpretations, which would still be necessary, even if one would

allow for the inspection of a reasonably efficient program 'behind' the terminal" (Wiener 1996 [1984]: 78).

Later and until recently, Wiener obviously considered the objection that Turing only sought to define "thinking" less important than the following: You can include into the simulation any argument you detect, which is missing in the simulation, simply because you are now able to formulate it. Wiener thus boils down the conclusions from Turing's test to two punch lines: "either Turing means that all efforts to structurally specify what can be justifiably called ‚thinking' are in vain; or you have to conclude that he proposes that the respective program embodies the best systematic hypothesis of thinking in order to permit tests of the best systematic counterarguments. In the second case, of course, Turing's test would be no more than a metaphor. At least one could extend it into a scientific, if curious, practice, because one may hope, after all, that each consistent debunking of a program leads to stronger hypotheses, as any systematic argument could be integrated into the program [at least according to the Church-Turing thesis]. It seems to me, however, that Turing simply preferred the first interpretation of his test as a sufficient criterion for attributing 'thought.' This can be inferred from his remark that the conditions of the test put the program at a disadvantage [as quoted above]: 'May not machines carry out something which ought to be described as thinking but which is very different from what a man does?' Turing's answer is typical of his thoroughly behavioristic attitude: 'if, nevertheless, a machine can be constructed to play the imitation game satisfactorily, we need not be troubled by this objection.' Turing seems to be satisfied by the indefinable 'intuition' of *functional equivalence* [emphasis TE] at the level of the screen symbols. To search the program itself for any structural similarities with human thought is thus out of the question" (Wiener 1996 [1990]: 246).

Wiener follows this direction by demanding a "structural specification" instead of "functional equivalence" as the definition of intelligence: "I tried to specify a *task*, which a machine has to fulfill, in order for me to begin to ascribe intelligence to it: to 'fold' strings under constraints. But for Turing's test not even this would be a reliable criterion. First, […] even humans do not always succeed in such 'folding,' and second, a benchmark for the difficulty of such tasks for humans – and for machines – cannot be effectively determined. Therefore, I took one step further and tried something like a *structural characterization* of my own thinking. Beyond this, I don't know further. If someone would present me with a machine, in which I recognize the same processes at work that I find in introspection, then I would just settle down to the opinion that it thinks just like me" (Wiener 1996 [1990]: 247–248).

Stephan, Achim, and Sven Walter, 2021. Nachwort. In: Turing, Alan M., *Computing Machinery and Intelligence / Können Maschinen denken?*. Ditzingen, 131–183.

Turing, Alan M., 1950. Computing Machinery and Intelligence. *Mind*, 59/236, 433–460.

Wiener, Oswald, 1996 [1984]. Turings Test. In: id., *Schriften zur Erkenntnistheorie*. Vienna, New York, 69–95.

Wiener, Oswald, 1996 [1990]. Probleme der Künstlichen Intelligenz. In: id., *Schriften zur Erkenntnistheorie*. Vienna, New York, 198–277.

Wiener, Oswald, 2007. Über das „Sehen" im Traum (Zweiter Teil). *manuskripte*, 178, 161–172.

TE

OW: Although I am able to define functional equivalence now, I couldn't have done so when I was writing the bio-adapter. The realization that functional equivalence exists was just shocking to me. The brain of somebody, who so far naïvely believed that every fact in the world is unique – who believed in absolute things, so to speak –, received a heavy blow. If there is functional equivalence then there is nothing real. That might be too harshly said but that's how I felt then. So I had to digest this notion first – that, for example, only a few conditions at a few nerve cell endings suffice to evoke in me the feeling of touching a sanded wooden board. This feeling can be produced in very many ways – with the wooden board but also with different stimulants.

One lesson was that what really matters is what I had understood about the organization of *my* organism. Where does the feeling come from, which I experience as a quale? Some philosophers assure us that this is a stupid question, but this doesn't help me. While it is clear that we are not talking about a topographical location here, the question remains as to which agency registers this feeling. One can even question whether there is an agency that actually feels. What would it look like? What does the path to this agency, that is not yet this agency, look like? As long as we don't know these processes for sure, we could imagine a lot of intermediate stages in between, on which one could evoke the same feeling at any time, without always implying the entire sensory apparatus.

In the *verbesserung* this shows in the following passage: "the adapter must furthermore be capable in any event of performing all sorts of operations on a body that, initially, is after all still human (amputations; organ transplantations; neurosurgery) and carry out the regeneration of any of its own functions that may be impaired or design and install replacement modules and, more generally, newly developed components. in other words, it modifies not only its programs, which must be interpreted as command sequences of 'material states,' but also, in the course of its self-adaptation, its physical modules, which, as program carriers, are what makes sequential control possible in the first place. in this regard, the latter are no longer in any way passive media of the operation but in fact determinant states; the distinction between hardware and software is solely didactic and without any substantial basis: the installation of a joint between shoulder and elbow will usher in a new era of back-washing."[19]
Ideas such as these brought me to the concept of the bio-adapter. In 1988 I commented on it in retrospect, noting that I later found a passage in the *First Meditation* of Descartes where he outlines the notion of a demon simulating the impressions and things you feel without them being present:

"I shall suppose that some malicious, powerful, cunning demon has done all he can to deceive me – rather than this being done by God, who is supremely good and the source of truth. I shall think that the sky, the air, the earth, colours, shapes, sounds and all external things are merely dreams that the demon has contrived as traps for my judgment. I shall consider myself as having no hands or eyes, or flesh, or blood or senses, but as having falsely believed that I had all these things."[20]

Without being aware of the text by Descartes, I had had exactly the same thoughts while writing the bio-adapter.[21]

---

the bio-adapter

"I began to write my book *die verbesserung von mitteleuropa, roman* as an honest attempt at finding man's soul, his freedom, as well as his exceptionality within nature. [...] Incommensurable images always boil down to the logical conclusion, by which they lose their disconnectedly individual character. Again and again it's only a re-folding of machines; deliberate and involuntary reshufflings always yield clear shapes, and what now is false by way of not being coherent with the new insight will not turn out to be heroically but only trivially false. Each personality desires at order because it is self-contained structure itself. [...] So the only source of a personality worth desiring would be the incomprehensible, because then one would at least manifest one irrational feature of any kind. Yet obviously, merely to think about achieving the unlikely, charisma, and the belief in the self is forbidden. Hence, one must not think about anything at all. The irrational would have to have an idea of me in order to be relevant for my consciousness. Then it could delineate the revolt, and my suffering would become its power. Therefore, the desire for freedom channels into movement, drive, rebound, the frenzy of intoxication, sex, and daze. Things become unintelligible because they happen so fast, and they have to be accelerated or, at least, blurred further as soon as analysis impends on them. Maybe this tempo can be reenacted into a frenzy of insight? The tentative signal stems from the unconscious: I got it!

Every intuition, every initial understanding, every feeling to have understood is a new beginning. Does the self manifest itself in the chaotic moment before the dust settles? But soon the effort to see differently turns into the desire, nay, the *compulsion* to see differently as one actually does and probably has been seeing before. So the capacity of re-interpretation is soon exhausted. What seemed to corroborate my ego – a paradox, a conflict – now is only evidence that I have not really understood. As much as I hate my abilities, the irrational remains nothing but my inability.

Okay, inability. Anyway, only trivial things touch me. Self-denigrated and indulged in the embarrassment of my own opinion and my own style I search for discomfort, which I shortly enjoy because at least now I seem to be the master of my triviality – *against nature* for the poor. One has to declare valid the very first impulse for action because trying to improve would only bring to light higher naïveties, which one can no longer easily undermine. Then again the insight that all this takes place merely within an imagined social world, and everything has always been motivated by the attempt to understand the rationale of the others. Since freedom merely means discarding what is understood, the final stage is the total demolition of all values. The desire for the impossible delivers me to the insight – I myself am a mechanism too. 'The self cannot be saved.' The only thing to be understood is the structure of the natural numbers, as far as I embody it.

That's how *I* arrived at the bio-adapter. It is an allegory for my mental development (the book is a novel of personal development [Entwicklungsroman]). Yet it also describes what I wanted the reader to experience, namely the same development – start and takeoff. Above all, however, it formulates the idea that the intuition of self depends on values prescribed from the outside but not realized at the inside. Only change is able to enrich me, but this change must appear as a coincidence because I do not yet possess its structure, and it must complicate me without destroying me.

About the same time, the English philosopher John Wilson considered 'eudaimonia machines.' Yet, he was not a pathological case such as I am, searching for a paradox, which would falsify an entire mode of thought and not just a single theory. He too wanted to save a piece of humanity but he was more modest. He saw the threat to personality clearly: 'A properly programmed machine could both know what we were like better than we did, and also make the kind of choice that we would make if we were not disturbed by the human obstacles of prejudice and bias or other obstacles such as lack of time, patience, or the ability to concentrate. [...] Now we are faced, not only by a machine that produces eudaimonia chosen by men, nor only by a machine that chooses eudaimonia for men, but also by a machine that alters men, perhaps to fit an extended concept of eudaimonia' (Wilson 1964: 230).

If we want to experience ourselves coherently, we should not think beyond epiphenomena. Only the inconsiderate will survive mechanization. Personalism presupposes something authentic. But it turns out that the idea of functional equivalence is no deception. The world is a measurement process of which every part can be substituted. My thought is such a measurement section, too. [...] Do I bet on a machine interpreting and complicating my appetites and values so that my intellect can follow? Or shall I be reduced to those nerve bundles, which mediate wellness so that I feel 'eternally' well? Is this idiocy all that remains authentic?

Maybe hopelessness. *die verbesserung von mitteleuropa, roman* aims at reaching escape speed in order to take revenge for the hopes of its author. All right – I am not planned but I have evolved. But fuck evolution! Is there a way of escaping it? Also the bio-adapter lies around somewhere and in the way, say, of a stone. But isn't that a nice step backwards in the end – adaptation [...] masking my further complication? No, it's not. If the bliss bundle is to grow irregularly, the adaptor must also communicate meaningfully with the world, and any mode in which this happens will also complicate the world. In the sixties I didn't grasp that yet. Only disintegration counts; and only to me. Furthermore I can only stop, if *it* stops. Worse, it does not matter to me or to it, only the sporty aspect remains. I am born into the adapter, so both more bliss and more hopelessness is inconceivable. Or is it?

My reflections during the past twenty-five years have led me to the conviction that, in order to correct me, the bio-adapter must itself be conscious and willful, maybe experience lust and pain, certainly have appetites and prejudices. Suppose a radical new science would make this possible. How will the bio-adapter itself cope with its personality? Will it build its own bio-adaptor? And how could I, its thalamus, profit from it − by a third-order failure?"

Wiener, Oswald, 1996. Notizen zum Konzept des Bio-Adapters (1988). In: id., *Schriften zur Erkenntnistheorie*. Wien, New York, 108−111, originally in: *Maschinenmenschen. Katalog zur Ausstellung des Neuen Berliner Kunstvereins in der Staatlichen Kunsthalle Berlin vom 17. Juni bis 23. Juli 1989.* Berlin.

Wilson, John. 1964. The Frankenstein Problem. *Philosophy*, 39/149, 223−232.

TE: Did you develop concepts such as functional equivalence during the writing of or the reading for the *verbesserung*?

OW: It had brewed up somehow − rather from the background readings for the *verbesserung*. And some passages, which obviously express what I have just felt, I didn't know at that time. Especially the quote from the *Meditations* of Descartes only later impressed itself on me. Probably I had even read it, but read over it at first.

TE: The essay on the "bio-adapter" stands out in the book because of its style. So it has often been considered a separate part. Do you see it as an integral part of the *verbesserung* or not?

OW: Unfortunately, it has been considered as separate, while I do see it as an integral part. Even more, it winds up an entire development, which didn't result from the work on the *verbesserung*. It rather took place in the general background of my life, which my writing only accentuated. The style of the essay is consciously parodist. I tried to mock popular science writing. That's why the section "Introduction" of "notes on the concept of the bio-adapter, essay" was so important to me, although it remains totally unacknowledged in secondary literature. The true core of my anarchism is formulated there. I even went so far as to nastily claim – nastily at least at that time –, that it would be better to be killed by a spree killer than to be put on the iron lung for a few years or to waste away as a state pensioner. I tried to show understanding for leftist young radical people of the time. All of this has to do with the bio-adapter, but perhaps in somewhat convoluted ways. For example, I already chose the quotes very consciously, say, the motto of Karl Kraus: "and let chaos be welcome; for order has failed." I find that great! Equally the quote of Schopenhauer: "where calculating starts, understanding ends." Or vice versa (laughs) ...

TE: In the bio-adapter, too, language and linguistics are often a major topic, even if not in a positive sense. You wrote, for instance, that only linguistics conceiving of itself as a part of behaviorist psychology will practically fulfill its fate.

OW: Yes, language does play a role. Back then I understood language in several respects as an instrument for mental engineering. This led me to ideas which I still find quite intriguing. Soon after I "perceived *language* as a part of the objective world, onto which I have to project my 'contents'."[22] But then, how does language as an external stimulus influence consciousness? Insofar as it is capable, like a visual stimulus, to cause the individual to change its orientation, language belongs to the environment just like any object in the external world, which, for instance, cast light rays on your retina. In the *verbesserung,* I tended to exaggerate this aspect and called language the only environment. Nonetheless, I already realized that linguistics evaded the actual problem, because "language" does not mean anything at all, as long as you don't know how it affects the brain (in thinking, understanding, and imagery).[23] The bio-adapter has only little matter at its disposal, so it must be very economical. As already mentioned, I then thought, that if one strokes a tabletop with one's hand, for instance, the bio-adapter would only surrogate the stimulus at those places where the surface is touched. Everywhere else nothing would happen ... there would be no table, of course, but only its sensation. At the first stage, before bio-adapter intervenes directly in the nervous system, it still has to work with matter in order to simulate it, and so the tactile receptors of the hand are stimulated – but only at the points where the finger really touches the tabletop. Things like that fascinated me, because they immediately imply the following idea: Probably the world in which we live is just the same! We have already been living within the bio-adapter for a long time! Thus the section "bio-adapter" ends with a sentence without period: "maybe we all are".[24]

TE: What remains? Not even a brain, but ...?

OW: ... something functionally equivalent.

TE: So that the medium of intelligence is irrelevant?

OW: Right. The premise is, of course, that this is possible in principle. Until today I am not convinced that it is. The remains of my philosophy of consciousness is, after all, supported by a slight doubt that simulation can never be pushed so far that it *actually* becomes what it is supposed to simulate but that some remainder cannot be simulated. This remainder, however, would constitute the essence of intelligence. These are doubts I harbored and still harbor, but I wouldn't want to call them claims.

TE: Would you say that the bio-adapter developed a radical utopia, which also plays a role in the following stages of your work but is questioned again and again?

OW: Yes. Even today the thoughts that led to the bio-adapter are important to me.

TE: Which authors were you interested in while writing the bio-adapter? All those named in the bibliography?

Cybernetics and automata theory

OW: At that time, I could no longer youthfully enthuse about other kinds of texts such as before those of August Stramm or, in particular, of Benjamin Péret. In the mid-1950s, I had read these authors in an entirely different mood than the authors I now read for the bio-adapter. Now, I primarily read technical works and I started to deal with automata theory. I was successful as an employee and so Olivetti paid me a trip to Milan. There I purchased a book, which marked the beginning of my ongoing and rather dynamic commitment to computer programming. The book was *Computer Logic: Functional Design of Digital Computers* by Iván Flores, and it proved to be equally serious as Boris A. Trakhtenbrot's *Wieso können Automaten rechnen?* (Why Do Automata Compute?) from the late 1960s on.[25] This paved the way for dealing with the concept of the Turing machine.[26]

At first I entered a prominent and rather fashionable field of the 1960s, namely content analysis, of which I read and also bought a lot. Some of these tomes I still own. I was very interested in it because this was a kind of beginning of artificial intelligence, only without computers. These attempts went in the direction of finding a definition of meaning, whereby meaning was to be determined by the detection of word accumulations, statistics, information-theoretical esthetics, and other fields fashionable then. The beginning of so-called content analysis was actually political, because its target was the analysis of Russian bureaucratic language. Of course, I was deeply satisfied when I realized this, since it supported my views about the connection between language and politics. As an example, let me quote from the *verbesserung:* "but the rest of us add forcefully: the words together with their use are inseparably connected with political and social organization; they *are* this organization; they *are* that *a priori,* about whose existence these idiots have used up so much thought; in truth they *are* only there to make idiots believe in reality as they did before believe in the hereafter; believe in the hereafter, so that idiots toil properly and become still more streamlined and more well-behaved [...]."[27]

Later, I put that into perspective. I doubted the relation of a word or a sentence to any content outside the apparatus that establishes this relation within the individual. Something like "content" or "sense" or "meaning" (all these expressions are the same to me) cannot be deduced from the words used. So the demand for "political correctness" of language use is built on false premises, too. In search of the conditions of the fact that contradiction-free interpretations of an arbitrarily large set of data are widely found, although infinitely many interpretations of this set of data, e.g. of a sequence of words, are possible, I concluded first: "As the main source of constraints we identified language (Whorf) and all social institutions, which (presumably) emanated from it. So the trajectory arcs back to politics; society's dominance over language must be countered by our own production, which we must not fall for either. From this standpoint progressive conservatives will define the 'politically correct,' except for the last remark."[28]

TE: What did you read about content analysis back then? Ithiel de Sola Pool?[29]

OW: This name was familiar then but only to people specializing in content analysis. I also dealt with its mathematical branch but not with factor analysis. That chastened me a lot, because I thought that by this they build up a concept of meaning without any reference to human thinking. On the one hand, this radicalism struck me as very attractive, but on the other hand, it seemed an unbearable anathema.

TE: Especially speech recognition is still applying vector spaces for so-called "latent semantic analysis."

OW: Yes, but the means are entirely different. Today, a lot of statistics and probability theory is used in connection with the language philosophy and technology of Bayes, which is equally fascinating for engineers. In 2017, I held a lecture in Cologne, where I tried to acquaint a larger audience with this fact, which seems downright monstrous to me – yet monstrous in an ambiguous sense, namely both positive and negative. The latest technical developments allow for the implementation of many tasks, which formerly only humans were thought to be capable of. But the machines fulfill them in a completely different way. We're witnessing a kind of "alien intelligence" there. I'll give one brief example that impressed me in particular because it has something to do with the bio-adapter. The task is speech recognition and translation problems that are solved in a statistical way. On the one hand, the tremendous capacity of today's mainframe computers in terms of number of memory locations is impressive. It reaches numbers that are no longer imaginable. Also the processing speed is unimaginable, especially if many processors are working in parallel. My example is the television quiz game *Jeopardy*. In 2011, a program called *Watson* won three episodes of *Jeopardy!* against the two current champions of that series. Compared to the ambitions of current projects, Watson was quite modestly equipped: only ninety IBM Power 750 servers with only sixteen terabytes of RAM, each server with only a 3.5 GHz 8-core processor, and each core could only process a maximum of four threads at a time.

Jeopardy has a lot to do with language, with linguistic wit, puns, and the like. A sentence is uttered and the participants have to invent a suitable question, which this sentence is an answer to. When they believe they have found a suitable answer, they have to press a button which makes a sound. From statistical measurements we know that the first to hit the button needs 3.5 seconds on average. Therefore, the engineers must design the machine according to the premise that the matching question is found in less than 3.5 seconds. So in only 3 seconds – I don't know exactly how many – billions of memory locations are read, compared, and merged.

But what does "compared and merged" mean? From an engineering perspective this is not so uncanny yet. But what is uncanny is the capacity, which makes the computation possible without seemingly any limit from the parsimony of thought. Insight – actually advantageous from a parsimonious point of view – no longer plays a role because of the machine's capacity and processing speed. Thus, if these machines would have something that I'd call insight – which they don't have yet, but let's just assume they will attain it –, then it would certainly *not* depend on parsimony. Let's take a closer look at how these statistics work. The sentences are "analyzed," but it would be better to say that word probabilities are measured. That is the most primitive way to approach the following question: What is the probability of a specific word occurring after a specific precedent word. For example, you say "because" and this predicts the probability that the word "that" will come next. This requires a huge corpus, on the basis of which nothing but measurements are made.

So far this was the preparation phase of Watson's *Jeopardy* performance: A gigantic collection of probabilities is created, not only for the respective next word, but also for the third word and so forth. At first I was tempted to shrug my shoulders and think: "What's the big deal, it's only probabilities?" But then it dawned on me what these probabilities result from. They result from texts that *people* have written, and it's quite clear that the statistics of their word usage somehow reflect, to use big words, the structure of the universe insofar as people have grasped or viewed it. Hence, it is evident that such an approach to solving tasks like the *Jeopardy* game, if pushed further, must necessarily be successful on a broader scale.

Are epistemology and cognition after all only a question of the technical progress of computing capacity? In a more general sense, I decidedly believe that no, it is not. For these machines do not invent anything at all. They have no ideas, they have no concepts, they have no structure – at least not how I define structure. They don't *build* machines themselves, and they don't use these machines. So they represent the surface of intelligence, which is structured insofar as there exist historical "channels" such as the text corpora in *Watson*. There exists a tremendous channel system through which very thick channels and extremely thin, even hair-thin ones are running. They represent millions, billions of historically established "associations" in the sense of connections between words and sentences historically uttered – including some in tasks of previous *Jeopardy* games.[30]

TE: But *Jeopardy* is often about mere puns. I could accept your stance if the machine's lexicon would consist of older puns that have been uttered and written down before. But what about creative or new word uses, newly generated wordplays or metaphors that have never been uttered in this way before? Of course one could opine that the fact that they have never been uttered and thus never appeared on the linguistic surface before does not imply that there might not be any so-called "conceptual mappings" underlying the comparisons made.

OW: It's mainly about puns indeed, and puns are, to my understanding, close to wordplays. You play with words and not with their meaning. The meaning of a pun is mostly either nonsense or corny. But even a corny joke is deeper than a pun, because it sometimes plays with word meanings. For a pun you exploit the ambiguity of a word in its current environment, so that a second meaning can also be attributed to it. Generally, the latter has nothing to do with the first meaning, but in some fortunate cases it indeed has. These are then particularly good puns.

To detect them is an ideal task for language statistics because the machine "knows" the different ways of pronouncing a word and compares billions of possibilities within an insanely short period. At the first stage, which takes half a second, it lists these billions of word combinations; then it detects those that become statistically conspicuous from the point of view of "searching for something that fits." All the dictionaries in the world that have anything to do with English have already been preprocessed and are thus available. So the statistics is already there; it doesn't have to be recalculated anew each time, but represents a gigantic corpus of statistical connections. That's the machine's memory, so to speak. Difficulties only arise if analogies at a deeper level of meaning play a role. But that's hardly the case with *Jeopardy*, which is a superficial game. Let me sum up what I want to say with this digression in one sentence: With such programs you create something similar to the bio-adapter! If I can no longer differentiate whether I am talking to a human being or a machine on the phone, then we *are* already in the bio-adapter.

TE: This hints at Turing's test, as you said.

OW: This *is* an example of Turing's test – it's about whether machine can be distinguished from man, and if so how. Turing's test is crucial for the bio-adapter, of course, although I didn't know that at the time. I got there by other means, or rather by my own means. As I said, the basic concept was "functional equivalence," and that was a real blow to me. This reminds me of how the poet Heinrich von Kleist felt the insights of Kant, if one can say so, were like a blow to his sensibility. To me it happened in a similar way – maybe not with such dramatic consequences as for Kleist, but in a similar vein. I felt an axe blow against my concept of the real, which until then had been one of my guiding notions.

TE: In the secondary literature about the *verbesserung*, there is controversy about the role that cybernetics, statistics, and behaviorism have played for you. Some say that the *verbesserung*, including the bioadapter, are prime examples of the view that human consciousness and intelligence will be suspended and replaced by cybernetics and cybernetic machines. Others, however, say that the book prophetically implies that behaviorism, which has been dominating the sciences from the beginning of the 20th century (just as the varieties of positivism did before), is a mode of thinking, if not an ideology, and will transform all science, medicine, and politics. So it will inevitably lead to the conditioning of the individual by the state and even to the loss of the remains of individuality. The concluding section of your book reflects this scientific stance, which in the 20th century (and also at the beginning of the 21st century) had risen to the status of an engrained theory of the world, as if it was a distorting mirror. According to this second view, statistics is neglecting details, and statistical correlations skip the description of the underlying processes. Yet intelligence precisely consists in reconstructing these underlying processes.

OW: Doubtlessly, both views hold true. A friend and esteemed colleague, Friedrich Wolfram Heubach, has recently written a book on dandyism,[31] wherein he wrote about an idea that he had already put forward at the time when both of us held joint seminars on this subject at the Academy of Fine Arts in Düsseldorf. The idea is that the dandy could be subsumed under the psychoanalytic notion of "identification with the aggressor," which has become popular under the heading of "Stockholm syndrome." Originally, the idea of identification with an aggressor stems from Anna Freud, I believe. This was pretty much true in my case at that time, and I would not hesitate to say that there indeed exists something like this syndrome. One aspect of dandyism surely is this identification with the aggressor; only that Heubach understands the concept of "aggressor" quite conventionally. A mother, for instance, could be such an aggressor. This is probably the way the concept was coined by Anna Freud.

In my case, however, the aggressor was behaviorism with all its implications. If I may dare to treat this intricate matter so trivially, the *verbesserung* expressed my idealistic attitude, which was, of course, anti-materialistic. So instead of behaviorism, which actually doesn't necessarily have to be materialistic, I ventured to postulate a blunt materialism right away. Most philosophers in Europe abominated behaviorism, and so did I. And consequently I also abominated the idea that machine could eventually replace man. Beneath it there is again the notion of the real, which I've already mentioned a couple of times in this conversation. So I think, I identified with materialism, as if suddenly a switch was flipped, and with it came a new sense of self: "Wow, now I'm a materialist, now that's so very bad – now that's the *radical chic*."

That's how the book should be understood. That's why it is so ambivalent: once this way, then that way. And that's why it was never really completed. For I never fully accomplished the transition to become the aggressor myself. There's always a relapse. I think that's how you should interpret it.

TE: And as a consequence you fully turned to automata theory? Could you see it like that?

OW: Well, you know that I don't belong to the species of unambiguous people who are capable of fully professing one thing. There is always a remainder, and sometimes quite a large one, which I can't overcome completely. And so I didn't change to the side of automata theory with flying colors. First, I hit an obstacle, because I had to find out whether or not it is really so important. So I had to learn automata theory more thoroughly in order to be able to judge it. Even now, I always return to one essential point: Efforts in the fields of behaviorism and statistics will fail. Although they will be able to replace man, they will do so only by functional equivalence and not in the sense of real man, if you will. Today, however, I can specify these matters better, namely: Machines on a behavioral and statistical basis will not have any *ideas* in the sense of what I call "proxy objects;" they will not *experience* what I experience when I work to solve a geometric problem, for instance. In fact, they will not experience anything at all, but still they will function. And yet I cannot say: Okay, that's enough for me. It simply isn't. At the end of the day, my last excuse when I feel really cornered, my last point of support is, that all I really want to know is how *I myself* think. How does *my* thinking function? After all, I'm not interested in anything else. But it's not about me alone, of course, it's about but how *people* do this – thinking. Today, I am convinced that it cannot be explained by former means – and these are computers. So the pendulum is swinging back again, so to speak, but over time these swings always take place at higher levels.

TE: But no previous level was without consequences, and you expect more insight every time you have passed through such a level, don't you?

OW: I guess that's what they called dialectics back then …

TE: But it is not only about a mere denial of automata theory and its offshoots, but also about what you can adopt from it and what you may have to supplement.

OW: Yes, plus now there are new imponderables: Certain programs, especially neural networks, can no longer be understood in terms of algorithms. Their programmers themselves no longer understand *how* their machines perform their tasks. Behind this lurks a threatening corollary: The machine isn't any different than man, because, after all, we don't understand how we function either. Yet, this seeming comparability must be harshly denied. We must show clearly how these two kinds of incomprehensibilities differ from each other.

Language and thought processes

TE: Back to the *verbesserung*. It seems that your attitude toward "language" as an instrument was in many respects very skeptical then. Which role did you attribute to language for thought processes?

OW: During my work on the *verbesserung* I also made initial attempts at introspection with epistemological goals. Every introspector notices that even before he uses a word or utters a sentence, there is something somehow mysteriously connected with the word or sentence. This something is *not* the word or sentence, but the general feeling that you *know* something without yet having actualized it consciously. I have recently begun to develop a theory according to which this knowledge can be unfolded, and that it then shows itself introspectively in concrete successive moves.

A simple example, which unfortunately can easily be doubted because of its obviousness, is arithmetic. If you mentally calculate, for instance, you must definitely execute each single step, as soon as the task exceeds the times table. When multiplying multi-digit numbers, every observer sees the same as Turing saw in the calculation processes of others: you "write down" numbers, then there is a pause, then you "write down" another number, and so on. If you do that yourself, then you know what happens in the pauses – at least you get the feeling for it. The final resolution of what we see here is that there is a process, a procedure, a method. It is in the nature of any procedure that it cannot be executed all at once while being present to the introspector. You can't play a melody by playing all the tones at once, because within that single concurrence of all the tones there are innumerable melodies. Even if you play some tones louder, there are still innumerable melodies.

This sequential way of proceeding or this procedural feature of thought is an important insight that I first had when I was working on the last parts of the *verbesserung*. It was the beginning of a way of thinking that later brought me to Piaget, because I was looking for psychologists emphasizing the active and dynamic aspect of thought.

Until then, I had only found static and statistical explanation attempts. Strikingly, scholars focusing on language, the philosophy of language, and on linguistics did not ask for the mechanism that leads to the very existence of the statistics of language use. Instead, they assumed that, by its sheer possibility and applicability, statistics is already self-evident. In their view, there was no cause why certain probabilities were distributed in a certain way. They did not even bother to look for causes. In contrast, I was convinced that there are good causes why thought is *not* statistical. Statistics actually only describes things, but does not unravel them, because it only describes their surface.

There is no doubt that language does play a role in thinking, namely the role of a stabilizer or an exoskeleton, if you want. Although it doesn't globally subserve "memory," if only because you would have to define the latter much more precisely, it does help with memory retrieval. When something does not come to my mind, I often find myself searching for a word denoting the thing that does not come to my mind. The fact is: In order for me to have the feeling that I have designated something with a word, I must first have another feeling, which is directed at something else, which is *not* this word. To put it somewhat self-tormentingly, there must exist something retrievable before the word. But how do I retrieve it? Unfortunately, we don't know yet. But if I have the *feeling* of "Ah, there is the hint of a thought!," then sometimes it wasn't a full-fledged thought yet that appeared. The thing that was meant was yet far too unclear. But still something was meant, that isn't new to me. At just that moment I have something that I can *name* with a word, and that is exactly where instrumental language use begins.

The mere existence of the word "retrievable" alone suggests that there is something worthy of that name. In this case you have to ponder a bit, but this pondering also belongs to the domain of knowledge. If you think about it a bit, you immediately realize: This "retrievable" does indeed exist, because you now remember that you have been talking about it before. Hence, you just recovered something that can be denoted. And if we talk about it very often, then we'll find a short word denoting the retrievable. In this sense, language is practically indispensable. Theoretically speaking, I don't think it is indispensable because, for example in mental arithmetic, "inner" words and symbols don't play any role. Mental arithmetic is a very strange process, adding up numbers, for instance. Even more striking is mental multiplication, because up to a certain point you learn it by heart. The multiplication table is so deeply entrenched into my brain that I no longer even notice what I'm actually doing when I multiply. So there is nothing left of the multiplication process. But how did I learn it in the first place? I have heard of children who wanted to understand why 3 x 7 is 21. In order to explain it, you must take pains to count aloud, then maybe to make dashes on paper. Dashes may be very practical under certain circumstances, but are perhaps not really necessary, not even at this level. And dashes are not words, mind you. A stroke with the pen can mean much more than a word ever could. You must already know what the stroke means in this context, that it stands for something that is pompously called a unit, as opposed to two or three units.

I base this characterization on introspection, which in this case, I believe, again offers the opportunity not to be misled or to be inaccurate, because the question is not about accuracy at all. The matter is simply to determine what is going on when I am mentally calculating. In the example of multiplying 3 x 7, I start by adding up three sevens, representatives of the number 7, so to speak. For me, the symbol is not the number. What a number is, mathematicians have disdainfully failed to tell us so far. So you have to develop your own ideas about it. Let me begin by stating that a number is a structure named with a number symbol. These numbers differ tremendously as far as their structure is concerned. If you follow Turing in one of his most difficult essays, you could even conceive of all human thought as number manipulation, but I won't go into that here. The piece is titled "System of Logic Based on Ordinals" and was written in 1938. In it, Turing conceives of logic as an ordinal number.

Anyway, what I said is actually quite simple: There exists something, which is different from words but can be named. Words hardly ever play a role in thought processes at all, except under very specific circumstances, for example when you have to repeat literally what has just been said. Try to repeat, for instance, the following sentence about an alleged "Pilsen beer stamp" by August Klotz, who is represented in the Prinzhorn collection [of outsider art]: "The Pilsen beer stamp does not lack the hair worm, it is itself."[32] In such sentences, words do matter, because very little can be associated with them. I for my part do have associations connected to this sentence, but of course I know that they have nothing to do with August Klotz himself. For example, the word "beer stamp" troubles me, but at the same time it reminds me of the word "beer brush," which is the name of a building in West Berlin. In my view, only the proverbial Berlin humor was able to produce that name.

TE: I don't really get it. Why beer brush?

OW: Well, very simply because of its shape [sketches the building on paper]. It looks like a tree and is located in the district of Steglitz near the Bundesplatz. It is slightly elevated and thus visible from afar. I think, there is a city railway station nearby, and in its building there is a restaurant where people drink beer. That is the beer brush.

TE: It's about the brush form, so to speak.

OW: I'd rather name it "beer tree." But if you think of a shaving brush, then "beer brush" fits quite well. And with this help I arrive at "beer stamp."

TE: I'd like to return to the role of language for thought from another perspective. In 1987, you wrote a short essay entitled "Wahl eines Wortes" ("Choice of a word"). Let me try to reconstruct this piece in the light of what has been said so far. Its starting point is that there are inexpressible sensations or intentions. Specifically, you wanted to specify one aspect of a landscape, or wilderness, in Canada. Since men enter it, it ceases to exist as wilderness or nature untouched by humans. The ideal, fitting adjective is on the tip of your tongue but won't spring to mind. In order to find it you tentatively try out several words. Finally, you arrive at "weakened," the connotations and etymology of which you list. Somehow, finding this word for a specific state of mind or sensation of how, as far as I can understand, you experience or want to see this landscape, satisfied you.

I want to suggest two things. Firstly, I can track very well what you described here. I can even track it better when I read your elaboration on how you found the word "weakened." The word alone impresses me, because when hearing it I get the feeling that I could eventually approximate your sensation. So the symbol that you present me with enables the communication of an experience from one mind to the other, so to speak. Secondly, I sometimes have similar experiences attempting to find an adequate word. By finding it, the fact that I want to describe something becomes clearer to me. Or rather, the corresponding state of mind only snaps in through the word. For me, this incremental search for a word feels different from the process of searching a word and having a still ambivalent, not yet fixed feeling. In such cases, it seems that words fulfill a bigger role than a merely mnemonic or supporting one, which you called an exoskeleton.

OW: I don't think that I can agree. Let's stick with the example of "weakened." How do I search for the word? First, I know that there is one. I think I can say that for sure. Then I don't search haphazardly but try to remember the features of the object in question, which made the biggest impression on me. I try to remember specific attunements in connection with the landscape in question, which should be "sublime," to use the old word. The Yukon wilderness does bear this aspect; especially up north it has attracted and impressed me beyond measure. When I stood there, I'd preferred to stand there alone – just to stand there and watch the wind blow! Only few creatures are able to live there. Now that only describes how I got there first but not the feeling I tried to find a word for. I am talking about Canada, where Ingrid and I lived for so long. That was the beginning. Okay, how do you get there today? By car. But there is only one road to the place where we lived. We had already been there in 1985, when I was 50 years old. I was very strong at that time and could go on long hikes.

Only 100 meters away from the road you became nervous on hearing a little noise, because it could have been a bear or a wolf or some other dangerous thing. This danger contributed to the overall attunement. I don't want to use this corny cliché, but you felt very small – no, that's not true, on the contrary: you felt tall because you were even able to feel that way! Central Europeans just don't know how the wind blows there!

In search of a fitting word, I first looked for a seed pertaining to this very attunement. As soon as I found the seed, the respective attunement already set in. Yet, in the short piece "Choice of a word" this attunement wasn't sublime, but referred to the fact that this wilderness is already ruined. There is nothing sublime left on earth because man pollutes everything. Then I imagined experiences that you have in this landscape. Amidst this wilderness, you believe, for instance, that the nearest house is very far away. You went out by car and then you walked ten kilometers into the woods. It's very difficult to walk there, for during summer everything is swampy because the permafrost soil is thawing. Finally, you stand there and you think: "Wow, that's it!" You look around, and all of a sudden you hear a loud noise. There's a helicopter flying very low over your head! Immediately you know that a government agency must have sent it. There's some government guy sitting in it and he's getting paid, for example for counting the wolves in the area. All of a sudden, you realize that nature has reached its endpoint. You turn around and leave, get in the car and drive home.

When I was there I felt exactly this attunement, but I couldn't name it. While writing the essay, I then searched for the word. I ruminated a bit about the meaning of the word "*to weaken*" – to make something weaker, to take away strength from someone. In this way, I reconstructed the attunement. This has only to do with language insofar as the word has several meanings. In actual fact, I am not searching for or by words at all, because I simply wouldn't know how to do so. If I searched by words, then I would have to proceed completely differently. I would say, for instance, "okay, the word begins with 'w,' and probably there is 'ea' in it." If my search really went like that, it would justify or corroborate the hypothesis, that words are essential for thought.

The entire passage in the essay "Choice of a word" runs like this: "In the first draft [of the addressed essay "Von der Freiheit eines Grizzlybären" ("On the freedom of a grizzly bear")] it reads: '... in an environment ... not contaminated by any consciousness ...' But the word 'contaminated' does not satisfy me. Without any ado 'devalued,' 'compromised' appear, but 'something is missing.' I have to ask myself what exactly my unconscious is referring to. The word 'un-authenti-cated' appears, together with the image of an almost transparent stone hill landscape superposed on this shoe rack there, juxtaposed to some-thing like myself standing three meters beside me as an enacting shadow. Not only do I seem to know which things these vague schemes refer to, but also what they mean. Something I imagine as being outside is relativized by being doubled – by being simulated. It becomes the simulation of its own mental image. It becomes a model of the theory, whereby its putatively autonomous status and its objective character are lost, or rather, reduced. I have known for a long time that *objective* is only a label attached to some of my ideas in contrast to others, and thus I am satisfied by the notion that here nothing happens but an exchange of this symbol between two ideas. On the other hand, I believe that this notion will threaten the feeling of orientation in others – which is exactly what I am poking fun at. Another aspect of it is that the 'matter' gets drawn into man's conceptual muck. Not only is it now nothing but my idea (it has never been anything else, only that I obviously must concretize this again and again), but it moreover nour-ishes the bullshit of the public castrating and spoiling my ideas in turn.

Of course, I didn't really *tell* this to myself then, I only *knew* it – and I tell it now. Immediately, the word 'weakened' emerged to satisfy me deeper. Yet my doubts still urged to be dissipated. I looked up the word in the etymological dictionary and indeed I find the meaning of 'diluted' as well as 'disgraced.' Only now I realized that another compo-nent had been in play, namely the sexual, which in the first draft was prepared by the words 'abstinence in thought,' delightfully referring to the Holy Spirit (only appealing to the philistine, by the way). The word 'weaken' was my 'solution' for the 'problem' of 'reducing the substance of something while curtailing its status plus libidinal compulsivity plus breaching a taboo.' Although my notion of the nature of this 'de-realization' remained unarticulated, I was determined to keep this word because, as it occurred to me, a brief account of its emergence will, as an appendix, illustrate what has been said in the text."[33]

In short, I believe that what you've just said about the supposedly bigger role of language is an illusion. I think it is reasonable "to understand 'word' as a central element of language very narrowly: we should use 'word' as neutrally as possible and restrict it to the acoustic stimulus (or grapho-visual stimulus of written words), insofar as we recognize it 'automatically' as a language element (and, to start with, nothing else). As a consequence, everything that words or word sequences trigger in the speaker or hearer belongs not to the word (and thus to language in a strict sense) but to thought."[34]
Already in the essay "subjekt, semantik, abbildungsbeziehungen" ["subject, semantics, representation"], I tried to show that there cannot be any semantics in the sense you suggested, namely as relations between words.[35] There, I argue that the representation of the world that the individual develops is independent from its linguistic representation (or, more generally, its symbolic representation). Furthermore, I argued in the 1970s that *"the use of symbols can absolutely not be grasped or explained by the symbols themselves,"* and that a symbol only symbolizes "through a mechanism that establishes a connection between the symbol and what it signifies."[36] Only then it becomes something that is supposed to refer to something beyond itself. Otherwise we would remain within the scope of statistics as described before, and statistics just have nothing to do with semantics. For me, semantics has to do with meanings, and meanings are not simply experiences, meanings are – and in this respect I have learned a lot more in the many years since then – complexes of structures, which one naturally cannot run simultaneously.

TE: To put it bluntly, one could also say that the entire evolution of language manifested, or sedimented, a lot of such feelings and attunements.

OW: I am convinced of that, if I understand you correctly.

TE: That's how it is sometimes conceived of. And that yields a pretty mighty archive already, an archive of acronyms maybe in your sense – of shortcuts.

OW: Certainly, I don't deny that. But at the same time, it is clear that there are a lot of duds among them. Elsewhere, I wrote the following on the role that words (as names) play in the thought process: "The meaning of a symbol is a model (a cognitive representation [...]), which the symbol makes ready to be run ('invoking' it); is the invoking symbol a stimulus, then I call it a name of the invoked structure [...]). [...] Since meaning is a structure it can only be experienced while operating, that is, as a stepwise temporal sequence. Meaning is never present 'as a whole.' This implies that a name only indirectly invokes a model, namely by way of changing switches in order to unfold ever more specific components of the structure according to their availability and the task at hand. As introspection shows (and parsimony predicts), these developments unfold by way of seeds. Thus, a name at best invokes the seed of a structure. In a narrow sense it *is* the name of the seed in question and its meaning *is* the meaning of the seed."[37] Although for many (most?) thought processes words do not play a role, they may appear at certain points within the process. Words are components of seeds "and the name of an [internally developed] object usually only appears at one step in the expansion of the seed." Conversely," the name of an [proxy] object usually invokes its seed."[38]

TE: But then, how do you explain that similar sounding names sometimes superpose, thereby blocking the attempt at remembering? Recently, I was talking to someone about the poet Hartmut Geerken, and when shortly afterwards we came to talk about an artist whose work strongly refers to commemorative culture and to monuments, we just couldn't remember his name. It turned out to be Jochen Gerz. Couldn't the phonetic similarity of "Geerken" and "Gerz" have blocked or superposed the correct word?

OW: I think it is obvious that phonetic similarities do play a role. If you consider that Anthony Marcel's research showed that every sound, which we apprehend as linguistic, triggers the machinery of meaning search.[39] At first, the multiple names, which a polysemous word stands for, momentarily activate several (if not all?) corresponding structures. But this isn't a feature of the word or of what is commonly called semantics. The initially unsuccessful search for a word, such as in your example, is rather the result of a mechanical blockade. In any case, the exact mechanism of this search process remains unexplained, to say the least.

TE: Yes, Marcel's work on the perception of ambiguous expressions is very exciting in itself. In the discussions of the results of his highly sophisticated experimental studies, he distinguishes between preconscious and conscious processing of visually presented linguistic stimuli. According to Marcel, word recognition is a complex process consisting of preconscious identification and conscious perception. Preconscious identification of (potentially polysemous) words proceeds just like the proponents of the so-called "non-selective view" describe, while conscious perception of (potentially polysemous) word stimuli follows the so-called "selective theory." The latter predicts that only one of the possible interpretations can be active at a time, whereas the advocates of the "non-selective view" assume that, at first, several (or all) of the lexical and semantic "representations" triggered by the polysemous word are invoked at once. Only then the context of conscious perception decides which of them is pursued further.[40] In principle, Marcel thus assumes a preconscious uptake of letter stimuli, which only in the following conscious phase – unfortunately he does not define the word conscious very sharply – are somehow integrated into and thereby disambiguated by a meaningful context. During the preconscious phase, everything that the letter sequences *could possibly mean* is still simultaneously activated, so to speak. This is what Marcel tried to test on subjects in his masking experiments. However, he did not record any phenomenal descriptions of the subjects' introspections, but only measured their reaction (times).[41]

OW: Well, that just comes from the scientific ideal. In this respect Noam Chomsky said something apt during an interview in 2012.[42] It touched me very much, because there he voiced a conclusion that I also arrived at on the same matter. He came under heavy attack by somebody working in the artificial intelligence business, but who, I believe, hadn't understood at all what Chomsky was getting at. As far as I understood him, he is concerned with a generative theory of language, that is, he wants to know the mechanism that allows not only new sentences to bubble out, but to understand the mechanism that generates meaning and significance. His critic is missing this completely. Chomsky criticizes that the people who develop today's translation or speech recognition software have no theory of language at all. The statistics they use does not amount to a theory, he says, and I could not agree more. At most, the critic could adopt the position that there will never be a theory of language because it is impossible in principle. And then s/he could argue that what we, the statistics programmers, do *is* already the theory. Our statistical trees *are* an, albeit very complicated, theory of language. On the other hand, Chomsky, who is an old-fashioned and honest philosopher and scientist, just makes the point that any theory must have something to do with Occam's principle of parsimony. So he is searching for a non-trivial structure (in my sense) and does not want to have a trivial structure in all its vastness put down as *the* structure of the thing.

This harks back to Chomsky's influential review of B.F. Skinner's book *Verbal Behavior*, which is in turn viewed as the beginning of cognitive science. In typically behavioristic style, Skinner had tried to describe linguistic competence by way of statistical "analysis" of stimulus and response, which led to, as Chomsky put it, "masses of unanalyzed data." In contrast, he insisted on the complexity of "inner representations" underlying language processes. Whatever he himself meant by that, they are what we are trying to elucidate more closely by our efforts. Chomsky explicitly stated this in his review: "One would naturally expect that prediction of the behavior of a complex organism (or machine) would require, in addition to information about external stimulation, knowledge of the internal structure of the organism, the ways in which it processes input information and organizes its own behavior."[43] As you know, I don't want to limit Chomsky's thoughts, which are close to me, to the subject of language alone. Let me quote internal notes of mine commenting on Yarden Katz's interview: "Chomsky says something more clearly than I have ever read before: 'The externalization [! he seems to mean the level of language/speech] is yielding all kinds of ambiguities but for simple computational reasons, it seems that the system internally [does he now refer to what he earlier called 'deep structure'?] is just computing efficiently, it doesn't care about the externalization[44] [...]. That tells something about evolution. What it strongly suggests is that in the evolution of language, a computational system developed, and later on it was externalized [if he refers to the thinking 'system' here, he means what we have 'always meant' – only that Chomsky still views it under the general heading of 'language']. And if you think about how a language might have evolved, you're almost driven to that position. At some point in human evolution, and it's apparently pretty recent given the archeological record – maybe [the] last hundred thousand years, which is nothing – at some point a computational system emerged w[hich] had new properties, that other organisms don't have, that has kind of arithmetical type properties … [Katz:] It enabled better thought before externalization? Chomsky: It gives you thought. Some rewiring of the brain, that happens in a single person, not in a group. So that person had the capacity for thought – the group didn't. So there isn't any point in externalization [! here suddenly language is left out]. Later on, if this genetic change proliferates, maybe a lot of people have it, okay then there's a point in figuring out a way to map it to the sensory-motor system and that's externalization but it's a secondary process'."[45]

In this direction – "the system is internally computing efficiently, it does not care about the externalization" – we must push on with our questions (which we already begun, cf. the following two conversations). I don't think that language analysis would be particularly promising for it.

1   Wiener, Oswald, 2001. Remarks on Some Tendencies of the "Vienna Group," translated by David Britt. *October*, 97, 124–126.

2   Adrian, Marc, 1980. *inventionen*. Linz, Vienna.

3   In: Rühm, Gerhard (ed.), 1985. *Die Wiener Gruppe. Texte, Gemeinschaftsarbeiten, Aktionen*. Reinbek, 297. Cf. Rühm's remark on the blueprint, ibid., 487.

4   The people sitting opposite the author in the semi-darkness move, turn their heads in conversation, and drink alcoholic beverages. One or two friends sit across from the narrator, who pays attention only to their shadows, which he gives names to ("kroneis," "otto," "elfie," "alma," "wilma," etc.). He describes how the shadows relate to each other in optical terms and speaks of them getting longer, shorter, splitting, expanding, etc.

5   Hogan, Patrick Colm, 2014. *Ulysses and the Poetics of Cognition*. New York, 6.

6   James, William, 1890. *The Principles of Psychology*, Vol. I. New York, 243. For a critique of James's metaphor, see Wiener's essay in this volume.

7   Bühler, Karl, 1909. Über das Sprachverständnis vom Standpunkt der Normalpsychologie aus. *Bericht über den III. Kongreß für experimentelle Psychologie in Frankfurt a. Main vom 22. bis 25. April 1908*. Leipzig, 94–130.

8   Stein, Gertrude, 1949. Four Saints in Three Acts. In: Vechten, Carl van (ed.), *Last Operas and Plays*. New York, Toronto, 440–480.

9   Wiener, Oswald, 1987. Wittgensteins Einfluß auf die Wiener Gruppe. In: Walter-Buchebner-Gesellschaft (ed.), *die wiener gruppe*. Vienna, Cologne, 46–59.

10   Ibid., 52, 56.

11   Ibid., 53.

12   Ibid., 53.

13   Ibid., 54–55.

14   Wiener, Oswald, 1998 [1982]. Eine Art Einzige. In: id., *Literarische Aufsätze*. Vienna, 43–85, here: 81.

15   Scheibert, Peter, 1956. *Von Bakunin zu Lenin: Geschichte der russischen revolutionären Ideologien 1840–1895. 1: Die Formung des radikalen Denkens in der Auseinandersetzung mit deutschem Idealismus und französischem Bürgertum*. Leiden.

16   Wiener, Oswald, 1969. *die verbesserung von mitteleuropa, roman*. Reinbek, XV.

17   Wiener, Oswald, 2007. Über das „Sehen" im Traum (Zweiter Teil). *manuskripte*, 178, 161–172.

18   Wiener, Oswald, 2019. appendix A: the bio-adapter, translated by Gerrit Jackson and Jakob Schillinger. *October*, 170, 51.

19   Ibid., 53.

20   Descartes, René, 1641. *Meditations on First Philosophy*, translated by Jonathan Bennett. www.earlymoderntexts.com/assets/pdfs/descartes1641_1.pdf (28 Apr 2023).

21   These and further aspects of Wiener's principal early work *die verbesserung von mitteleuropa, roman* are discussed by Nicola Cipani in an extensive commentary, including a theoretical introduction: Cipani, Nicola, 2022. *Zur Theorie eines ", roman". Oswald Wieners "verbesserung von mitteleuropa": Ein Kommentar*. Baden-Baden.

22   Wiener, Oswald, 1987. Wittgensteins Einfluß auf die Wiener Gruppe. In: Walter-Buchebner-Gesellschaft (ed.), *die wiener gruppe*. Vienna, Cologne, 46–59, here: 48.

23   Cf. Eder, Thomas, 2013. Nachwort. In: Wiener, Oswald, *die verbesserung von mitteleuropa, roman*. New edition ed. Thomas Eder. Salzburg, Vienna, 207–220, here: 213.

24   Wiener, Oswald, 1969. *die verbesserung von mitteleuropa, roman*. Reinbek, CLXXXIII.

25   Flores, Iván, 1960. *Computer Logic: Functional Design of Digital Computers*. Englewood Cliffs; Trachtenbrot, Boris A., 1959. *Wieso können Automaten rechnen?* Cologne.

26   Wiener, Oswald, 1996. *Schriften zur Erkenntnistheorie*. Vienna, New York.

27   Wiener, Oswald, 1969. *die verbesserung von mitteleuropa, roman*. Reinbek bei Hamburg, CXXIX.

28   Wiener, Oswald, 1998. Bemerkungen zu einigen Tendenzen der „Wiener Gruppe“. In: Kunsthalle Wien, Fetz, Wolfgang, and Gerald Matt (eds.), *Die Wiener Gruppe*, Vienna, 20–28, here: 27.

29   Sola Pool, Ithiel de (ed.), 1959. *Trends in Content Analysis*. Urbana.

30   Cf. Wiener, Oswald, 2015. Kybernetik und Gespenster: Im Niemandsland zwischen Wissenschaft und Kunst. *manuskripte*, 207, 143–162. See the unchanged text also in this volume.

31   Heubach, Friedrich Wolfram, 2017. *le dandysme*. Hamburg.

32   August Klotz quoted in: Jadi, Inge (ed.), 1985. *Leb wohl sagt mein Genie. Ordugele muß sein. Texte aus der Prinzhorn-Sammlung*. Heidelberg, 215. The entire text passage is: "The Pilsen beer stamp does not lack the hair worm, it is itself. / a) (am no beer agent) / and red tail grass comports itself handpurely essential like fibers / b) ad=acquisition bottles (beer (ad bubbly) quittance bottle (?0) / thicket of ivy yeast through mountain water of the nose tips:" [„Dem Pilsener Bierstempel fehlt der Haarwurm nicht, er ist es selbst. / a) (Bin kein Bieragent) / und Rothschwanzgras führet sich handrein wesentlich wie Fasern / b)ad= acquisitionsflaschen (Bier- (ad Sekt)-) Quittungsflasche (?0) / dickicht der Efeuhefe durch das Bergwasser der Nasenspitzen:"].

33   Wiener, Oswald, 1998. Wahl eines Wortes. In: id., *Literarische Aufsätze*, Vienna, 111–112.

34   Eder, Thomas, 2015. Selbstbeobachtung und Sprachverstehen: Beim Hersagen eines Gedichts von Paul Celan. In: Eder, Thomas, and Thomas Raab (eds.), *Selbstbeobachtung: Oswald Wieners Denkpsychologie*. Berlin, 315–371, here: 315–316.

35   Wiener, Oswald, 1970. subjekt, sema[n]tik, abbildungsbeziehungen. ein pro-memoria. *manuskripte*, 29/30, 45–50.

36   Wiener, Oswald, 1975. Was ist der Inhalt dieses Satzes, was du draus entnimmst, was hast du draus entnommen, wirst du dir auch das Leben nehmen, den neuen Salat probieren, erröten. Lecture at the colloquium *Die Sprache des Anderen [The Language of the Other]* by the Société Internationale de Psychopathologie de l'Expression. In: *Gedanken* (ed. Brus, Günter, and Oswald Wiener). Berlin, Oct. 22 1975, 23, 24, 27, here: 23.

37   Wiener, Oswald, 2008. Über das „Sehen“ im Traum (Dritter Teil). *manuskripte*, 181, 132–141, here: 133–134.

38   Wiener, Oswald, personal correspondence, 2014.

39   Marcel, Anthony J., 1980. Conscious and Preconscious Recognition of Polysemous Words: Locating the Selective Effects of Prior Verbal Context. In: Nickerson, Raymond S. (ed.), *Attention and Performance VIII*. Hillsdale, NJ, 435–457.

40   Ibid., 436–437, 453.

41   Cf. Eder's essay in this volume.

42   Chomsky, Noam, and Yarden Katz, 2012. Noam Chomsky on Where Artificial Intelligence Went Wrong. Noam Chomsky Interviewed by Yarden Katz. *The Atlantic*, 1 Nov 2012, https://philpapers.org/archive/KATNCO.pdf (28 Jan 2022).

43   Chomsky, Noam, 1959. Verbal behavior. *Language*, 35/1, 26–58, here: 27.

44   The example brought up by Chomsky shortly before in the interview is this: "There are cases where you find clear conflicts between computational efficiency and communicative efficiency. Take a simple case, structural ambiguity. If I say, 'Visiting relatives can be a nuisance' – that's ambiguous. Relatives that visit, or going to visit relatives. It turns out in every such case that's known, the ambiguity is derived by simply allowing the rules to function freely, with no constraints, and that sometimes yields ambiguities. So it's computationally efficient, but it's inefficient for communication, because it leads to unresolvable ambiguity." Cf. Eder's essay in this volume.

45   Chomsky, Noam, and Yarden Katz, see note 42.

From Machines to the Psychology of Thought

A Conversation between Oswald Wiener
and Thomas Raab

After having abandoned his literary collaboration with the "Vienna Group," Oswald Wiener was hired in the 1960s by the Italian office machine company Olivetti as a corporate salesman and data engineer. His involvement in book-keeping machines and punch card procedures led him to the then new field of cybernetics, which left its traces in the concept of the bio-adapter in *the improvement of central europe, novel.* The essentials of computation as elaborated by Alan Turing dominated the next step of intense study. Soon, the definition of structures as Turing machines became the fundament for all of Wiener's further ideas on the theory of thought and artificial intelligence. Since the end of the 1990s, Wiener regularly worked with a group of scientists and artists on introspection experiments in the psychology of thought and neighboring fields. Among them are Benjamin Angerer, Nicola Cipani, Thomas Eder, Tanja Gesell, Thomas Raab, Stefan Schneider, Cornell Schreiber, Michael Schwarz, and Johannes Ullmaier.

Structure

TR: Your definition of structure has not changed since the 1980s and 1990s, when your theory revolved around notions such as model and (internal) screen. Also today, while you are mostly speaking of seed, assembly, and orientation, this definition stayed the same: "A structure of a string is a Turing machine generating or accepting this string."

OW: Yes, in the *Materialien* book from 2000, I already quoted this from my earlier work. The definition had been printed for the first time in my 1988 paper "Form and Content in Thinking Turing Machines."[1]

TR: Although this definition of structure, which serves as the "anchor" of your theoretic construction, is stringent, it is not provable. Yet, it is intuitive because nobody can deny *perceiving* patterns and regularities in nature. And these are structures or, at this level of description, "forms." We never *experience* anything formless and cannot conceive of a non-form. Nevertheless, you can't prove your definition because it is epistemological and not scientific!

In the introduction to our introspection book, I suggested that with this kind of theorizing you fall between the cracks of science on the one hand and the Romantic "cult of the ego" on the other. Your definition is objective insofar as it can be materialized on computers and yet it stems from epistemic intuition, that is, from introspection.[2]

Beside this peculiar – or should I say timeless or, even, far eastern – feature,[3] psychologists or philosophers cannot readily see how to *apply* this notion of structure. Did you hit on the "structuralist" Jean Piaget, whose developmental ideas lurk in the background of your thinking, for that reason?

OW: What you say about structure may be right, but I discovered Piaget later. In fact it's the other way around: Only when I had found my notion of structure could I productively understand Piaget's whirling ideas.[4] In *Materialien,* I quoted only four of his works because I didn't know many more then. *Play, Dreams and Imitation in Childhood* sparked my interest. The rest of his oeuvre I later read step by step. My interest culminated around 2005 to 2007 and in any case *after* working on my book *Vorstellungen,* which I never finished.

TR: Anyway this Piagetian background warrants that you can build up a psychological theory from simplest organisms to epistemology *without having to postulate anything ontologically new* on the way.

OW: I had the same idea before. What I found and still find important in Piaget is that he stresses the processual character of knowing as well as of motor processes at the expense of sensory processes. His problem of the figurative, which I also touched on in the *Selbstbeobachtung* book, shows me, that he himself had no clear notion of the biological aspect of thought but got stuck in teleological description. Animals are controlled by instincts and so their behavior heads for an objective "goal state." Obviously this is not the case in human thought, at least not in a direct sense.

TR: So Piaget first of all only tried to specify which tasks a person is able to do at which developmental stage and how s/he learns to cope with them?

OW: Yes. In doing this he established that there are no "mental images" in the sense of Kosslyn,[5] which he rather harshly dismissed in his and Bärbel Inhelder's *Mental Imagery in the Child*. But he had the same difficulties as I had, namely explaining to himself why we undeniably seem to *experience* images. I know only of a few introspections by Piaget but this problem always pops up there. One could show that the notion of mental image has not been passed down from one author to the next but obviously is the first, albeit primitive, step towards introspection proper.

TR: Do you believe that everybody naturally believes in mental images?

OW: Yes. The "mental image" as well as the "inner eye" are common figures of speech, which no one ever invented. They simply suggest themselves because we can't compare our "inner" experience with anything else. According to our experience, to imagine something is similar to perceiving something.[6] Moreover, people who don't think much about such matters tend to believe that they don't see things but images of things.

TR: Oh, I never thought so. Does this result from the epistemologically naive notion of pictures on the retina?

OW: Yes. I too wrote in 1969 in the *bio-adapter*,[7] that you don't see your legs, for instance, but their image. This might be true as far as my concept of the *bio-adapter* is concerned but it is utter nonsense as a psychological proposition.

TR: So Piaget, who came to deny mental images, and his notions of schemas as well as of genetic epistemology were already on your mind when you released *Materialien* in 2000?

OW: Yes, but first I had to understand what a schema is. So I made shifts by conceiving it as an automaton.

TR: Fair enough, but where does one schema end and another begin? At least we have the intuition that "one movement" stops and another starts. But does this intuition suffice for theorizing?

OW: As of today we don't know. But conceptually there is no other way than postulating such simplifications, because otherwise one can only ramble on about epistemology. You must begin by tentatively defining phenomena.

TR: Okay, now I can say that my orientation consists of sensorimotor schemas, which is no doubt correct at this level of description. But I don't know how these schemas are organized, so it doesn't help a lot.

Schema

A schema (term first used by Kant, cf. Lohmar 1991) is an idealized sensorimotor control unit converting (preprocessed) sensory signals into effector control signals in order to reach a situational "goal." Unfortunately, the concept of goal is ambiguous. On the one hand, it denotes a material counterpart on which the schema operates — the target or object. On the other hand, it denotes temporary physiological "satisfaction" yielded by the fulfilled action. This ambivalence of "inner" and "outer" goal refers to the conceptual problems at the core of the notion of schema to be listed at the end of this note.

The fine-tuning of the execution of a schema occurs "online," i.e., by continuous adjustment to the feedback from kinesthetic, proprioceptive, visual, auditory, etc., signals to the schema itself (Desmurget and Grafton 2000). Arbib (2003) located the power of this theoretical concept in the fact that, because of its functional definition, one is able to desist from considerations on its physical realization. Thus, it can be applied likewise to psychology, AI, and neuroscience in the hope of future convergence.

By yet another idealization, a schema can be conceived as a machine controlling an "action" in definable steps, which are fine-tuned by continuous sensory feedback (Wiener 2000). This interpretation builds on the introspective intuition that each and every body movement has a beginning and an end, the latter by reaching the aforementioned double goal.

As an example for both the power and the problems of the concept of schema, I want to briefly discuss the crucial "grasping schema." Its execution tentatively begins with the movement of the entire arm towards the target object, let's say, a cup of tea. The latter is the goal in the first sense, that of target. The goal in the second sense is the somatically marked state of, say, "having quenched thirst." The description of the somatic goal is, of course, too complicated to be put down here.

Now the execution of the crude steering of the hand toward the cup is ballistic, even if small adaptations of direction and speed are possible depending on situational change. Near the target, the arm movement slows down and the hand opens slightly. Only at this point do visual feedback seem to become prominent. The necessary fine control of the fingers does not start until there is tactile contact. This "clutching" is once more definable as a distinct phase of the schema. It lasts until the hand clutches the cup firmly enough to lead the cup toward the lips. This is marked by an "okay-feeling," which is registered most saliently when the cup, for instance due to its geometry, has to be stabilized by the pinky.

The fact that this schema, whose fine-tuning is certainly very complicated in terms of physiology, can be denoted by a term and its execution described by words seems to make it, at least didactically, definable. In short, a schema is the prototype of its particular execution, which is adapted on the fly by sensory and somatosensory feedback (time pressure, somatic and other biological parameters), in order to reach its target and goal.

The execution thus affords a dynamic embedding of each focal schema into the current *dynamical hierarchy* (aka heterarchy) of other schemas. However intricately interlocked this embedding might be and however many potential interruption points exist in the schema's execution, my remarks so far exclusively concern the control of schemas from the "outside" — by exteroceptive and proprioceptive signals.

At least in humans (and probably all higher primates) this execution is further embedded into an historical, social, and mundane *orientation* characterized by intermittent thinking, i.e., assembly and *figurative proxies* of partial aspects of the current situation. These control signals, registered as "motor impulses" or "seeds" (Wiener 2015a) control the ballistic schema execution according to more long-term "psycho-economic" goals inhibiting instinctual and physiological goals.

Already in attentive perception you can observe that again and again inactive schemas are "called" by stimuli at the fringe, although the focus of orientation remains at the target. For example, I sometimes spontaneously register a muscular impulse onset in the shoulder while observing the narrow flight curve of a bird in front of my window. My body seems to spontaneously "imitate" the bird. Sometimes, such an irritation might even serve as the unexpected trigger of an idea for a current problem I am facing. Although motorically generic, the schema output may thus become the seed for a productive thought if embedded in an adequate running environment. Attending more carefully, one is able to register such seeds several times a day.

I believe Wiener's ideo-motor theory of thought to be so parsimonious because in the dynamics of a productive construction environment controlling the assembly process, the *same* schemas are at work as in perception and locomotion, although they are now used to habituate new structural complexes. In order to do so, they have to be temporarily retained in a running environment by a "task pressure." So the preconscious parts of orientation now become a construction environment serving as "working memory" (for the "secondary process," as Freud [1953] named it) and enabling new sub-structures and schema connections. No less parsimonious is the fact that in this theory both the "figurative" aspects of thinking, that is, "mental images" as surrogates of objects, as well as their manipulation can be interpreted as motor signal sequences.

Despite all caveats, the following result of introspection on formal tasks (having solutions coherent with accepted formal premises) seems clear: Both processes of type 1 (surrogating the object) and processes of type 2 (surrogating the action on them) operate on the *initial impulses* of schemas and not their ballistic execution (Wiener 2015b). In introspection as well as in thought (as a subcategory of introspection, namely without psychological goal), we inhibit and thus affectively register the onset of action. Thought does not use the resources of schema execution, let alone their entire control and feedback signals, to heuristically find solutions or avoid errors. Hence the noticeable effort to fixate aspects of the proxy object during processes of type 1 in order to operate on their output during processes of type 2.

So much for the heuristic merits of the concept of schema as far as they are relevant for psychology and neuroscience. Now for its main problems:

1. The dynamics and plasticity outlined suggest that the demarcation of "single" schemas seems intuitive but, in terms of physiological implementation, arguably fictitious. Not only is their coordination controlled by the interplay of many, if not all and even the "highest" cortical regions. It is even unclear whether or not they would allow for the heuristic distinction between afferent and efferent, which is so central for both physiology and contemporary cognitive science. Which region inhibits which, and which excites which? From a neurophysiological perspective schemas certainly do not originate in the motor cortex and end in sensory fields. There simply is no sensor/motor "interface" (Freeman 1995).

2. Introspection even during "purely" formal tasks shows that assembly is not working with "pure" schemas which are somehow "stored" in the construction environment. On the contrary, subjects report that the schema-output observed as intuition is always embedded in a "symbolic" and autobiographical environment which might interfere with the current assembly process (Wiener and Schwarz 2023). In short, assembly is subject to "primary" condensation, displacement, and repression processes (Anna Freud 1937). By way of functioning as an analogy, these at times "auto-symbolic" quasi-images (Silberer 1909) may even be productive for the thought process (Schwarz 2015, Gentner et al. 2001). Yet, more often this – in relation to the task at hand: – "psychoanalytic noise" distracts or misleads. Here the lack of a plausible theory of memory both in general psychology and psychoanalysis becomes painfully apparent (cf. Raab 2023).

3. A relative, but not congruent, much underestimated aspect is addiction. Schemas get fixated first by reaching their instinctual and later derived goal (in the second sense above) reinforced by external and later internal gratification. Their "pathways" habituate by positive feedback through endorphin release. This addiction learning is necessary insofar as it provides for the *functional* stability of schemas, which is restored by "neural plasticity" even after fairly grave physiological failure. So the mere use of a schema is often experienced as positive (Piaget's "functional pleasure"). This again is a cue to why it is difficult to decouple schemas, which is necessary for the ideomotor thought process. Everybody knows the experience that thinking has to proceed against some inner resistance, against mind wandering, against phantasies, against the urge to move. Thinking is effortful. A corollary of this observation is that nobody ever seems to get "addicted" to thinking. On the contrary, entropic mind wandering seems to be the baseline behavior of waking consciousness both in perception and thought. In contrast to thought uninhibited sensorimotor behavior such as sport, making music, and so on can very well be addictive (Becker 1992).

Summary: For the scientific theory of schema so crucial for general, and personality psychology, we dearly lack specific guidelines of the neurophysiological realization of schemas as well as more precise introspections of the "psychoanalytical noise" of underlying motivational layers of thinking (of the "primary process" in Sigmund as well as Anna Freud) accompanying formal and everyday tasks (the "secondary process").

Arbib, Michael A., 2003. Schema Theory. In: id. (ed.), *The Handbook of Brain Theory and Neural Networks*. Cambridge, MA, 993–998.

Becker, Gary S., 1992. Habits, Addictions, and Traditions. *Kyklos*, 45/3, 327–346.

Desmurget, Michel, and Scott Grafton, 2000. Forward Modeling Allows Feedback Control for Fast Reaching Movements. *Trends in Cognitive Sciences*, 4/11, 423–431.

Freeman, Walter, 1995. *Societies of Brains*. Hillsdale, NJ.

Freud, Anna, 1937 [1936]. *The Ego and the Mechanisms of Defence*, trans. Cecil Baines. London.

Freud, Sigmund, 1953 [1901]. *The Interpretation of Dreams*. In: Strachey, James (ed.), *The Standard Edition of the Complete Psychological Works of Sigmund Freud*, Vols. 4 and 5. London.

Gentner, Dedre, Keith J. Holyoak, and Boicho K. Kokinov (eds.), 2001. *The Analogical Mind*. Cambridge, MA.

Lohmar, Dieter, 1991. Kants Schemas als Anwendungsbedingungen von Kategorien auf Anschauungen. *Zeitschrift für philosophische Forschung*, 45/1, 77–92.

Piaget, Jean, 1951. *Play, Dreams, and Imitation in Childhood*. London.

Raab, Thomas, 2023. Fantasy, Repression, and Motivation in an Ecological Model of Memory. In this volume, 273–302.

Michael, Schwarz, 2015. Introspektive Aspekt des Operativen und Figurativen in Bezug zur Laufumgebung. In: Eder, Thomas, and Thomas Raab (eds.), *Selbstbeobachtung: Oswald Wieners Denkpsychologie*. Berlin, 165–189.

Wiener, Oswald, 2000. see note 1.

Wiener, Oswald, 2015a. Glossar: Weiser. In: Eder, Thomas, and Thomas Raab (eds.), *Selbstbeobachtung: Oswald Wieners Denkpsychologie*. Berlin, 59–98.

Wiener, Oswald, 2015b. Glossar: figurativ. In: Eder, Thomas, and Thomas Raab (eds.), *Selbstbeobachtung: Oswald Wieners Denkpsychologie*. Berlin, 99–141.

Wiener, Oswald, and Michael Schwarz, 2023. Pleomorphism in Thought and the Computational Metaphor. In this volume, 101–163.

TR

OW: Absolutely true. The main question remains: How do we get finished structures by this improvising and obviously tedious construction in "living thought," as Piaget says.

TR: Is this tediousness also an aspect of the widespread impression of experiencing "mental images"?

OW: Yes. First we need to possess prototypes,[8] that is, coarse versions of the finished structures, to control construction during the thought process. And secondly this construction cannot function without quasi-images because the latter enable creativity by letting different schemas react on them.

TR: These quasi-images are not images proper insofar as they do not have a sensory mode, but are rather hinges connecting different schemas. So are they "amodal"?

OW: At least less naive introspection suggests so. We experience schemas as quasi-visual, quasi-acoustic, and so forth, but only due to our perceptual habits of controlling orientation by stimuli.[9]

TR: But still you believe that this approach is more productive than the ones in academic psychology, because the formalization of the notion of schema by structure bridges the gap between the "idealism" of Kant's schema notion and ethology as well as, further on, psychology?

OW: Sure, but it remains a postulate as long as the human organism is not properly understood in crucial respects such as the psychological one.

The intrusion as an example of a seed, and its development through assembly

TR: In *Materialien* you conceived of (insight) learning of a new model, i.e., of a new regularity describable as a structure according to the definition above, as a constructive process. Within the running environment consisting of schemas, you discern a construction environment consisting of schemas primed so as to be possibly interconnected to form a new model during the thought process. This conception is akin to the one of biological constructivists such as Humberto Maturana. Back in 2000, I think that I understood your concept of "model" quite well, as it was formally defined in Turing machine terms, but in contrast to Maturana it seemed not so well grounded in the more biological strata of orientation. By introducing the intuitively catchier notions of seed and orientation[10] you accommodated your ideas to the flexibility of biology and physiology, I suppose. How did this step come about? Do these newer concepts stem from introspection?

OW: Yes. I had similar ideas before, but, as far as I remember, the term seed (in German "Weiser") did not yet occur to me. Still, I remember having already used it in conversations with my friend Helmut Schöner in Dawson City during the 1990s. But my concept of it was still too blurry to adapt it to the theory.

TR: Wasn't the concept of seed in the beginning synonymous with "imageless", i.e. amodal or quasi image, which hundreds of years ago led to heavy and unproductive controversy in the German "Denkpsychologie"[11] or psychology of thought?[12]

OW: Yes, but in turn the concept of seed helped my introspection to better attend to phenomena which I call "intrusions" – sudden "mindpops" experienced as images. Some intrusion experiences from that time I still remember quite clearly.

Intrusions are very brief. Just *how* brief one can only estimate, but certainly not longer than one second. Nevertheless, one gets the impression to know exactly what the intrusion is about. At times, this might even be a very complex relationship.

Here, many questions come to my mind. One question is whether or not these intrusions are connected to the events registered in the seconds or minutes before.[13] Our introspections have already shown that this question has largely to remain open. However, there are rare cases in which a hypothetical connection can be established. Such connections have much to do with mechanisms also active in dreaming. An intrusion may, for instance, illustrate a word. In this respect I still find Freud's ideas very productive.[14]

I'd like to recount an intrusion I had in Canada during the 1990s. I registered the seed of a nightly scene which had left a deep trace in my memory. Sometime in the 1950s, I drove together with my first wife, Lore Heuermann, from the Olivetti headquarters in Vienna back to Judenburg in Upper Styria where we lived at the time. Many kilometers ahead of us, we already saw a flashing indicator in the clear but moonless night. It took us fifteen more minutes to get there. When we arrived we saw a truck set aside on an overpass. Probably the driver had parked it there to be maximally visible. A small Fiat had driven into it from behind, and behind the steering wheel of this car sat – dead – the village doctor. The turn signal was blinking on and on. I could still provide many more details of this scene.

What is important though is that the seed experientially already implied the entire episode.

TR: When did you have the intrusion?

OW: Many years later, in the 1990s. I can't remember the occasion because I am so used to this kind of experience. I guess we have such intrusions all the time but mostly they just go unnoticed.

If you want to develop the seed, as I began to do with my short account, it is clear that you have to *build up* the entire complex. In doing so you clearly notice that this affords some effort. You put something into a sequence, not only because you use language which is inherently sequential, but also because there is no other way to capture the meaning of the scene in order to let it have the same effect on you as it had in the first place. This construction process suggests the concept of assembly.

TR: That means you have to assemble if you want to reconstruct what you have "seen" in this short period of less than one second?

OW: No, you have to already assemble even if you only want to simply *know* what this seed was about! At first you only notice: Hey, there is something familiar! I know that the intrusion means something but I don't know *what*. At first I merely experience an attunement, a "complex quality."[15]

Inner models (psychological aspect) experienced as regularities (epistemological aspect) to be represented as Turing machines (formal aspect)

TR: An assembly thus serves the stepwise clarification of something seemingly determined from the outset, when it emerges as an intrusion, for instance. Otherwise, you could not reconstruct the details because you wouldn't know which one fits and which doesn't. Functionally, the registered attunement or intrusion hence points toward a prototype of its detailed readinesses (of schemas), which have to be arranged to a whole?

OW: Concerning the concept of prototype: Quite early on I realized while programming a Turing machine that this machine epitomizes what one commonly calls a clear thought. You begin with simple programming tasks such as a copy machine or, even simpler, a finite automaton computing whether the number of symbols on the tape is even or odd. The latter you can manage by programming a TM with three states. *How* you interlace these three states is just what I termed "representation of the representation" in 2007.[16] Now you can denote exactly what the machine does: It reacts in *one* way, if the number of symbols is even, and in the *other* way, if it is odd.

TR: So you came to this concept, which you first called prototype, while programming?

OW: No, at first it came to me while scrutinizing Turing's famous paper of 1937. It's not very easy to understand and so it took me several attempts. At first I didn't catch what Turing meant by "cycle-free machine" because he formulated very clumsily, which is often the case with pioneers of his stature.[17] I always fell back on his claim that a human being who calculates, i.e. his "computer," can be formalized as a read/write-head with inner states. Besides I believed from the outset that he didn't abstract this concept from the observation of other people but from his own introspection. Furthermore, I instantly doubted the extreme polarization of the process into symbols on the one hand and machine on the other.

In the course of the paper, Turing explicitly desists from human experience in favor of technical feasibility. In my second essay on dreams I thus quoted him: "*the use of more complicated states of mind can be avoided by writing more symbols on the tape*" (250).[18] Therefore, the most complex computation is but a sequence of most elementary meaningless actions of only two kinds: change of symbol on the current cell on the tape or change of cell (251).

In my exegesis, I continue by criticizing his method: "But to substitute the process by description does not get rid of the dynamics, which now resides in the agency controlled by the description; and although it proceeds in sequences consisting of simplest states, it cannot circumvent the problems of complexity: although complicated states have been replaced by sequences of simplest states, the specifics of the process must be retained in the specifics of the respective sequence."

TR: Behavioristically inclined as he was, Turing thus wanted to reduce the number of distinct (mental or mechanical) states in order to transfer complexity to the machine's tape – in other words: to its environment. The machine description becomes smaller and smaller, but the numbers of both symbol types and the length of strings written on the tape become larger and larger.[19] Does your criticism pertain to the fact that thereby the computation itself does not become easier?

OW: You just shouldn't forget that by shifting the trade-off between outer and inner complexity, you might conjure away the actual problem![20] For the true question remains: *How* do these elementary states follow each other? Turing charmed away this question. First you had one very complex state and now you have sequences of very simple states. But there are infinitely many of them! Why this sequence and no other? The very effectivity of the machine results from finding the correct sequence and not from the sequence itself.

TR: So Turing already killed meaningful structure by brute force computation just as in today's machine learning?

OW: Yes, Turing let structure just vanish! This is exactly the problem of applying Turing machines to the psychology of thought. The engineering "solution" of the problem of intelligence simply conjures away intelligence because it shuns introspection and numbly stares at "adult," i.e., fully learned behavior. Without introspection there will never be any progress in psychology!

TR: In other words, Turing's view is too abstract because it does not encompass the *development* of structures! Viewed from very far away it may well be just as he described it, but psychology cannot afford this view from afar because it deals with concrete and biologically constrained events, which we register only in introspection. Is Turing's level of observation just empirically beyond reach?

OW: That is exactly my opinion! In the aforementioned essay I thus continue: "So Turing's analysis is far too abstract for the psychology of thought. Crucial is the *genesis* of such sequences depending on the *physical implementation* of these simplest states, which introspection identifies as those *foci* 'of only two or three most simple elements.' (...) We have to understand, how these sequences emerge as configurations of *modules* or subsequences. For Turing, these are all but *strings*, i.e., sequences of names of the standardized elementary actions."

So, as quoted before, Turing reduced complexity by increasing the symbols on the tape. By this he meant the description of a specific Turing machine written on the tape of a universal Turing machine.

Just as almost all AI researchers following him he conjured away the true problem. He presupposed that such machines and their descriptions simply exist. But who brought them? The Easter Bunny?

TR: So Turing's problem was not only that he was behavioristically minded as proven by his famous test, according to which a machine is intelligent if it *behaves* like a human.[21] He also misinterpreted the core function of intelligence, which is active structure *building* instead of structure *application*? And you believe that his misinterpretation is the result of failing to observe how he himself solved problems?

OW: Look, I always came back to the fact that a string of symbols does not do anything! It just exists somewhere. What is the essence of a Turing machine description? It is itself a string of symbols. But if this is so, then of course it *is not* the structure itself.

Already as a computer science student at the Technical University of Berlin at the beginning of the 1980s, I had the idea that the table of a Turing machine is the "content" of the string on the tape which it accepts. Then I compared that to my introspection and finally made up my mind. One thing is certain: If I understand something clearly, then I can program a Turing machine representing it. Therefore, Turing machines must be *products of intelligence*! And structure is what such a machine is doing *from the perspective of an observer*.

That's how I arrived at my basic definition of structure.

The problem of describing "living thought"

TR: Let's pin that down: There is a stringent definition of structure but in "living thought," as Piaget called it, we hardly ever experience anything stringent. Instead, our mind wanders, we get distracted, tired. One could even say, our brain "struggles" against insights. But if, as you say, understanding human intelligence crucially depends on introspection, how can we describe this chaos as adequately and, above all, as realistically as possible?

In retrospect, it seems no wonder that the descriptions of introspections in your partly idiosyncratic terms had a difficult birth. Everyday language or auxiliary drawings represent objects and not experiences. Once you start describing the latter, you instantly have to rely on the cloudy concepts which haunt psychology to this day: perception, emotion, attention, cognition even, etc. Mental phenomena have no analog in the objective world, and so introspections are obviously so hard to describe that the body revolts against it. In this view, Turing only followed "common sense," because the products of intelligence can be described as objects, that is, as machines.

Do you believe that one could somehow shortcut your decade-long struggle with concepts and their interaction with introspection? That would be nice for those who newly want to embark on introspection. Is there a way to faster unlearn the aforementioned natural attitude towards thought?

OW: If we had a dogma, this dogma would be the shortcut. But we don't have a dogma. It is important to me to let the difficulties that I have and had in understanding these things show in everything that I utter. That's why my theory always remains tentative. Concepts such as seed, orientation, assembly, and attunement which only gradually came to the fore, are quite obviously not the ultimate concepts of a viable theory of thought.

TR: Why is the central new concept of seed so important?

OW: Crucial for me was the insight that a seed is not a string but the beginning of an assembly. This meant a true progress but still it's not enough. We need much more detailed knowledge how the brain "implements" seeds.

TR: But shouldn't the first step be to describe seeds better as an observational category?

OW: Well, that is what we tried in the 2015 book *Selbstbeobachtung*. But as we observe internal structures while thinking, and the habitual description of the outer world provides for sensory metaphors only, our descriptions turned out quite clumsily. Maybe that's why the almost synonymous notions of attunement and complex quality became so prominent lately.

TR: Could the notion of attunement as a generic structure accepting very many to all objects serve as a theoretical link between orientation and seed?

OW: To me an attunement is a mixture of readinesses, that is, of sensorimotor schemas that became preconscious, so that you are able to register them. As for now the notion is not so much a theoretical as an empirical link.

TR: Sometimes you use attunement like psychotherapists in the sense of mood, that is, as an affective category. Yet sometimes you use it more in the sense of prototype, as a still undeveloped seed. In the latter use, the emotional or bodily aspect sinks into the background. Could you elaborate on this?

OW: Well, because of its linking character attunement has both a theoretical and an empirical aspect. To put it a bit coquettishly: for the good of the theory of thought based on introspection attunement can be partially "operationalized," as psychology has it. Thus it's (self-) observable. With due reservations, of course.

TR: One last aside concerning the established psychological terminology where "attention" can be either "overt," that is, measurable as
saccades, or "covert," that is, unmeasurable.[22] Does "attention" always
presuppose assembly, both in perception and in thinking?

OW: At least attention and assembly have common aspects. Yet they
are not the same. For me, attention is not a separate entity. We are
always attentive to something. Once you realize this, it becomes clear
what attention is. It isn't assembly as such but the current running
environment as part of overall orientation. Eventually, the running
and construction environments determine what I register and what
not. This *is* attention. Attention *is* a specific combination of readinesses. The more of them are fixed in the current running environment, the more "precise" is attention. If fewer are fixed, orientation
becomes more generally "vigilant."

Fake intelligence by enumeration algorithms and big data statistics

TR: You claim that the halting problem of Turing machines made
obsolete the utopia to build a machine able to construct an adequate
machine for any arbitrary well-defined task by sheer enumeration,
i.e., uncreatively and unconstructively. Humans construct struc-
tures/machines by a process, which is not "executed" but strongly
interacts with the environment. For this interaction you introduced
the concept of "coincidence" or "guided chance." "Guided" means that
chance is produced by the interaction of two fully determined constellations – namely, of the outer world and the structures in the
human organism – so that in the latter a constructive dynamics
ensues. This is a very productive idea, I think, because the entire psychology of everyday life comes to bear on the otherwise too inflexible
mechanistic notion of intelligence.

 Did you find out early on that *what* influences model construction
from the environment can, if at all, only be figured out by introspec-

tion? Or did it dawn on you gradually? Or did you even gather it from Freud's *Interpretation of Dreams*?

ow: Just like everything else I realized this step by step, I think.

Here we touch on something which also comes up in an interview with Noam Chomsky.[23] There he claims that the language-producing apparatus is not algorithmic. Without doubt he means exactly what you say: We have a malleable material, certainly specified by its internal laws of behavior, and yet it doesn't produce machines algorithmically but is guided by environmental bombardment. New machines are not computed or enumerated but emerge through interaction with the outer world.

What would be the opposite? We have often discussed the immense computing capacity of today's hardware constantly growing further at an enormous rate. By computing capacity I mean computation rate as well as storage space. Without much ado we can imagine a future phase of technology, when this capacity becomes larger than in today's computers by so many powers as the latters' now is in relation to the very first digital computer.

In my textbook, I have detailed out how a machine produces new machines without any insight.[24] I did this to help laypersons understand a few computational proofs. I showed, for instance, that one can put all Turing machines in successive order for the sake of enumerating them. Then I brought in a machine able to run all these machines on all strings on the tape, which is basically unnecessary because the empty tape suffices for the proof. This procedure can again be sequentialized and enumerated following Cantor's second diagonalization method. The entire procedure affords a terrible amount of computing capacity but it will also yield very complicated machines.

TR: How to assess all these machines?

ow: That's exactly the point! Of the thus generated machines those which will halt at some time can be used. But only if you already have an idea *what for*! In other words: you must *interpret* them. And this interpretation is impossible without internal models. There still remain those machines which have not halted (yet), but the others you can enumerate as a very special (sub-) set. The only bottleneck is the capacity for the enumerating mechanism.

This fits the allegory that even an army of apes will eventually write all the works of Shakespeare if only they are given enough time. Or Borges's *Library of Babel*. But this would only be possible if there is infinite time at one's disposal. It's impossible to enumerate all machines, but it isn't necessary because we only need those machines that fulfill specified tasks.

We have already mentioned the objection to this allegory. How are we supposed to know what tasks they are able to fulfil? Let's assume that such an enumeration procedure produces a Turing machine with a million states computing something. How can I find out *what* this is?

TR: So basically you don't know its application. In this respect, all fake intelligence has the same problem as Turing already had. An artificial neural net trained by machine learning to compute specific input-output relations also needs a human interpreter who knows what the input and what the output is supposed to mean. It may well be that big data programs operating on statistical premises handle specific tasks better than any human could ever do, for example in pattern recognition. But still it is humans who specified the task in the first place.[25]

OW: I say it again: In order to know what a machine does, you have to have a model of what it is good for. At this point Chomsky cannot help us either because he derived his concept of structure from linguistic syntax. The latter also includes an operand (the "subject" of a sentence), which is operated on (by the "verb"). Although it can thus be viewed as an analog to a finished thought object, it represents the *end result* of thought just like in AI. It too leaves out the living and messy construction process of thought.

Let's return to the simple machine computing whether the number of symbols on the string is odd or even. It is the end result of a model of this computation in the programmer. But as an observer I too must possess a model of this machine in order to know that I could use it for this specific task.

OW: I have to know what an even number is, for instance.

OW: Yes. But you can also state that the machine does different things under different perspectives.

TR: I understand: The environment of the machine specifies its function.

OW: Exactly. This might be unlikely with a machine as simple as the even-odd decision machine. Then again, it has been shown that there are machines with only five states which cannot be interpreted by human observers. I also explained that in the textbook on Turing machines. In the meantime, it has become a real sport to write the smallest possible machine writing as many characters as possible on the blank tape before it halts.[26]

TR: Let's note: Fake intelligence based on "genetic programming," "big data," or "machine learning" is seductive and gets confused with human intelligence all too easily because it always computes well-defined tasks. But if they have to stand the test in tasks that have yet to be found and defined, which in humans is often the most important step towards solutions, they fall way behind the universality of intelligence.

OW: Right.

Additional new concepts

TR: Let's move on from such basic thoughts about the difference between machine and human intelligence to the newer introspection concepts we have been developing during the past 20 years or so.

Flipping through the glossary of the *Selbstbeobachtung* book I discover quite a few new terms. In particular, there are several words starting with an "i" – intuition, irritation, intrusion, idiosyncrasy (laughs).

But seriously: These concepts developed, because, due to the slowly improving modularization of the problem of thought, introspection became more precise, too. Hence, in the background lurks a criticism, which certainly is all too familiar to you, namely that of the "theory-ladenness" of introspection. How do you respond?

OW: You can only see that coolly. "Theory-ladenness" pertains to all sciences. Why should it hinder psychology?

TR: I think that today I understand better than before that one of the main problems you had during those many years working alone was finding tasks suitable for introspection. We, the younger ones, have benefited from being given tasks that you had already digested during the last 20 years.

The difficulty of introspection with formal or semi-formal tasks lies in the fact that you must have understood many aspects of the tasks beforehand in order to then pass them on to others. Otherwise, you would not know whether or not a task is psychologically productive. Furthermore, it should neither be too difficult nor too easy. So it isn't easy to find tasks at an adequate level of difficulty, which are productive for all introspectors in a group.

Is there a way to reduce this effort?

OW: As we go along, we should develop a task catalog, out of which everybody interested can choose one out of this or that task domain according to his or her interests and knowledge. At any rate, comparisons of introspections are necessary as a corrective.

We also need more introspection from everyday life. With more discipline and courage one could certainly accomplish something in this respect. Then we could better define these newer "i"-words.

TR: Would you have termed irritations differently, say, 20 years ago?[27]

OW: As a start, you have to register that something is happening at all at the "fringe" of consciousness, as James called it.[28] My older term "error signal" denotes a special kind of irritation, for instance.

TR: With regard to your definition of attention above: Does that mean, that you already have to have a psychological theory of thought in order to be able to observe an irritation?

OW: Yes, of course! But then everybody solving problems by insight must necessarily introspect, albeit mostly without realizing it. The same is true of intuitions. What is an intuition if not a partial fitting of a regularity into a task environment?[29] It's a partial fitting, which alarms the thinker by signaling: Hey, there is something! Oh, it's an analogy! The analogy might not lead very far, but at least you are on the way towards an insight.

In this respect, I have experienced absolutely fantastic things while introspecting. Suddenly, you get an intuition of how to solve a mathematical problem but it doesn't function. Nevertheless, I have the feeling that it must function somehow! Sometimes, many days pass in which intermittently the same intuition occurs. At the end, maybe something else will work but quite often I am able to recognize this first intuition in the final solution.

TR: So whether an intuition, that is, a sensorimotor schema lending itself to thinking about a problem,[30] is right or wrong only becomes clear after a solution is found. The mere fact *that* an intuition occurs is often so satisfying that we don't want to let go of it. Art virtually thrives on intuitions and analogies, albeit often epistemically unproductive ones. Is it possible to recognize beforehand whether or not an intuition will lead to a new structure or not?

OW: I don't think so, because we don't get the new structure at once but have to sequentially fit in parts of it while controlling whether the whole remains coherent, etc. While doing so, you might easily have the impression that everything fits well but only later discover that this can't be true. Furthermore, you may find a false solution without ever discovering that it's false!

TR: Yes, in my case study in the book *Selbstbeobachtung,* I made an error which a reader pointed out to me only after publication.[31] I was even able to track down this error. Two intuitions became prominent while solving the problem but only one of them was right. And I followed the false one.

OW: You confused tangent and sinus, didn't you?

TR: Yes, but the crucial thing was that I had the wrong intuition of the relevant right triangle. That's why I identified its hypotenuse as a leg. I even remember having had an error signal when I was preparing a sketch of this intuition for the book with a CAD program. I couldn't draw the respective line so that it wouldn't cut the circle. Yet I brushed this error signal aside by convincing myself that my CAD skills just were not good enough.

OW: Everybody makes such mistakes. There are other cases as well. You might find the wrong word, for instance, thereby spoiling an insight. You mean sinus but you write down tangent instead. Or you mean left but write down right, which is a very common mistake when logging introspections. Then the error is not due to the intuition but to what you continue to do with it. I often err in this way. You end up empty-handed because you cannot reconstruct the original impulse of how to proceed. You have "thought it away," so to speak – in fact "wrongly thought it away."

All these things are concomitants of the non-algorithmic construction of machines, although parts of it do remain algorithmic, namely the already established structures you apply.

What next?

TR: One last question. What do you see as the main problem of the theory right now? Where should we proceed in order to make a step forward?

OW: I believe the most important thing would be to better clarify and instrumentalize those few terms that seem fruitful to us.

For example, we would need to gain a clear picture of what a "readiness" is. How do degrees of readiness manifest themselves? I fear that introspection doesn't lead very far here. That's why our work seems to stagnate. This problem cries for help from physiology. Neurophysiologists would have to instructively tell us: "Look! What you call readiness, is this or that in the brain. These nervous excitations mean this or that. If you perform the first step in an assembly, then this happens, afterwards this sets in" and so on.

I can obviously only provide metaphors, of which some are certainly true but others are certainly *not* true. To me, orientation is a "landscape" of readinesses – but I don't know exactly what I mean by "landscape." A current orientation seems like a topography in which I move around, and this topography represents some specific relations in a problem. To put it a bit more abstractly: My orientation is a structure of sensorimotor schemas. My current readiness consists precisely in the fact that this topography controls chance. Chance hits at a specific point just like a quantity of water which then follows the topography for some time while changing something in it. Unfortunately, I still lack more persuasive metaphors.

TR: One move of a thought, which in introspection appears as an episode with a beginning and an end, is just like this quantity of water gravitating through this landscape until it hits an obstacle and stops. In thought, this obstacle would be the capacity constraints of the construction environment. You don't find that accurate enough?

OW: No, I rather find that falsely accurate. It is just a crook suggesting itself – which already seems suspect to me. The fact is that I myself suffer most from the lack of a definition of (action) readiness. I always imagine that ensembles of nerves are partly "charged," and that the readiness is implicitly due to the fact that these "charged" ensembles function as switches. If a seed emerges, I just register that some *interaction* of readinesses is taking place.

A seed sets switches which control the following course of quasi action. But this is too imprecise.

1   Wiener, Oswald, 2000. *Materialien zu meinem Buch VORSTELLUNGEN*. In: Lesák, František (ed.). *AUSSCHNITT 05*, Vienna; id., 1988. Form and Content in Thinking Turing Machines. In: Herken, Rolf (ed.), *The Universal Turing Machine: A Half-Century Survey*. New York, 631–657.

2   Eder, Thomas, and Thomas Raab (eds.), 2015. *Selbstbeobachtung: Oswald Wieners Denkpsychologie*. Berlin.

3   In the central sutra of Mahayana Buddhism, for instance, we find the sentence "Form is emptiness, emptiness is form." Everything we experience is undeniably structured but at the same time always meaningless since skewed by the current jittery motivational background: "whatever is form, that is emptiness, whatever is emptiness, that is form. The same is true of feelings, perceptions, impulses and consciousness" (Conze, Edward [ed.], 1954. *Buddhist Texts Through the Ages*. Oxford, 152). This aspect also found its way into academic cognitive science, most notably into: Varela, Francisco J., Evan Thompson, and Eleanor Rosch, 1991. *The Embodied Mind*. Cambridge, MA.

4   According to Jean Piaget, the human child develops ever more intricate sensorimotor sche-
     mas, at first building on genetically pre-determined reflexes. In permanent interaction
     with the environment (assimilation and accommodation of objects), these schemas are
     "broken," i.e. at specific points hampered by external stimuli, and then viably recombined
     (cf. the box on "Schema," 75–80). Without having to postulate an ontologically different
     entity such as "mind", these schemas develop through a sensorimotor stage (from birth
     to ca. 2 years of age) via a pre-operational stage (ca. 3 to 7), a concrete operational stage
     (ca. 7 to 12) to a final formal stage (ca. 12 to 15). In the course of this development, in which
     phases dominated by play (assimilating habituation) or by imitation (new accommodation)
     alternate, the brain is gradually enabled to run schemas internally, that is, without the cor-
     responding objects to be manipulated. Schemas thus begin to mutually effect "themselves."
     By this process, schemas are "reconstructed" at a control level that inhibits motor activity
     and can run "offline" as structure. This functionality is experienced as "thinking."

5   Kosslyn, Stephen M., 1980. *Image and Mind.* Cambridge, MA, and London; id., 1996. *Image
     and Brain.* Cambridge, MA, and London.

6   Generally perception is broadly defined as all physiological, psychological, and social pro-
     cesses absorbing stimuli in order to regulate behavior. Wiener's definition is narrower,
     namely all processes, which lead to a conscious registration of some outer and inner sti-
     mulus as a seed for assembly.

7   Wiener, Oswald, 1997. notes on the concept of the bio-adapter. In: Weibel, Peter (ed.), *The
     Vienna Group.* Vienna, New York: Springer, 666–686 (originally published 1969 in German
     as part of *die verbesserung von mitteleuropa, roman*).

8   A prototype is a structure sufficient only to *identify* an object in perception or reproduce
     it as an idea by embedding it into a coherent running environment – but not more than
     identify. In introspection it is registered as a seed or attunement and has a "gestalt-like"
     quality. The observer knows "what" the seed means but has not yet specified this "what."
     If you want to specify a prototype, that is, detail it by thinking in order to gain a model of
     it, it has to be embedded in a construction environment by way of assembly. The latter
     affords some effort.

9   Amodal: When registered in introspection, seeds conceived of as "motor impulse patterns"
     cannot be assigned to specific sensory modalities (visual, auditory, gustatory, olfactory,
     tactile, kinesthetic, vestibular). The undeniably sensory impression seems to be due to
     "emulation," which is the habitual rash assignment of experiences to sensory channels. In
     addition, it is somewhat uncanny to admit to oneself that one is observing "pure struc-
     tures" such as in mathematical thinking, and not images. Helmholtz was the first to point
     out such "tacit assumptions" of sensory modalities in perception: "we always believe that
     we see such objects as would, under conditions of normal vision, produce the retinal image
     of which we are actually conscious." (Helmholtz, Hermann von, 1885 [1884]. *Popular Lec-
     tures on Scientific Subjects,* Vol. 1, New York, 307)

10   For the German "Weiser," see Wiener, Oswald, 2015. Glossar: *Weiser.* In: Eder and Raab, s.
     note 2, 59–98. To our knowledge, the respective English term "seed" was first used in:
     Neisser, Ulric, 1978. Anticipations, images, and introspection. *Cognition,* 6, 171: "A seed is a
     highly structured set of anticipations."
     Orientation: all currently active phylogenetic and epigenetic structures, from inherited to
     formal, controlling behavior in the current stimulus situation. If the situation changes
     abruptly, we partly lose orientation and have to act (motorically or quasi-motorically) in
     order to try to reinstall it. Orientation has a *hierarchical* aspect, insofar as a certain affective
     tone is a motivational condition for problem-solving, and not vice versa. Within the hier-

archy, each phylgenetic- and epigenetic "structural layer" has to be dynamically (heterar-
chically) organized in order to warrant effectivity, speed, and plasticity of action and, especially, of thinking.

11   The psychology of thought, narrowly: "Denkpsychologie", was a term used by the
      Würzburg school going beyond the psychology of problem-solving to include questions
      of concept formation and logical inference as well as the latters' embedding in situational
      and personal determinants. Beyond the general functional description of problem-solving
      of formal and semi-formal tasks, the research group around Wiener also tries to introspect
      and document individual "thinking styles," psychological and bodily resistances, and envi-
      ronmental influences on thought.

12   "Un-intuitive thought," German "unanschauliches Denken." As a young psychologist, Karl
      Bühler (1879–1963) noted on introspections of philosophical comprehension tasks that solu-
      tions sometimes come suddenly and "imageless." The subject merely realizes the solution
      as an "aha experience" and is able to formulate it instantly. Lacking the concept of seed,
      which in the simplest form is the affective registering of a prototype, Bühler was expecting
      to experience "mental images," the absence of which he rightly noted, but formulated so
      provocatively that in return, his senior Wilhelm Wundt and many others opposed the
      experiments of the Würzburg School in general. In the following, introspection was briskly
      devalued by this dispute within psychology at large (Bühler, Karl, 1951 [1908]. On thought
      connections, trans. David Rapaport. In: id. [ed.], *Organization and Pathology of Thought.*
      New York, 39–57; Schwarz, Michael, 2015, Wendepunkte in der historischen Debatte um die
      experimentelle Selbstbeobachtung. In: Eder and Raab 2015, s. note 2, 389–441).

13   Mandler seems to believe a priori that there is *no* such connection while für Freud it must
      always exist (Mandler, George, 2005. The conscious continuum: from "qualia" to "free
      will." *Psychological Research*, 69, 330–337). In the respective literature, intrusions or, in
      Mandler's diction, "mind-pops" sometimes also go with the name "involuntary memories"
      (e.g., Salaman, Esther, 1970. *A Collection of Moments: A Study of Involuntary Memories.*
      London).

14   In *The Interpretation of Dreams* (Strachey, James [ed.], 1953 [1901]. *The Standard Edition of
      the Complete Psychological Works of Sigmund Freud*, Vols. 4 and 5. London), Freud expli-
      cated his concepts of displacement and condensation which often suggest themselves in
      introspection. Also assembly is regularly interrupted by intrusions. Cf. Wiener, Oswald,
      and Michael Schwarz, 2023. Pleomorphism in thought and the computational metaphor.
      In this volume, 101–163.

15   The notion of "complex quality" was introduced by Felix Krüger (1874–1948) to denote
      vague orientational impressions mostly with hardly noticeable influence on the global
      attunement.

16   Wiener, Oswald, 2007. Über das 'Sehen' im Traum (Zweiter Teil). *manuskripte*, 178, 161–172.

17   Turing, Alan M., 1937. On computable numbers, with an application to the Entscheidung-
      sproblem. *Proceedings of the London Mathematical Society*, 42, 230–265.

18   See note 16; the page numbers in this paragraph refer to Turing's paper, s. note 17.

19   Wiener, Oswald, Manuel Bonik, and Robert Hödicke, 1998. *Eine elementare Einführung in
      die Theorie der Turing-Maschinen.* Vienna, New York, chap. 10 "Zwei Zustände genügen."
      Engl. "Two states suffice."

20   "A trade-off in the sense of automata theory means the ratio between the length of the
      alphabet used by a Turing machine and the respective number of states in its table or, as
      a corollary, ratio of table length to used tape length. In German "Schnitt": cf. Wiener, Bonik,
      and Hödicke, s. note 19, chap. 12 „Universal Turing machines".

21   Wiener, Oswald, 1984. Turings Test. In: id., 1996. *Schriften zur Erkenntnistheorie.* Vienna, New York, 69–95.

22   E.g., Goldstein, E. Bruce, 2010. *Encyclopedia of Perception*, Vol. 1. Los Angeles etc., 74f.

23   Chomsky, Noam, and Yarden Katz, 2012. Noam Chomsky on Where Artificial Intelligence Went Wrong. *The Atlantic*, 11.

24   Wiener et al., s. note 19, chap. 16, 160ff.

25   Cf. table 1 on page 2 in Hsu, Chih-Wei, Chih-Chung Chang, and Chih-Jen Lin, 2004. A Practical Guide to Support Vector Classification. *Technical Report, Department of Computer Science and Information Engineering*, National Taiwan University. www.csie.ntu.edu.tw/~cjlin/papers/guide/guide.pdf (4 May 2022). It lists evidence for the power of "support vector machines" in classification tasks in contrast to humans.

26   Such a Turing machine, called "busy beaver," is supposed to write as many symbols on the empty tape by as few internal states as possible and then halt. The states thus must be heavily interlaced. But *how* they are interlaced is not intelligible to the observer. In short, he or she can't give its operation any "meaning." For five-state Turing machines, the current world record is 4.098 symbols in 47.176.870 steps (Marxen, Heiner, and Jürgen Buntrock, 1990. Attacking the Busy Beaver 5. *Bulletin of the EATCS*, 40, 247–251).

27   Irritation is the term for a seed ephemerally registered "at the fringe" and "imageless" like an attunement (cf. note 9). Contrary to the latter, it is noticeably tied to a specific assembly. The metaphor of "fringe" pertains to its emulation aspect in relation to the "focal" processes, which leave just enough energy for the irritation to be registered. In the course of assembly, it may serve as a "reminder" to be expanded later. At times, an irritation might remain "blank," and the observer just knows that "there was *something*" – an error signal which can't be specified any longer.

28   "Let us use the words *psychic overtone, suffusion*, or *fringe*, to designate the influence of a faint brain-process upon our thought, as it makes it aware of relations and objects but dimly perceived" (James, William, 2012 [1890]. *The Principles of Psychology*, Vol. 1. New York, 258).

29   As the output of an offline sensorimotor schema an intuition provides for the dynamics of an analogy to be used in the assembly process. As such it is crucial for thought's creativity. As stated in the box on "Schema" (75–80), it also often carries everyday associational "noise" (cf. Wiener and Schwarz, s. note 14).

30   Cf. for instance, "phenomenological primitives" or "p-prims" of Andrea A. diSessa in: Phenomenology and the evolution of intuition. In: Gentner, Dedre, and Albert L. Stevens (eds.), 1983. *Mental Models*. Hillsdale, NJ, 15–33.

31   Raab, Thomas, 2015. Selbstbeobachtung zu einem Diktum von Helmholtz. In: Eder and Raab, s. note 2, 217–236.

Pleomorphism in Thought and the Computational Metaphor

Seed, Symbol, and the "Grounding Problem"

A Conversation between Oswald Wiener
and Michael Schwarz

^{MS:} In our conversation I would like to refer to your sketch on the "computational metaphor,"[1] which you wrote by the end of 2018 to initiate a discussion.[2] You intended the text to be a basis for a comparison of different formal descriptions of natural thought by means of concepts from computer science, which you tried to track in its history, with results from introspection. You begin by emphasizing that these attempts conceive of token or symbol too statically.

^{OW:} Yes, with its symbol concept, computer science polarizes the dynamics of natural thought into static symbols on the one hand and transformation rules on the other. The symbols thus become the atoms of the respective formal system. They have the structure of their corresponding read-write-head only,[3] and "symbol structures" are defined by the transformation rules only. If these *rewrite* rules are themselves implemented as token strings, then all strings have the same structure, namely the structure of any suitable universal machine. I wanted to call attention to this loss of structure.[4]

^{MS:} If I understand you correctly, you aimed at extending the dynamics, which we experienced in introspection and then critically related to the all too static and sensualistic concept of mental image (as exemplified by several contributions to the book *Selbstbeobachtung* of 2015[5]), to the question of "internal symbols" compared to the symbol concept in computer science.

^{OW:} That's right.

^{MS:} Time and again we found, that even the image-like impression/ memory is, as Frederic Bartlett had already emphasized, pre-structured and schematic. Above all, it presupposes the temporally dynamic process of *assembly*. The reproduction of closed line sketches, for instance, depends on amodal, i.e., meta-sensory operations. I am thinking of my study on the PELOT figures in the book.[6]

^{OW:} Any critical introspection immediately shows that connecting imagining to perceiving (*emulation* of perception) by positing its pictorial character, e.g., "thinking as the manipulation of images," is misleading. Instead, the often cited "vividness" of imagination basically

depends on how many details the current running environment has. So it's not a matter of richness of the mental image.

MS: In your glossary entry on the seed,[7] you elaborated on such dynamic relations registered in introspection. They enable us to even understand and specify the historically first criticisms of the notion of mental image in the psychology of thought of the Würzburg School.

OW: Yes, you could see it that way. However, there adequate introspection to sufficiently illustrate the stages of expansion of seed phenomena and their functional embedding, for example, is still lacking. Some specifications remain at least didactically helpful, such as the distinction between "implication," "irritation," and "quasi-image" …[8]

MS: The second crucial point in your sketch pertains to the "grounding problem" (Stevan Harnad) at the foundation of artificial intelligence. Roughly speaking, the problem is how thought (or its formal description) relates to the environment, or rather how the formalism itself relates to the environment, especially if we don't want to conceive of the relationship as a mapping.

OW: The "grounding problem" is anything but only a problem of "purely symbolic models of the mind" (Harnad), that is, of symbol systems. It equally (and in an interesting way) affects "connectionism" too. Structures are always virtual structures residing in the head of the observer, who can at least attribute them to physical processes discerning tokens (at the level of the read-write head of a Turing machine) and strings (at the level of the transformation rules of a Turing machine). But s/he cannot relate these distinctions ("is accepted by transformation rule no. k") to entities outside of the respective formal system. This would require other virtual structures, which the observer must assign to the strings.

MS: I find it very exciting to discuss these two aspects, since I have been trying for some time to trace the origins of this relation on the basis of Jean Piaget's descriptions of the formation of "symbols" in children's thought. While researching this topic I got surprised by Piaget's interpretation of Sigmund Freud's notion of "symbolic thinking" in some of his early writings on psychoanalysis,[9] and also how close Piaget's interpretation gets to the concept of seed phenomena.[10]

The computational metaphor

MS: Maybe we could begin with the computational metaphor. How do you think it relates to so-called Artificial Intelligence (AI) today?

OW: In a narrow sense, the computational metaphor has been advanced by many authors based on Allen Newell's and Herbert A. Simon's "Physical Symbol System Hypothesis" (PSSH). Additionally, I also include all attempts to create mock intelligence by means of statistics under the general heading of "shallow formalisms" because they shallowly map the causal relations of human thought onto a formal description. These include the "neural network" hypothesis, information theory, and Bayesian philosophy, and even more so the project to save the PSSH by combining it with artificial "neural networks" to hybrid models.

MS: Nevertheless, you believe that automata theory – and the PSSH is based on the idea of a *universal formal system* – is crucial for the understanding of productive thought because it provides a frame of description in terms of effective procedures (in the form of Turing machines) as epitomized in your definition of structure.[11]

OW: Yes, the notion of *formal system* is immensely important for conceptualizing human thought. Both working on the construction of formal systems and symbol manipulation are characteristic activities of human intelligence. Obviously, the notion itself derives from the observation of human behavior – in particular from idealizing regularities, which the individual grasps in his or her own thinking. If you analyze any achievement of human beings, no matter what kind, you are forced to conclude that we build machines in the sense of Turing. That doesn't necessarily mean that these machines take on the form of a Turing machine. Nonetheless, it is the biggest flaw of artificial neural networks so far to be unable to construct formal systems.

MS: Do you mean the fact that such nets cannot produce Turing machines by means of their method of "learning"? And do you want to contrast the creation of recursive procedures performed by someone observing the sequence of events in the machine and relating it to its environment with the statistical mapping methods you dubbed mock intelligence?

OW: Yes, exactly. The creation of recursive procedures is the core feature of human thought. Yet, the question remains, whether the apparatus creating these constructs and manipulating them is itself a formal system (which seems be the most obvious hypothesis in the sense of Occam's razor). To what extent can it be described as such a system and how detailed would the description have to be so that it performs equivalently (as a program of a universal machine)?

Alan Turing's Behaviorism

MS: By referring to the observation of human behavior, you alluded to Alan Turing and, in particular, to his "discovery" of the universal machine relating machines to thought?

OW: Yes. More specifically I mean section 9 of his paper "On Computable Numbers."[12] There, Turing talks about a man who computes. He indicates clearly that he himself observes this "computer" from the outside, thereby realizing what he is doing in behaviorist fashion. He observes how the computer reckons with pen and paper, draws symbols on the paper, reads and rewrites them – while multiplying two numbers, for instance. What is happening inside the computer, Turing does not mention. But I believe nonetheless, that of course there was also a big portion of introspection involved.

MS: You mean Turing overlooks the cognitive experiences we ourselves found and described in living thought? Even while multiplying two two-digit numbers you can make a wealth of observations, which should, when inspected more closely, totally amaze you. This is lacking in Turing's paper ...

OW: Generally speaking, behaviorism developed during radical times in psychology. So Turing didn't want to talk too much about "states of mind." Of course, the notion of state of mind is indeed dubious. That's why he replaced it by the table of a Turing machine. Yet, we have to emphasize that he does not say a word about *how* the notes of instructions in the table come about. In short, he does not say anything about the creative aspect of formalization and how it looks like from the inside. Turing said and wrote not one word about it, in none of his writings.

MS: Another essential aspect you keep emphasizing is that Turing decomposes the behavior of the computer, or rather his computations, into static "symbols" and dynamic "operations." These symbols and operations are supposed to be so elementary that you cannot decompose them further.

OW: I believe that the concrete steps of the run of a Turing machine are overly concrete in a way. In any case, you need some ingenuity in order to implement, say, the search-and-find of an analogy. Yet, in human thought this kind of recursivity is obviously a primary and main feature.

MS: So an analogy is recursive because it is repeatedly applied to similarities across several phenomena. As humans we are able perceive analogies and use them instantly. But we would have to explain how analogies and detection are to be implemented.

OW: Yes, because that is a fundamental feature of the human mind. But however the implementation takes place, this does not affect the fact that the implemented process must result in the representation of a recursive procedure. Therefore, my definition of structure still stands. It is not devalued by the fact that in introspection we do not find structures as concrete ready-to-use processes. So it would be necessary to sketch what one should do in order to find something corresponding to recursivity and to the concept of structure in introspection.

MS: Certainly one problem is Turing's convention of description. Do you believe that, if we introspect objects or internal proxy objects and then try to describe them, recursion must inevitably occur in the description. Like: "there on the top right is something similar as further down" etc.?

OW: Exactly. In introspection we do discover sub-modules for multiple use just like in computer programs. If the concept of the Turing machine is a description of the notion of computation, this is a formalization of observable processes, as Turing observed in a person who computes. But tacitly he also relied on formal descriptions or assumptions, which aren't observable in the external word and, therefore, not in a behaviorist fashion. The point is that Turing's description is lacking this internal component about what is going on in the head of his computer. That is missing completely.

MS: I think there is a good way to observe this primary factual "effectiveness" of living thought we experience before we formalize it by a symbol system. Like everybody else, Turing initially had to learn the application of his general descriptive convention for machine operation on strings. Only after that was he able to perform any arbitrary run of a special machine presented to him (in the form of a table) on any tape (with pencil and paper). Consequently, he had developed a scheme of action corresponding to a Universal Turing Machine (UTM). He had become a UTM.

OW: That is entirely correct Manuel Bonik, Robert Hödicke, and I already wrote about it in our introduction to the theory of Turing machines.[13] I used the argument you just brought up to prove by way of the Church-Turing-thesis that a universal machine must exist. The proof goes like this: I myself am able to run any Turing machine table, so I am able turn myself, so to speak, into any arbitrary effective machine. And since the way I handle the tables is effective, there must be a machine that does the same.

MS: Yes, I got the example from your book! I mentioned it, because it clarifies that *first* I formed the universal procedure as an embodied action scheme. Then I understood this action scheme intellectually, *before* I was able to formalize it into a general descriptive convention on the basis of introspections and a lot of effort. After all, you did just that in order to be able to write your textbook. You wrote down (pro-grammed) a UTM in the form of a table, which then operated within your convention on that section of the string intended to represent the Turing machine "tables." The rules therein are applied to the other section of string intended to represent the input of the computation. Yet, as you just indicated, the steps you translated into this convention are "overly concrete" because the fairly simple sensorimotor content of an elementary action, e.g., replacing one token on the tape with another, has to be broken down into quite a few smaller mechanical sub-steps on the linear tape. It requires a lot of concentration to even recognize these original processes in the run of your UTM, although they seem so simple to us.

OW: That's right! Universality follows from the basic idea that you can code the description of the machine on a tape, and that there exists this universal machine, which is only universal because one can write any description of any procedure or of any calculation on the tape or indeed of any finite description out of the recursively enumerable infi-nite set of descriptions already existing or yet to be invented. That's why the machine is "universal." But to represent a universal machine is only one of our manifold human abilities.

The symbol concept of the *Physical Symbol System Hypothesis* (PSSH)

MS: That's right. Moreover, the operations of a UTM are not even com-plex. But you just referred to Newell and Simon, whose definition of the PSSH aimed at suspending the strict separation of data into tokens and processes. So they wanted to extend the dynamics to the "control system" itself. Practically, this means to permit the rule-governed change of the TM tables.

OW: Yes, I refer to Newell's and Simon's definitions of the concept of symbol using the computational metaphor, as exposed especially in their 1976 paper.[14] The state of the art in artificial intelligence at that time had been physically realized by LISP machines that were specifically optimized to run LISP programs. Their typical *symbols* were John McCarthy's symbol expressions (S-expressions), which he had developed together with the LISP programming language. Some years ago, I held a seminar introducing "PC-Scheme," a current LISP dialect, to students.

MS: Yes, this is a purely procedural language in which everything is formulated in bracketed *expressions*. The *expressions* are "lists" nested in parentheses containing arbitrarily chosen *symbols* (atoms). This "structure" (binary trees) specifies the order in which a mechanical "interpreter" computes the lists. Since the contained *symbols* are able to denote *expressions, strings,* and also *procedures* to *transform expressions* (of the lists), they are no longer "symbols" in Turing's sense, because they can also be considered pointers to operations (machines). Turing's symbols neither designate TM tables nor point to operations producing, copying or transforming them!

OW: You see, that is how Newell and Simon must have understood the notion of symbol at that time. As an *internal representation* (in the physics of the machine), these *expressions* must be retrievable and modifiable as "list structures" and the *symbols* as "pointers" to other *expressions*, implemented as *memory addresses* in a random access memory. Thus, processes for generating and modifying expressions can already be carried out as transformations of the pointers. The symbols are nothing other than variables for the operations possibly referring to other expressions and operations. Since the symbols must be universally applicable, they must not have any additional function (no meaning) beyond simply referring. They must only be distinguished from each other to be unambiguously assignable. Put simply, the arbitrary *symbols within this metaphor* are both pointers to operations and the operands of operations.

Of course, the physical symbol system has to be an instance of a universal machine. So Newell and Simon hypothesized that such a system has the *necessary* and *sufficient* means for *general intelligent action*, as they put it!

MS: This remains a matter of discussion to this day. So the hypothesis is that any *general intelligence*, also in the form of "artificial" machines, *must necessarily* be based on the very class of symbol systems we just defined, and that every adequately organized (correctly programmed) symbol system of this kind is *sufficient* to display intelligence! The little word "action" indicates that its interaction with the environment is also intended. But isn't this formulation a bit shortsighted from a psychological perspective?

OW: In my opinion, it would be a mistake to deny any merit to this kind of Gordian solution attempted by Newell and Simon. It helps my understanding of conscious processes in natural thought about as much as the idea of "neural networks" helps my understanding of the "encapsulated" sensory domain. This is no small feat, if I take into account the evolution of my views while dealing with these hypotheses. Yet, apart from the engineering problems of implementing them, which would probably determine their success or failure, they omit the crucial part of the more abstract problem, namely all the parts between the first stages of perception and the use of language, which are so essential to natural intelligence.

MS: That was precisely the reason why I dedicated myself once more to the psychogenesis of the symbol in the child to write a separate chapter for this book.[15] So far we do not have much more than a universal framework for description, the core of which is captured a little differently in your own *definition of structure*. After all, the formalism *producing* such recursive processes is not yet included in the definition of the PSSH. And if I interpret the more speculative parts of it generously, these processes are understood (in anticipation of an implementation) as "sensorimotor" actions denoted by symbols, the dynamics of which should also serve to adapt to the environment. Yet, nowhere do I see an adequate psychological model for the transition from these behavioral processes to the processes of imagination and thinking.

Formal description and AI – Searle's problem of "causal powers"

OW: That's why I speak of procedures only as far as they are clearly captured! So now our problem is exactly the problem of the cognitive genesis of structure. Like many other problems it can be traced back to one question: How far must formal description go in order to achieve the same as the formalized system?

MS: You mean, how far does the formal description of the processes seen at work in human thought or, say, the processes attributed to thought by neurology, have to go in order for the formalized to perform equivalently to human thought?

OW: There are two methods to achieve artificial intelligence. One is to describe thought while expecting that the description – which of course would have to be very concise and consistent to be transformed into an executable computer program – is performing just like the thing described. In contrast, the other method is to formalize an idealized description of neural information processing. It seems that psychology has engendered the PSSH, while, in turn, the neural net hypothesis (NNH) inspires psychological theories mathematically.

MS: Some linguists still believe that thinking is a matter of words, i.e., of symbols, and that insight is structured in language. But if thought consisted only of sentences to be transformed into new sentences via transformation rules, and the new sentence is supposed to be the result of thinking, then it seems easy to believe that the simulation performs equal to the simulated, e.g., such as in Joseph Weizenbaum's "psychotherapy" program ELIZA. But between a question and the answer there is a cognitive process engaging all of my brain resources by regrouping my entire orientation.

OW: Against this background, I would like to mention John Searle's notion of "causal powers." By the latter I, and probably Searle too, don't mean anything metaphysical at all. The "causal powers" seem to reside in a level not yet co-formalized – in a carrier level, so to speak. Regarding this, we are used to thinking about objects by decomposing them into levels: molecules, then further into atoms, and so on, for instance. Then we stipulate one of these levels to be causally effective for a given problem. But we can ask: How does the underlying level, which seems to produce the laws of its upper level, function, and so on?

In his book *The Sciences of the Artificial,* Herbert A. Simon described such decompositions into levels as something we apply to everything we see.[16] As examples, he mentioned the levels of nucleons, atoms, molecules, molecular complexes, cells, or the hierarchies of social organization, in which the stronger social binding forces, e.g., the emotional ones, are used up in the smaller units. For this, Simon found an ingenious simplification.

He thought that this is due to the fact that there are essentially different kinds of forces, such as in physics there is the strong nuclear force and the weak nuclear force as well as the electro-dynamic force and gravity. These four are, I believe, still the four basic forces of physics. Simon now believed that the strongest binding forces neutralize each other to form an atomic nucleus. The forces effective at this level hold the elementary particles together so that one does not notice anything of them at the next level, which is the level of the weak nuclear force. Similarly, electrodynamics does not apply at the level of the gravity at all, but rays of light are deflected by a mass. At this level, it becomes irrelevant what light rays or matter jets consist of. And since the consumed binding forces do not penetrate to the upper levels, you are able to describe each level separately by its respective "shallow" formalism.

Yet, this model describes a basic feature of our operational thinking. As we apply it to everything, I think, one should scrutinize it more precisely. This way of thinking just *creates* the hierarchies defining the elements to be made visible by measurement methods and to be arranged by the respective formalism. It seems to me that these are essential problems.

MS: Yes, you had already interpreted not only Turing's test this way[17] but also symbolic AI research, which tries to clarify intelligence at the isolated level of a "language," thereby ignoring "deeper" levels such as the thought relations experienced in introspection. They then implement searches for relations, which, as you say, generate a correct answer in the form of a sentence defined as a subset of all possible sentences within the linguistic domain. So your point is, that explicitly observable phenomena of thought such as seeds or even words, and what is implicit, i.e., what is implied by my orientation, cannot be decomposed easily into levels to be formalized independently. Do you think that Searle means something similar with his notion of "causal powers"?

OW: The fact that we are thinking in this way, conceiving of things in, say, effective levels that are hierarchically ordered, is obviously inherited. Maybe this is the reason why we are unable to understand some crucial relations. The ideal model for such a *decomposable system* is the layered structural concept of computer science, where each layer performs its own elementary operations. On top of the machine code sit the assembly languages, on top of which the higher programming languages up to normal user programs operate. But in introspection not all our ideas appear decomposable. Again and again we experience surfaces, whose "main body" remains unconscious. In the essay you mentioned I said:[18] We have to assume that a large part of the work of consciousness consists of attempts to represent these surface points of a model, whose largest part remains unconscious, as a decomposable system. But this is not a property of language, but of the models.

"Causal powers"

By introducing the concept of "causal powers," John R. Searle initiated a discussion on the scientific foundation of the concept of "intentionality," which has been widespread in phenomenology since it was first formulated by Franz Brentano. Searle locates these causal powers – as a necessary condition for "intentionality" – in the chemical and physical processes that, as "a product of causal features of the brain," exist only in humans and animals. Since these "causal powers" are found only in a *"certain sort of organism with a certain biological structure, and this structure, under certain conditions, is causally capable of producing perception, action, understanding, learning, and other intentional phenomena."*

In his 1980 paper "Minds, Brains, and Programs," Searle didn't aim at clarifying the concept of intentionality, but at juxtaposing intentional phenomena, which are supposed to be known by every human consciousness, in particular the phenomenon of *understanding* (a language, for instance), with the execution of *purely formal processes* (e.g., translation following formal rules). Based on his famous "Chinese Room Argument," he pleaded that machines without such "causal powers," i.e., machines operating exclusively by computational processes over formally defined elements "instantiating a computer program," are principally unable to generate something like intentionality. A computer program alone does not need the same "causal powers," but only enough of them to induce the next level of formalism, when instantiated. Therefore, according to Searle, the causal powers of a formalism can also be implemented by all sorts of materials, just as Joseph Weizenbaum sketched out how to construct a computer using a roll of toilet paper and a pile of small stones. But all powers beyond that, e.g., the ones necessary for understanding, the formalism cannot reach. Thus, only a machine having the biological structure of a brain is able to produce them.

"And that is why strong AI has little to tell us about thinking, since it is not about machines but about programs, and no program by itself is sufficient for thinking" (Searle 1980: 417).

Searle, John R., 1980. Minds, Brains, and Programs. *The Behavioral and Brain Sciences*, 3, 417–457.

MS

MS: Some pioneers and supporters of the PSSH, e.g., Nils J. Nilsson, wrote that Searle's criticism of the meaninglessness of formally manipulated symbols and of the lacking foundation of symbol systems is unjustified. I suspect, however, that these reactions fail to take into account that his objection was not only aimed at the lack of inter-action between a physical machine and its environment, but at the *nature of their relationship* ("intentionality")! This is how I understand why you also include an "observer" in your model. Now do you believe that the main question is: Down to which carrier level and which biological structure must our understanding and formal description of intelligence reach?

OW: Logic represents a formal description of the very highest level, so to speak. Logic does not think. It will never think, because it is an abstraction on a level lacking Searle's "causal powers." What is the level directly below?

MS: Well, we have been working at this level for years. It's the level of experiences, which we observe in introspection (attunements, seeds, quasi-images, and so on). It is also significant that, according to Piaget, purely formal thinking constitutes the last developmental stage and that symbolic pre-conceptual as well as intuitive thought develops much earlier. I also hesitate to locate the formal description of neu-rons by artificial neuronal networks (ANN) at the level directly below without first considering the complex issues of biological and psycho-logical structure.

OW: The question is this: Down to which level do you have to go with your description, so that the description thinks by itself? It seems clear that we don't have to go down to the individual atom, but I'm just guessing. I am not completely, but ninety-eight percent, sure that we don't even have to go down to the big molecules. But then we might have to go down to biopsychology and nerve cells. I am sure you know that huge efforts are currently being made in this direction. On the other hand, Michael Nielsen, for example, talks about billions of "units" in a single artificial network. I bet that this technological development will still go on for a while. The technological equipment will get even cheaper and even faster, and even smaller... At the end, parsimony – both in Occam's sense and in the sense of material econ-omy – could be simply out of the question. Then, understanding intel-ligence and recursivity won't be a scientific goal any more.

MS: At this point, let me pin down that through introspection you have taken up the topic of "symbols" in thought again, that is, the topic of seed phenomena, because it is impossible to reduce such phenomena to the PSSH's narrow definition of symbol! There, symbols are arbitrary and function as pointers, which make them unsuitable for descriptions of introspections. Furthermore, the question of grounding these systems remains unanswered.

OW: Yes! Well, the dynamics of the processes – including assembly, scaffolding, even our notion of attunement – are far too complex to be reduced directly to the symbol concept of the PSSH. Without a model of the "symbols" in *human thought* these theories remain stranded. In this regard, I would later like to add something on the topic of how to approach the unfolding of "inner symbols" via *bootstrapping*.

But again, this is not to say that the problem cannot be formulated at all on the basis of a PSSH. This is exactly what the "Church-Turing thesis" amounts to, which in my version goes like this: Everything that I understand clearly, I can represent as a Turing machine, and thus also in a von Neumann computer, which is in fact a Turing machine. This implies that, if I understood exactly what thinking is, then I should be able to implement it with a von Neumann computer. Conversely, if my program cannot think, then I have not yet understood (and formalized) thinking adequately!

MS: Yes, especially if you also consider the formalized portion of thinking in its interrelation with the environment. In the 1990s, Searle's criticism and this question of the "causal" interrelation with the environment made connectionist networks fashionable. Until then, this method had been somewhat ridiculed by "symbolic AI," but from then to the present day it has been on a "triumphal march" based on a wave of technological progress. "Artificial Neural Networks" began to "recognize" objects in photos, steer automobiles, and play out their superiority over humans in board games and quizzes. This certainly leaves an impression on the general public.

Artificial Neural Networks (ANNs), hybrid models of thought, and the "grounding problem"

OW: It was clear from the outset that the performance of today's neural networks would not be sufficient for intelligence. Of course, pattern "learning" and "recognition" is a part of intelligence, but not without rhyme or reason like here. First of all, it is clear even to everyone tackling ANNs optimistically, i.e., especially to the people who make money with them, that human thinking does not follow a gradient descent algorithm. I think this is evident, and it is already a serious disadvantage of the neural network metaphor for intelligence.

MS: But scruples about the "grounding" of symbol systems being decoupled from the environment, as well as about the lack of coordination of ANNs triggered the development of hybrid systems trying to circumvent Searle's criticism. ANNs should play the subsymbolic, causal part providing both "meaning" and "grounding" to the arbitrary symbols of the PSSH part. Thus coupled with the environment, these systems should be able to yield higher "symbolic representations." But the metaphor is misleading, as you suggested, and the "grounding" of ANNs remains absolutely inexistent. In my opinion, the statistical evaluation of sensory data does not yet enact causal experiences, which are necessary for any formation of grounded sensorimotor schemas. Moreover, phylogenetically acquired as well as inherited schemas enabling intentional action are still missing. Representations binding together sensory "elements" only cannot be expected to be able to anticipate the behavior of objects.

OW: Most of these researchers refer to a paper by Stevan Harnad proposing hybrid machines.[19] If my interpretation is correct, Harnad still meant that all these processes, which he called bottom-up processes, can be implemented by connectionist networks. These include not only sensory invariants, but also "categorical representations," which can be trained to identify objects as members of a category. All these processes should yield symbols conceived of as mere names, but which should suffice as "symbolic representations." Actually, this sounds a bit naive. I don't see any "representation" in such a system at all. All information is lost, and what I understand by representations, i.e., what I have called "models,"[20] is entirely missing in this bulk of literature.

In this context, we must also mention Geoffrey Hinton, because he had concurrently pointed out the almost insurmountable difficulties inherent in such a transition from parallel to recursive processes, if the ANN approach is taken seriously.

Hybrid models of cognition

After the criticism of Searle, who measured up freestanding symbol systems to the "causal powers" (and the performance) of animal and human consciousness (intentionality), researchers at the end of the 1980s proposed hybrid upgrades to the concept of symbol. The arbitrary shapes of a symbol system's tokens were supposed to be "grounded" by a non-symbolic, causal nexus to the environment. In 1990 Stevan Harnad, for instance, outlined a hybrid *non-symbolic/symbolic model* of the mind.

According to Harnad, *non-symbolic representations* also comprise of the *sensorially invariant* features of object and event categories (both innate and learned) computed in a bottom-up manner. Built on connectionist networks (such as in trained image recognition), his model yields symbols enabling *iconic representation* by distributed processes. For Harnad, it is only the symbol designating the representation that allows for the comparison of sameness, distinctness, or the degree of similarity of objects. However, Harnad thinks that for *categorical representation* (identification of an object), icons are useless, since they must first be selectively reduced to invariant features in order to reliably distinguish objects as members of a category from non-members. According to Harnad, this selective abstraction process would also lie within the technical scope of connectionist processes.

For Harnad, the elementary symbols computed by bottom-up processes are mere "names" to be used by the higher-order operations of *symbolic thought.* Their "intrinsic meaning" refers to the objects and categories of objects, from which they originate. For representations to be recognized as symbolic, the criteria of a "physical symbol system" must be met. Among others, the symbols at this level can be arbitrary and thus denote anything, but have to follow explicit rules that are part of a formal system. Additionally, their syntactic manipulation must be semantically interpretable.

It remains unclear whether Harnad, by equating "intrinsic meaning" with Searle's "intentionality," implies that the "causal," "non-symbolic" processes already effect the aforementioned "causal powers." It also remains doubtful whether Harnad's notions of iconic and categorical representation, which yield symbols as mere "names," suffice for object reference, especially when the objects referred to are out of the sensors' ranges. Furthermore, it is difficult to judge whether such symbols allow for becoming aware of one's own intermediary means in goal-directed action, which, e.g., Jean Piaget postulated as a necessary condition for "intentionality."

Harnad, Stevan, 1990. The Symbol Grounding Problem. *Physica D*, 42, 335–346.

MS

MS: You mentioned that the physical symbol system must be an instance of a universal machine. You also mentioned that Turing conceived of the UTM and its rewrite rules as a common structure of all strings on the tape. Why do you think this is relevant?

OW: It is relevant because there is no other structure![21]

MS: In this regard, you say that an "observer" is necessary, who relates any formal system to entities outside of it.

OW: Yes, entities outside the formal system just *are* the grounding problem! How does a formal system relate to "reality," so that it plays the same role as a cognitive system or, better say, as in man. Harnad tries to construe this with rather casual methods. But then any effort to understand starts at a simple level ... You have to ask the correct questions. How is human language founded on reality? How does this come about? Questions like these we have been asking ourselves for a long time: What is an object? What takes place if you say: This organism "internally" manipulates a proxy of an object?

MS: I agree. In my view, Harnad doesn't realize that it's he himself who relates his "causal" "nonsymbolic mechanisms" to an environment and not the mechanisms of his "symbolic representations." He does not even intend that, not least because in his sketch there are no internal models at all (no representations in your sense), which could be related to the environment.

OW: I think, grounding simply means that a human being, who is grounded in or based on reality in the aforementioned sense, must have a representation of this reality. And the fact that this representation is similar to or, in some respects, even isomorphic with reality, which can be judged by a third person, is already sufficient to satisfy this grounding.

MS: I also have the impression that in Harnad's model the entire content of the "representation" is lost as soon as its object is no longer within sensor range. In one example, he speaks of a "symbolic representation" of a "zebra" produced by a linkage of the symbols "horse" and "stripes," if these two symbols are "subsymbolically" grounded. This means that for him they are grounded both in an "iconic" and a "categorical" way, that is, they are recognized and assigned to their class by ANNs. Then he is talking about the fact that a person, who has never seen a zebra before, but who possesses the grounding of both elements as well as their linkage, will recognize a zebra with the help of this "symbolic representation" even at the very first encounter. But he doesn't mention whether or not he could put a pencil or a piece of clay into the "hands" of this physically grounded symbol system, which should then, even without ever having experienced a zebra, draw or form a clay model of this linkage. Could it even get a vague idea of this combination? Something quite normal for a human being is missing here!

OW: Yes, that's right. To have a proxy of an object means to have a representation of the object just in the sense I have described in my glossary entry *figurative*.[22] You have to have processes of type 1 and of type 2 within a running environment. That already suffices to make the emerging object become a proxy. Therefore, a being that doesn't have the same depth of representation as I do – of this lamp, for example – cannot have the lamp as a proxy in this sense either. But does a dog have the lamp as a proxy? That is hard to judge, but I suspect, to a certain extent, yes! The dog will not only recognize the lamp, but it will perhaps even be able to do something with it. Now what about a fly? In this case, I am rather inclined to say a fly does not have objects as proxy. And I am totally sure that until this day no computer has one either.

MS: Yes, and it is just this mental model which the "observer" can relate to the event of coming up against a zebra in reality! Naturally, he or she can judge the adequacy or inadequacy of this model by reference to the real zebra.

OW: In a certain sense, a fly is also grounded in reality, of course. It can also handle reality, but it is questionable whether one should use the philosophical word "grounded" for an organism, of which one does not expect to have ideas, for example, and to which one therefore does not attribute thought. In any case, I wouldn't say categorically that you must not call a housefly grounded. I suppose groundedness is gradual. The fact that my behavior fits the world is already a matter of groundedness. I can deal with the world by somehow making it compliant to my goals. At least, I can try to. And I fit into the world insofar as I can predict what will happen. I can imagine, for example, what might happen, if I drive carelessly down an icy road. All of that is part and parcel of my representation of the external world. If I have such a representation, then my thinking is grounded in reality.

MS: Harnad's model already fails on the basic level because the content of the symbols is lost. As we have just said, we cannot compare its symbols with what one could hesitantly call "symbol" in human thinking, namely all seed phenomena.

OW: Well, the problem becomes evident in artificial neural networks. Let me briefly explain. It is claimed that in ANNs information is distributed, but the computation surprisingly yields a discrete statement. In face "recognition," for instance, all sorts of things happen in this network, but we have no coherent understanding of what exactly happens. The bottom line, though, is that the net computes that it's Mr. A's face. Or that it's an elephant, but the elephant itself, of course, is obviously as opaque to the net as anything else in it. Yet, to the human observer it's more than just an output string.

Now, if you claim that there are "patterns of activity" in the net, and these "patterns of activity" are either already a structure on the level we are interested in or on a level below, only that it is "subsymbolic," then in my opinion this amounts to admitting that the net is a black box for you, of which you just cannot say anything at all in terms of its function. Especially concerning the latest developments of ANNs, which are so successful, this is the biggest mystery.

MS: I think, from the perspective of introspection we can say quite a bit more about the "subsymbolic." At least we can intersubjectively talk about concepts such as *attunement, seed,* and *expansion* on the basis of our experiences. According to the computational metaphor, a linguistic or informational "token" or "symbol" would actually reside on a superordinate level of these processes. Does it reduce the entire content of a human "symbol," which is embodied in a seed and its elaboration, to a naked token?

OW: Many are perplexed by such questions, since hardly anyone uses introspection. I think we can already say a little bit more about this matter, but we'll get to that later. I'll only give an outline here.

For example, a neural network performing face recognition or so-called object recognition could also be conceived of as executing a superposition of images, because a specific input image yields a specific output, e.g., the word "elephant." It does so just like some other input image, although both images look completely different. In a first approximation, one could say that the two inputs are superposed in the network, which is of course only a manner of speaking. But at least they can then be sorted out afterwards! What is missing completely in cognitive science are human construction processes. What is called –

I think: wrongly called – distributed information in ANNs in fact represents those traces you need to achieve an assembly. The information, if you even want to call it that, doesn't exist yet, but enables a kind of "bootstrapping," that is, the construction of a situation. And this assembly is, by its nature, a very different process than a mere unifying computation of distributed information. Because what we need in order to build a model is, after all, already unified information. We want to have the elephant and not a symbol string or even sub-symbolic entities, which amount to even less than a symbol string. What we need to deal with an elephant has to be bundled so that we can apply it by translating it into motor activity. Above all, then, this means that we can apply *ourselves* to this object. In short, our representation of the elephant starts with a collection of readinesses for action. And these readinesses are seeds for running environments, so to speak!

MS: That's why we have always talked about orientation. By observing the first formation of symbols in children like Piaget did, interpreting it with the help of your concept of prototype, i.e., the elaboration and, later, the evocation of typical situations (in the absence of the object) connected to the actual orientation, we perhaps get a little closer to the psychological concept of symbol or seed.

Bootstrapping and symbols conceived of as formalized seeds

OW: I think that symbol or token was intended to theoretically formalize what I call a seed, which is the internal counterpart of a symbol. As it were, the symbol can even function as the name of a seed. What I mean by seed I have already explained in more detail elsewhere.[23] A seed is the incipient unfolding of a system of readinesses for action, which makes it possible to construct – in the process whose formal description is called "bootstrapping" – a problem as well as the means to solve it.

MS: Maybe you could briefly explain your idea of bootstrapping. You mean an equivalent to the process of "booting" a computer?

OW: Yes, to me bootstrapping is a term from the same area of computer science as "stack," which we should also talk about later. Bootstrapping is happening every time a computer boots up. It consists of simple, very elementary algorithms being executed, which then step by step do not install the entire operating system, but activate it and set it up, so that simple operations create complicated contexts, in which you are then able to work.

MS: It sets up the running environment in which a computation becomes executable?

OW: Even more than that. The computer has to get set first so that it can start to operate. Bootstrapping manifests itself in the time it takes to read in something, calculate this or that, or move data. This method is cheaper and better than storing the full content. So, there is a whole period of time that passes before the computer is even ready-to-operate. Everything that happens during that time is called bootstrapping. It formalizes, I think, the intuition of what I call "expanding" or "assembling." Formalizing means that formal computer processes simulate introspectively experienced processes. That doesn't mean that the formal description captures the essence of what is formalized. It captures a particular feature of it, and only in a particular respect. Bootstrapping captures that there is something not yet ready in terms of random access memory, but made ready in the process. The computer sets up a running environment to create the most urgent, but by no means all, conditions so that the project, which had begun by a mere seed, can now be tackled thoroughly.

MS: Maybe it would be helpful to bring up an example for a seed phenomenon from living thought. Here is the description of a typical episode from my introspection. The question emerged as to whether a particular screw-nut runs clockwise or counterclockwise? Now, while I try to orient myself mentally, I experience a *seed* suggesting a situation, which in turn assures me that I am able to answer the question. However, the seed isn't the answer yet. The following development ensues: Suddenly, I find myself in a situation in front of a bottle with a screw cap, in fact ready to screw it *down.* To do so, I know how I would have to grasp the bottle and in which direction I would have to turn the screw cap. And I know that this direction it is called right-handed. So while discussing this with you, I expand crucial details of the task through knowledge actualization. The situation or mental episode now represents the question of the nut on the thread of the bottle. Yet after that, further mental tunings are necessary to adjust the situation to the question of whether the screw cap functions clockwise or not. Only by assembly can I try to figure out that, if my hand rotates in "this way," then it is just like the hand of a clock moving "this way." So further mental coordination is necessary to answer even this simple question.

OW: Yes, that is a good example. The most important conclusion is that there are no internal symbols, but only processes, which themselves – and that's why I had to go into some detail here – run deterministically nonetheless. Therefore, in a lower level something must be static and fixed. Some memory must exist, otherwise bootstrapping would not be possible. In any case, something must be stored in the sense of Bergson's *Matter and Memory,* in order to make bootstrapping possible, that is, a constant expanding of seeds and assembling of running environments. That is necessary, even if doubtlessly a lot of processes support themselves reciprocally, or perhaps support themselves in parallel. It is even certain that the construction process begins in parallel. What is constructed then influences in one way or another what happens in other places of the running environment. All in all, the process already has similarities with the "settling" of a neural net,[24] i.e., at least it takes on the form of a gradual grinding in of parallel processes.

In the end, however, very concrete clues and determining procedures have developed. But as far as I can tell from introspection, things always have to be constructed or assembled first. Moreover, in my experience, this constant construction process almost always goes *from the general to the specific.* Something begins totally vaguely, and already I believe I have reached the goal. But it depends on what this proxy under construction must ensure in the following. It is a matter of how many details I have to construct, so that I can use the proxy further. A lot can often be done even after the very first steps of expansion. Let's ask ourselves, for instance, how much twenty-eight times twenty-eight is. If I only have to estimate the product's order magnitude, then I can immediately answer: Well, it will have three digits, I suppose. But if I want to compute the product exactly, I am forced to go into the exact details of the calculation.

MS: Yes, I can confirm that. In my example above, the first step of problem-solving was also a very general analogy, namely one between nut and screw cap, of which I knew the correct sense of rotation. This embodied "semantic" parallel is sufficient as an interpretation to take the first steps towards a solution. What I did not mention before, however, and what became clearer only during my follow-up concretization, was how the bottle situation was given to me in the first place. How did I experience this episode?

It was instantly clear to me that I had not really *seen* a bottle, not even my hands. Rather, I found myself adequately postured in front of a red screw cap. A quasi-image was also present. While introspecting I asked myself just which cap it was. Immediately I noticed that I found myself already amidst a kind of dream analysis, i.e., the situation was given to me just as like a dream fragment, as it is the case so often. I wondered if it was the red lid of a Coke bottle, but knew instantly that there was more to it – that there was some pattern on the lid and that there was also something white on it. So I wondered from what time in my life this "memory" could originate from, and now found myself attuned to the time of the 1972 Olympics, when I was five years old. It dawned on me that the pattern on the lid was related to the Olympics logo, a sort of fanned out rosette. And suddenly I remembered exactly which lid it was that I was fixated on. It was the round tin lid (with a red and white pattern) of a can for dark block chocolate that my mother had bought at the time, even if not for me. It came from the child's desire for chocolate, which was denied (Zeigarnik effect[25])! So you see, I'm already moving into psychoanalytic territory. It is very important, I think, to address these aspects. You have spoken so often about similar experiences, too. I discover them all the time, perhaps more often when I have an introspective attitude.

OW: Yes, of course! Your story reminds me of my example of a "hypnagogic quasi-image" in Silberer's sense,[26] which I reported in said glossary entry for "seed." There, I described the connection between quasi-movements when cutting a bacon rind ("Speckschwarte" in German) and huge tomes pejoratively called "Schwarte" in German.

MS: What is so often overwhelming in such situations is its *overdetermination*, even if one can only sometimes decipher it. In my case, I had to research the Internet to find out what kind of chocolate can it was that I had experienced. And I found it! Its lid has a fanned white rosette, very simple in design but similar to the 1972 Olympics logo. On the can it reads "SCHO-KA-KOLA. Die Energie-Schokolade. 16 Ecken · Zartbitter" (CHO-CA-COLA. The energy chocolate. 16 slices · bittersweet). This I did not remember! Caffeine! That's why my mother did not give it to me! I'm not sure whether or not the can had a screw top or whether or not turning it right applied to it. But here one can observe how deeply rooted in my orientation its prototype is. It became actualized when I had the task to identify the rotation sense in an almost egocentric situation. This little episode alone is full of condensations and displacements (in the Freudian sense), because in German the word for screw-nut is "Schraubenmutter," i.e., "screw-mother" playing a double role here. Furthermore, not only the two emblems are similar, but also the word "KOLA" on the lid resembles a Coke screw cap and so on. So the seed is quite personal, too. No one except me is able to fully understand it. And it is a symbol because it functions as a quite general analogy to the screw-nut-turning problem. As a prototype it is only the tip of an iceberg of schemas, and perhaps this depth was not even necessary in order to solve the problem by assembly. In any case, this kind of symbol is absolutely not arbitrary, nor can it be separated from personal experience.

Assemblies are slightly different every time

OW: The development from general to more concrete is perhaps more than the mounting of a structure, because the individual additional accommodations of orientation are already moves of a machine. During construction, that is, during assembly of the running environment, there is already an ordered procedure at work. However, the assembly is slightly different every time one works on the same problem, because there are so many inputs, so that they can probably never be exactly the same. Yet, certain essentials remain and just change over time.

MS: Yes, the assembly of seeds and prototypes into a scaffold is not a process always developing the same way. The more general the analogy discovered, the easier it fits all sorts of problems.

OW: Anyway, this constructive assembly may be the counterpart of "distributed information." It is, of course, a very different process from linking distributed information in ANNs, where distributed information means the distribution of weights of the "units." In a neural network it is always crucial whether it is in the learning mode, as it is called, or whether it is in the working mode. The working mode is totally uninteresting, because nothing changes within the net. A completely normal function has converged, stubbornly computing an output for every input. The only interesting thing is the learning phase. What does "information" mean here?

From the general to the specific

MS: It's highly mysterious that, as you emphasize, every assembly develops from the general to the specific. The *running environment* has not been calibrated yet, but the first step is a seed. Or just *clutter*, that is, an unordered group of seeds, which are then accepted or discarded during further assembly. You once said, and I found this very apt, that the origin of assembly in the seed is a very *general* but *not a* *reduced* description. Basically, it is not a description at all, but the initial setup of a running environment, which is so general that practically any further development is possible.

OW: Yes, the seed's function resembles the function of a stem cell, to engage another analogy. It can take a lot of developments depending on which features are carved out. I think this has a lot to do with two papers of Anthony Marcel, which are very important to me.[27] Although he was not really able to prove it, Marcel argues plausibly that truly understanding a word implies a processual development from the general to the specific. During this development, a whole range of directions inchoately start off, which would lead to different interpretations. But in the end, the entire apparatus of understanding yields *one* interpretation. As it is clear that the entire setting is involved, we could compare Marcel's results with our concept of running environment. Different running environments translate the same task into different results. I think this is comparable to results of introspection, when a seed begins to expand.

MS: The fact that different running environments yield to different results already ran like a golden thread through the experiments of the members of the Würzburg School. Their concept of "task" may even be considered an antecedent of our concept of orientation. Only their experiments have perhaps been too much focused on words and laboratory conditions. From today's perspective, you could criticize that they have not been enough founded in the "ecology" of living thought? Yet, Narciss Ach conducted experiments with unconscious tasks. And looking at the introspective analyses of Karl Bühler and Otto Selz one can only be astonished by how much important material they discovered. Bühler, for instance, already spoke of the temporal aspect we just mentioned, of successive experiential episodes until a "finished thought" emerges.[28]

Expansion and assembly

OW: I draw the following distinction. The *expansion* of a seed comprises those processes already included in the seed, i.e., which runs without any constraints of a "task," if you will (anyhow, task was much too narrowly defined by the Würzburg School). Perhaps that is its most general meaning. Then, during *assembly* the constraints of the momentary situation and of orientation take effect: "Well, okay, but I still have to consider this and that... and that too." Expansion pertains, so to speak, to the level of sensorimotor schemas, and assembly to the level of additional constraints, which these sensorimotor schemas must satisfy. In the course of assembly analogies always occur in specific running environments, because the only important fact is *that* an analogy emerges – or is rather suspected.

MS: What strikes me is that you say that there are different levels. I also often find this kind of over-determination in seeds that serve as analogies. There are different areas that coincide, connections that I discover only later and under specific circumstances, that the observed analogy meant something else still. These observations seem important to me.

OW: Yes, exactly, but that is already included in what I said before. Whether or not you see a specific analogy depends very much on the stratification of your current orientation and on said process of development from the general to the more specific. If an analogy is very general, then it is perhaps only distinguished from other analogies by the fact that it takes place in *this* specific orientation, and that the general meaning needs a few moves to become specific. So on the same level of generality analogies to entirely different things may occur. According to Anthony Marcel, this is also the case in the process of understanding a word. Instantly, perhaps within a tenth of a second, the word activates five or six different interpretations at once. These *are* precisely different analogous objects. Sound alone may also serve as an analogy, so it suffices that the objects have acoustically similar names. I think that is quite clear.

MS: The assembly process is rather different from expansion, as you have indicated before. One intervenes in the process of a seed expanding to become more concrete, partly by practical-logical considerations, by rejecting developments that seem to lead nowhere, or by starting to construct something anew. Often while expanding seeds, though, many phenomena and analogies occur, which you just haven't observed before or which you only recognize as such in retrospect. Assembly seems rather like a purposeful shaping and synthesis of this richness of phenomena.

OW: I think that is quite correct. One could add that assembly means, in a sense, the perspective of the running environment while expansion means the perspective of the seed. That again implies, I would say, that assembly and expansion are basically two aspects of the same process. On the one hand, expansion extends the seed, that is, clarifies and holds together what has appeared in the first instance. At the same time, however, as the running environment somehow consolidates, something becomes explicit by establishing the aspects, which the specific running environment is supposed to represent. But it is the same process. The development from the more abstract to the more concrete obviously passes through a phase, during which a lot of analogies are possible.

Pleomorphism, i.e., potential polymorphism

OW: We could give this phase of potential polymorphism the name pleomorphism. As far as I know, this phase has never been included in any technical token or symbol concept, let alone implemented. There has to be a transition from the stage of attunement (more about it in a moment) to the stage of *proxies* (of objects).

MS: I think that what has been said so far concerning the expansion of a seed culminating in its pleomorphism, as you call it, overlaps with Freud's notion of "symbolic thought." Or rather it represents an approach to clarify his notion as well as what Piaget has observed on the psychogenesis of the "symbol" during children's development. Piaget called this the infantile "syncretism."[29] For it is clear that where analogies are diverse because of the generality of the thought, contradictions, condensations and displacements accumulate.

Freud believed that the distortions necessarily resulting from this generality serve to make a wish unrecognizable and are even produced especially for this purpose by an unconscious agent (named censor). I think that this finalistic interpretation is at best superfluous, but, considering my previous example, understandable. My "problem" of the screw-nut and the seed for opening and closing a Coke bottle lid as an analogy, which in retrospect turned out to be ambiguous, clearly refers the biographically earlier "problem" of opening and closing of the KOLA chocolate can, which indeed represents a denied wish. However, it seems inevitable to me that any theory of the "cognitive symbol" must at least potentially model this kind of deeper content in order to meet the minimum requirements of a psychological explanation.

OW: Well, on the polymorphous character and the loss of dynamics I have written the following in the style of a manifesto: "I don't have any 'internal symbols, signs, or tokens;' if I talk of symbols in order to mean something specific, I mean marks on paper, which not only I am able to see, but which other organisms can see too." This is my definition of symbol. And that's why it was mistakenly believed that the 'internal symbol' is just a mark, not on paper but somewhere else – in my mind. Yet, I don't have such marks, but all that I observe is always processes, attempts at reconstruction or construction. Everything happens in a specific constellation of constraints which enable me to infer, in a multiplication for instance, that the product is, say, 56. During the process I have the lightning-fast illusion that I see number 5 or 6, of course. But I know that I don't really see them, and certainly not as a symbol.

Just as we believe we see something in the mind, we believe that there is a symbol as soon as we want to identify something constant in thought. But all that is constant is the process. And there is absolutely no doubt that written signs, marks, or symbols *help* thinking.

But given this interpretation, there are no "internal symbols." There is the written symbol, the written word, the written sentence, and when reading them these symbols evoke seeds in me. These seeds are the essence of thought, while linguistics believe that it's words. Words are symbols, but seeds are not.

If the Physical Symbol System Hypothesis wants to offer something tempting, the seeds must not be "pointers" either. The seed is the process itself but not yet in full progress. It is present as a growth impulse. So the excitation of specific pathways is there, but this excitation is not enough to concretize the machine that is supposed to run. Yet, together with the rest of the environment, it is enough to construct this machine, lightning fast – or rather more or less fast, to say it cautiously.

MS: It is also very hard to imagine how the kind of ambiguity we mentioned, which begins with a seed, could be reduced to a pointer whose essential property is to be unambiguous. I have taken the habit of using "cognitive symbol" instead of the term "internal symbol" in order to at least imply its processual aspect. It is clear that this will again lead to misunderstandings, but *seed* is opaque to anyone not accustomed to our terminology, while symbol in common language carries such an enormous literary ballast that it shouldn't really be used anymore. Ultimately, after all, we want to distinguish this unfolding of an insight from the conventional use of the word "sign" or "symbol."

Symbol in thought (cognitive symbol)

When a "cognitive symbol" becomes manifest, it means the beginning of the actualization of recognition or of knowledge of an intentional *situation* with a proxy object from the past (memory). According to Otto Selz, this amounts to a "knowledge actualization." As soon as this remembered and directed activity/method for achieving a goal becomes focal in thought, the actualized aspect enables a new view onto the current relationship under scrutiny (thought or action). In the best case, the current orientation will offer a solution to a possible perturbation or gap within this relationship. When a cognitive symbol becomes conscious in action or perception, the current situation is grasped, recognized, or interpreted under the aspect or schema of an earlier situation. This enables anticipation as well as pre-practical choice. However, if a perturbation or gap occurs in thought or action as a result of a current relational complex, which the cognitive symbol cannot *reproductively* remedy, a *productive* process of problem solving or construction may ensue. Such a dynamic cognitive process allows for "gedankenexperiments" by selecting and expanding the cognitive symbols and their assembly into running environments with which problems can be solved.

The cognitive symbol in introspection

In introspection, a "seed" and, more broadly, the connection between attunement, irritation, manifestation, expansion, and assembly potentially enable the *unfolding* of a "cognitive symbol." On the basis of several examples, Oswald Wiener suggested that seeds are not *pointers* to something recognized but the nucleus of the recognition process. Furthermore, the cognitive symbol is neither a symbol in the sense of computer science or mathematics nor a sign to be assigned arbitrarily. Nor is it a symbol of social origin, although it might emerge from a social conflict.

Wiener, Oswald, 2015. Glossar: Weiser. In: Eder, Thomas, and Thomas Raab (eds.), *Selbstbeobachtung: Oswald Wieners Denkpsychologie*. Berlin, 59–98.

MS

OW: To sum up: By comparing crucial concepts of the computational metaphor with insights from introspection, we can show that, contrary to living thought, "symbols" (in the sense of the PSSH) are nothing but *external*. "Internal symbols" are not symbols at all, but representations, i.e., structures in the making. What folk psychology calls "internal symbol" or "mental image" is the nascent understanding (e.g., of a word) in the form of the corresponding seed, especially if it occurs in thought without external symbols. This comparison particularly shows that in this perspective the computational metaphor of the PSSH cannot help, as Newell and Simon believed, "to gain a rather deep understanding of how human intelligence works in many situations."[30] On the contrary, it has prevented and still hinders a deeper understanding of thinking.

Attunement, complex quality, and orientation

OW: Several terms that are of great importance to me, although they are unexplained or largely unexplained, have not even been mentioned in our discussion so far. One of them is *attunement* (or mood; *Stimmung* in German). You have talked before about such an *attunement* episode from your childhood. That brings me to the following which may seem unrelated but isn't. I've been doing some digging in the literature to try to solidify the concept of *attunement* a bit, and was struck by things that probably mean something similar. Above all, I am thinking of the term "complex quality" frequently used by Hans Volkelt. Yet, Volkelt was an avowed Nazi and, therefore, later excommunicated from the "society of democrats." Of all the writings of Friedrich Sander, Felix Krueger, and others, I consider an early work by Volkelt to be the most interesting: *Über die Vorstellungen der Tiere* (*On concepts in animals*, 1912).

MS: Yes, Volkelt was a problematic person, a big shot in National Socialist pedagogy. I have read some writings of the authors you mention. I believe it is his dissertation you're talking about, which he submitted to Wilhelm Wundt in Leipzig. It is certainly indispensable to comparative psychology.

OW: In it Volkelt frequently talks about the concept of *complex quality*. I believe that he meant what I call *attunement,* but his choice of words is interesting because he uses quality obviously in the sense of quale. Since I myself also ponder on qualia, this immediately appealed to me. He means the overall impression of a situation, which you cannot articulate, but experience as a quale, that is, you know it without being able to articulate it. This is exactly what we call *attunement.*

MS: Yes, in his dissertation he also deals with a form of conscious regulation of actions in animals, which is not structured by proxies. He is concerned with behavior that "instinctively" depends, so to speak, on the overall situation but does not yet necessitate thinking or imagining and not even an object transcending perception, i.e., a proxy. Yet this behavior, Volkelt believed, is neither controlled by the sum of sensations, but by an *attunement* or complex quality attributable to the overall situation.

OW: Yes. Very early, already in an essay in the seventies or even earlier, I speculated that an *attunement* is the preform of a concept, and I still believe this is right. But what does it mean?

MS: Yes, that was in your essay on "Why art at all?"[31] That is a very important text of yours which also serves as an introduction to aesthetics, because much is anticipated in it – from the idea of aesthetics as "being touched" to the idea of orientation and its loss. I read it now and again with art students.

OW: If we could define the word *readiness* a little more precisely, we could just say, an *attunement* is a specific, but yet unorganized mixture of readinesses, similar to a seed, but without quasi-sensory components. A seed may, of course, be part of it, but then seeds appear momentarily and disappear immediately, while attunements sometimes last for longer, possibly for a very long time. Attunements, in this context, are part of the cognitive development of structures. They are at its beginning, on the "first day of the creation" of a concept, to speak ironically. Where heaven and earth are hardly differentiated yet, or only a little differentiated, and where perhaps already water and land exist, but not much else has happened.

Complex quality

With the term *complex quality* Hans Volkelt refers to primitive consciousness – predominantly ascribed to "lower" animals (as exemplified by his experiments with oak spiders) – but not beyond. It pertains to a consciousness of unstructured "feelings" (*attunements*). Volkelt conceives of these mostly hereditary qualities as "generic perception" of "vitally important facts" (situations and objects), which he denies have any object character. Volkelt showed that for the *recognition* of an object (e.g., prey, which to the spider would be a mosquito) the behaviorally effective situation is the decisive trigger, i.e., the mosquito in its specifically vibrating web. If the spider encounters the mosquito outside this situation, e.g., as a visually presented object, it will not recognize it as an independent object, and thus the prey schema won't be activated. In "vitally indifferent situations" we cannot detect any "object-like" or cross-sensory constants, which the animal follows. Yet, these constants are part and parcel of human imagining. Just like Ehrenfels with his "gestalt qualities" Volkelt declines to explain such qualities as the *mere sum* of sensory data or unstructured sensations. For the complex quality is, beyond the conception of Ehrenfels, "*a psychic whole other than the sum of its parts*. The primary complex has its peculiar quality, namely its 'complex quality'."

Ehrenfels, Christian von, 1890. On Gestalt Qualities. In: Smith, Barry (ed.), 1988. *Foundations of Gestalt Theory*. Munich, Vienna, 121–123.
Volkelt, Hans. 1912. *Über die Vorstellungen der Tiere: Ein Beitrag zur Entwicklungspsychologie*. Leipzig.

MS

MS: If we define *attunement* as an unequivocally attributable consciousness of specific action readinesses occurring before the development of any proxy functioning as an object, we should perhaps conclude that attunements arise *before* the aforementioned ambiguous phase, i.e., *before* pleomorphism. So we could hardly speak of ambiguity in attunements, could we? If in human thought "symbols" (in the form of seed phenomena) are much more complex than the "symbols" of the PSSH, why not assume that attunements are such symbols? Yet, you immediately see that attunements are even less arbitrary than seed phenomena. The PSSH postulates symbols, which according to introspection only exist at the end of an entire development. They are general abstractions from expansions and assemblies. Just like you said before: Logic itself does not think but is an abstraction of thought processes.

OW: In particular, it would be important to specify the word "quality" here. A quale is, by its very definition, so to speak, an atom – something that is not further analyzable. The epitome of a quale is, for instance, a color experience, where one says in the vast majority of cases: Okay this is, say, green. At most you can say: Oh, that's this specific green, and then you might have names for it such as olive-green or frog-green or whatever. But that's it. I have been doing such qualia studies again and again for years, such as listening to tonal dyads. Among them there are some that I hear as a quale, i.e., I know immediately what kind of dyad it is. The easiest for me is the tritone, which I hear quite clearly. My quale of a fifth, however, can easily turn out to be a fourth. Sometimes I confuse them. These tonal qualia are experiences that I don't have to decompose to identify: the tritone dyad, for example. But others I do have to analyze. I necessarily have to decompose major and minor sixths, for instance. I have to sing the two notes, and then I may find out that this is not a minor sixth, but a major sixth. For the quale itself is not clear, not precise enough. So on the one hand, there is something like atoms, as in the case of the tritone, because I don't need to seek out its two component tones separately. On the other hand, in the case of the sixth, there is such a quale impression too, but nonetheless I have to dissect it at times. Then the two separate tones are the qualia, and the dyad is a mixture of these two qualia. I think, you have to conceive of attunements quite similarly. What are these smallest atoms of experience? Well, they are not analyzable only regarding conscious access, only for conscious analysis. For the physiologist, however, they are of course analyzable. So you must conceive of qualia as being relative, I believe.

MS: Let's pin that down. If thought begins with an attunement, or the *attunement* is the origin of a thought already leading into a certain direction, which is clearly differentiated from other possible directions, but without yet becoming a proxy object, then the question is: To what extent can I make the attunement itself a proxy for "conscious access"?

You just talked about sensually imaginable qualities, which beyond a certain point evade conscious analysis. They are encapsulated. But there is sensorimotor conduct, which feels exactly the same way. So are there "instinctive" qualia of actions? Plus there are all those sensorimotor acts being learned and developed every day. Basically, I want to refer to your concept of *prosthesis* and that qualia can be trained. Automated schemas of thought and action such as learning the small multiplication table or handwriting – do they too become qualities by such training?

Prostheses

OW: Yes, this concept is very important to me and it applies here. If some behavior is automated, you might be able to remember how you learned it, but this isn't necessary. On the contrary, it would impede behavior greatly if you had to constantly remember how you learned it. For instance, you don't even think about how multiplication works. You just seem to have memorized a ready-made table. But does that mean that it's made of symbols? No, it's *not* symbols but sequences of transformations that take place. Seven times eight is fifty-six – that's not symbols, that's a movement, a kind of trivial Turing machine.

MS: In order to enact some behavior I don't have to remember, how and where I've learned it. But while introspecting, it often strikes me that, as soon as the thought process falters and I am unable to expand the seed in the desired direction, because I can't find the necessary means to do so, a specific place comes to my mind, where I have seen or learned what I now can't remember. Sometimes, it may even be a passage in a book where I could possibly find the missing "sense." So perhaps here the orientation to an already known problem becomes conscious again. As far as the difference between conscious and automatic processes is concerned, something is on the tip of my tongue ... But maybe you could meanwhile elaborate on the concept of *prosthesis*?

OW: In the language of Turing machines, this is quite clear. A *prosthesis* is a read-write head, and there are many of them. So they depend on the existing hardware, e.g., on upstream sensors and their input-output relation to their connected unchangeable structures. But for the most part they can be conceived of as software read-write heads, which can very well be changed or newly created – like programs running in a universal machine, in a computer. We can describe the concept of prosthesis as a simple Turing machine. In our Turing textbook, for instance, I gave simple machines that translate from one positional notation system into another, e.g., from unary numbers into binary or decimal numbers.[32] Now imagine a "meshed" (non-modularized) Turing machine, which reads a binary number, transforms it into decimal form for a more essential machine only beginning its operation when it reads decimal numbers on its tape.

The aggregate machine can be viewed as two separate devices. The upstream one does nothing but read "one zero zero one," for example, and return "nine" in the decimal system. The downstream device then reads this number to process it further. So the first device functions as a *prosthesis* for the second. It doesn't have to be visible at all for the downstream machine, which computes, say, a multiplication. For the latter, the upstream machine is *transparent*. This kind of modularization we can now generalize, because in between the two machines we could put additional read-write heads, and the multiplication machine may also serve as a *prosthesis* for downstream machines, i.e., mediate between machines. Put slightly differently, you could also think of it as a camera, in front of which you strap one lens and then another lens, and so on, until finally a picture appears at its back.

This is how you should see it if you want to formalize our experience of, say, the process of reading. When we read a narrative, we *experience* the situation described in it. Every clue in the text may mobilize seeds, change my orientation, or be integrated into my attunement built-up so far. However, what is entirely transparent in the consumption of the story are all processes of deciphering letters and words, the structure of sentences, the sounds that are pronounced – everything that I once learned with great effort. You will surely remember how laborious it was as a child to decipher one letter after another. Then you formed words from the letters already mastered. Then you had to bring homework to school and so on. I remember that well.

MS: Yes. In the beginning, reading is even tied to sound production, which only disappears with a lot of practice. In the end, you are able to read completely without moving your lips or tongue. When paying attention to it, I sometimes perceive motor rudiments even today.

OW: Okay. So as an adult the reading process has become transparent. Now a *prosthesis,* viz., a software prosthesis has been constructed. I am usually not aware of it today but – and this is of utmost importance – I am able to give attention to the task of deciphering. If I do so, something interesting happens. If I attend, for instance, to the shape of single letters, then I often miss the meaning of the text. It's simply not passed on. Or some meaning somehow reaches me, slips in like "oh, it's about a man who apparently has red hair" or so. It all depends on how intense my concentration on deciphering is. So the processes seem to be connected in series. This is why I named the transparent processes *prostheses*. Because the underlying meaning of the *prosthesis* is something that is strapped on.

But that is only one example. So the question, which we always try to come back to, is how to relate our concept of structure to what we really experience in introspection without skewing what we observe, as the PSSH does by frivolously applying the concept of symbol to thinking.

MS: Earlier I tried to differentiate between "conscious" thinking, where the term "conscious" is but a crutch, and the transparent automatic run of a Turing machine. The moment I look at something consciously, I still have access to what the prosthesis does – to what lies beneath.

OW: Yes, that's right, and that is not a crutch. As I said, you can draw your attention to it. Then the situation is different because you don't use the prosthesis anymore, but you make it the proxy object of your thinking.

MS: Yes. In your description I find this aspect of making something the proxy object very important. Although it somehow digresses from introspective experience, you could connect that to Piaget's attempt to look for the origin of symbolic thought in the genesis of children's play and imitation behavior.

After all, what has been said so far would mean that I am nowhere near being conscious of an action itself, even if I'm oriented to a specific situation and possess a specific attunement to the respective action complex, because I become aware of the action execution by (repeating) the consequences (the results) of it. In order to become aware of my learned or inherited prostheses, I must not simply use them, but make them the proxy object, i.e., draw attention to them, as you say.

Here I see a connection to Piaget's descriptions of a child playing an action "as-if" instead of executing it on the object itself. This may serve to transform these prostheses and their readinesses into a proxy object, so that the child would be able to analyze them and "construct" a prototype of the attunements related to them. This would yield to a "symbolic schema," as Piaget called it. He uses the term symbolic, because these schemas act in place of the "real" action situations in the absence of objects. Perhaps, then, a mental reproduction of the prototype could reenact the orientation to a past situation, i.e., evoke a complex of attunements.

OW: So far it is correct that orientation is first directed to the result of an action, especially in learning movements and directed action. It is directed to establishing the relation between cause and effect. I have also called this relation "servo-mechanism," because you don't know, for instance, all the muscles enacting a movement with the right strength and in the right order. You only know the effects of your action on the senses including the kinesthetic sense. Hermann von Helmholtz already stressed this in his description of the relationship between "motor impulse" and its "result." By result ("Erfolg" in German) he means the first change to be perceived by the sense organs, just as I alluded to earlier when speaking about the musical tone, which I can intonate and sing, and then, in a strange way, identify whether or not the sung tone I now hear is correct. But all the mechanics in between – of the involved laryngeal musculature, for example – is lacking completely. This is very important for the theory of thought. For what we are, at best, able to mentally represent is the immediate relationship between the impulse (the attunement) and its result. In between there is a cascade of events within an encapsulated realm, which we are unable to reach even when trying to attend to it.

MS: Okay, there are limits to conscious analysis. What you experience, when you reach them, can only be called a quale, as you said. But then there are also complexes, which you are able to isolate from the overall situation by thinking. In the psychogenesis of play, the child from a certain point on is able to ignore the execution of an action on the object. This enables it to analyze and isolate its own action. According to Piaget, this behavior is the prerequisite for recognizing the same action performed by someone else. But Piaget went on to observe and describe a second type of behavior in the child. He called it "imitation," that is, behavior which looks for similar motor results in order to relate the initially isolated prototypes of one's own action to the action perceived in others. The child tries to repeat sounds, syllables, and gestures, which, once recognized, it reproduces and imitates with its own body. The development culminates in the objectification and internalization of imitation. In my view, this amounts to the "symbolic thinking" of possible situations.

This could be the incipient development of what you called a *model* (or *processes of type 1 and 2*, respectively). However, it's still a long way. I also wonder whether what we call *assembly* comes about gradually at a more advanced stage of mental development. But at least the kernel of the most important structural relations is already there. Unfortunately, these are neglected in the sensualistic hybrid models, I think. What develops is the "symbolic" representation of a situational orientation in absence of the "real" situation. Thereby the child is able to relate a "model" to "reality"! Moreover, by this process the minimum requirement of what Piaget calls the *semiotic function* has emerged, because from this stage on the child is able to master language and the use of linguistic symbols.

The psychogenesis of symbolic thought

According to Jean Piaget, during psychological development the first *symbolic behaviors* (symbolic play) yield "symbolic schemas" playfully reproducing own actions as prototypes instead of performing them on real objects. Yet, by progressing to "imitative schemas," actions of *others* become related to the child's own prototypical actions. Thus it becomes able to reproduce them as well. Such behaviors reach from body movements to facial expressions to the imitation of action results, that is, of sounds and more complex sensorimotor relations.

It is likely that these new prototypes, as already grasped schematic contexts or aspects, continue to closely interact with the *orientations* of the original sensorimotor actions, because they have been constructed from these orientations' action readinesses. By this postponed reproduction of prototypical imitations, the episodic situations of interest to the child can become actualized without the situation's object being present. The prototypical action just mobilizes the corresponding orientation or, as is the case with the complementary type of imitation, represents the object itself. Initially, the analogy is limited to the action of others alone, i.e., to the production of their sounds and movements. Later, it pertains to the imitation of situations and things themselves too.

The formation and application of these two types – symbolic schemas and imitative schemas – are not designed for the use of objects, but of their proxies. They *are* symbolic surrogates in their internal realization. In their "artificiality" these schemas first serve the separation of subject and object (of action on the one side and object on the other). I say "artificiality," because the first type of schema substitutes the real act "as if" it was performed, and the second type of schema acts "as if" it brings forth the physical object.

In advanced symbolic play, both types of imitation intermingle more and more. They are projected or transferred to the most diverse objects (toys now "walk," "cry," "eat," or even imitate actions of people). Thus, schemas further detach from bodily imitation, i.e., from the child's own actions. However, before they become internalized as prototypes, i.e., before they are episodically "imagined," "remembered," and no longer executed, the formation of prototypes extends to all possible things. They become objectified, that is, constructed on the fly and independently of habitual action schemas. As such, they finally become internalized *cognitive symbols*. These symbols, however, "unfold" prototypes of orientations. Thus, they are not symbols in the conventional sense. They are bound to the overall orientation of sensorimotor development, from which they receive meaning and true depth.

Already in symbolic play it becomes evident that the child again and again imitates the (prototypically "reproducible" or "recognized") episodic relations impressing on it. It does so for various reasons, e.g., for wish fulfillment, compensation, or anticipation. Due to the projections already used in play before, it notably becomes able to easily transfer "similarities" to various relations. So it projects own actions to the actions of other people or things. The action of others is not only imitated, but also projected onto the material world. Moreover, objective relations stand in for bodily ones (or vice versa), prototypical relations from one object reappear in others. By this a "syncretism" develops, which flexibly culminates in the largely implicit orientation of "symbolic thought," which functions at quite a general level but is nevertheless rooted in sensorimotor schemas.

Piaget, Jean, 1945. *La formation du symbole chez l'enfant: Imitation, jeu et rêve – Image et représentation*. Neuchâtel, Paris (Engl.: *Play, Dreams and Imitation in Childhood*. London 1951).

MS

OW: Let's get back to our specific questions. What I meant earlier is that, if we conclude that a seed or an intrusion could be interpreted or viewed under different aspects, then you have to ask yourself: Okay, but why then is it in reality viewed under *this* one specific aspect?

MS: In introspection I mostly experience what you are referring to as a seed feeling over-determined. Of course, this pertains especially to dreams, perhaps because there the running environment doesn't restrict thought so much. In any case, I experience that the seed already seems to appear together with structural relations presumably used to support the overall situation. Yet I don't necessarily become aware of the content of these relations. Perhaps they are pre-conscious, so that I usually notice them only in retrospect. In dreams, however, it is almost the opposite. After waking up I experience almost exclusively relations of content, whereas the structural or formal relations are either captured immediately after waking up or otherwise only by willful analysis. That's probably the reason why Freud believed that the manifest content of dreams only is the surface, whereas the images dreamt are symbols encoding the true or latent content.

OW: As such, this is hardly surprising. I have already attempted to explain the pleomorphism of the phase in which many analogies are possible. Moreover, we must not forget that the experiences from the recent past continue to live on in us all the time. They constitute an extended running environment, so to speak. Things we talked about yesterday, for example, still make up a background today. This background will weaken over time, but parts of it will remain effective. What is important is this embedding of the incident, which we are momentarily conscious of. This embedding makes the incident appear different from all other incidents. This is, of course, the premise of our thinking to be clear. Often, however, we do realize that something is constantly taking place in this staggered background, even if our thinking seems very focused.

Let me give an example. The other day I took on a task from recreational mathematics: a sequence of numbers, where the first five members of the sequence are given, for which I had to find the law of formation. So it was a very common problem. I sat down with the intention to introspect and tried to write down everything that went through my mind while solving it. One of my first thoughts was: "Alright, I actually know quite a lot about sequences, not about this specific one, but…" These were wordless thoughts, of course. The numbers already reminded me of something, because there is not only a two in the sequence, but even two twos next to each other. That is remarkable and unusual, because normally in a sequence, each member is different. So I had already registered these two twos as something strange, and this fact alone already determined that I would come back to it – that with every conjecture coming to my mind from now on, I would have to test it on this pair of twos. Although that was implicitly established, I noticed it. And suddenly it dawned on me out of nowhere: "That's like my new neighbor." Period! Well, I had to think about this: Two or three houses down the road, a new neighbor had moved into a house that has been empty for a year. But "the new neighbor" is actually a married couple! So here it came: I already knew quite a lot about the new neighbor, though nothing concrete at all. But at least I knew which expectations he could fulfill and which not. This was the connection to the mathematical sequence: I know what a sequence is, and I approximately know what is to be expected. The same holds true for the neighbor. Certain things that I saw – that his car has an English license plate, for instance – made me think: "Ah, that's probably an Englishman." Then this was confirmed. It doesn't amount to much, but at least I knew much more than before. The woman is from our region here – and already the draft of a romance emerges, to speak poetically: A southern Styrian woman meets an English gentleman, or something like that …

MS: Yes, yes, I know exactly what you want to say! I also regularly register such analogies which abruptly contribute to my orientation and which determine an order. These may be incidents, which have stuck to me only recently or a week or a year ago, but quite often they even stem from my childhood.

OW: All the time this couple obviously exerted an influence in the background, so that when I seemed to focus on the mathematical problem, it was projected onto the sequence of numbers. So the quite global relation intruded: "That's just like my neighbor."

But this means only that the overall problem-solving attunement grounding the "construction site" of the running environment and its current proxy object is completely open. But it may concretize in the blink of an eye, if some specific aspect becomes salient. This aspect is only potentially part of the running environment, but then all aspects are only potentially there. That's exactly why we have to scrutinize what the proxy object exactly "looks like." Above all, these potentialities are also graded, i.e., certain aspects are realized more easily than others. In principle, a small change within the broader running environment seems to make an aspect virulent, which before had hardly any chance to become actualized.

MS: Well, all these aspects are preconscious, that is, accessible to consciousness in principle, if one may say so. I realize the relations within the proxy object if I rethink what connections had already been anchored before.

OW: Yes, you realize this in retrospect. It is not clear from the beginning that my new neighbor has something to do with this mathematical sequence, that he shares a similarity with my situation facing the problem. In retrospect, however, I can see that similarity quite well, because I have tried to reconstruct it to some extent. You see, what is similar is really very global. The neighbor intruded because he was already there in the running environment, albeit not in connection with the number sequence, of course. But this can only work at this very general level, at which so much is possible. With regard to your mention of over-determination earlier: one thing determines the other. The running environment "new neighbor" determines the running environment "number sequence" to such an extent that, as soon as a similarity is discovered, it breaks through into consciousness.

MS: That sounds reasonable to me, and I don't see that such a phenomenon could even possibly be implemented in artificial neural networks. That's why I talked about conscious access. If I *recognize* a similarity, then usually I am able to explicate it. I am able to express it in some medium, to describe it, just as you now did. The minimum requirement to call something *recognizing* is probably to register an *attunement* just as you described. I have to be able to analyze a distinction within the current readiness enabling me to reproduce what I have recognized, just as in your example of the tonal dyad.

This is the case even with the simplest figurative analogies. For instance, if I try to feel out a cut-out figure in the form of a boot, blindfolded and with my hands only, "Italy" comes to mind. But the same is true when I see the same two-dimensional figure. This explicit knowledge transfer between different sensory modes, in this case between palpation and vision, won't be possible by merely hearing the word or seeing the written word "Italy." So in my opinion it cannot be done by an ANN either. Of course, one would have to ask exactly whether and if yes, how this could be related to a "symbolic expression" of the PSSH.

OW: In ANNs, this would only make sense at all if there were a device belonging to the network, which makes these "patterns" effective, i.e. ensures that the patterns that "light up" within the ANN are rendered a causal factor for further developments. But in neural networks there is nothing that reads these patterns. Moreover, there would have to be a device that takes these different patterns as examples to find a common structure of them, that is, a structure accepting all these patterns and only them or only those, which also refer to an object. Such a machine is completely missing in ANNs. Yet a human interpreter is able to see patterns and say: "Ah, this time this and that has lit up, so the net's output was that one," or ask: "This is the same object, but in this case the node weight distribution is completely different, so what do these patterns actually have in common?"

MS: So now you are talking about assembly and the invention of recursive procedures? But your example with the neighbor again shows that the most general features, which appear almost together with and become tangible by the seed, are present as prototype. It would be very interesting to know how these original relations of objects came about.

Variables and prototypes

ᴼᵂ: I have already pointed this out with respect to bootstrapping: What neural network developers call *distributed information* would, according to introspection, be a candidate for those clues that one uses to assemble a running environment. After all, the clues *are* not the running environment; they just determine the proxy object indirectly by creating the preconditions for it. This is achieved by modeling out, for example, the implicit laws that govern it, but we do not yet know this. Thereby, a coarser form of it is provided. The coarsest form of a proxy object we used to name *prototype*.

Furthermore, we should not forget that the gradual construction process automatically settles the question of variables. It is quite clear that the *prototype* has an internal dynamic, which, unlike common formalisms, does not depend at all on the assignment of variables. Relations already exist, although what they constitute does not. Assembly, hence, always proceeds with potential extensions, whereas all formalisms so far functioned by assigning variables.

ᴹˢ: What do you mean by being unlike common formalisms?

ᴼᵂ: I mean programs such as WolframAlpha, a well-known tool on the Internet, which draws graphs of arbitrary functions. Programs like that are able to differentiate, and that is all in the sense of other kinds of formalism. Programs such as these compute difference quotients, and for this they use variables effectively like we do, when we make calculations with x and y on a sheet of paper.

ᴹˢ: By "differentiate" you mean deriving mathematical functions? That again has to do with the symbol concept of the PSSH, because as far as I know, McCarthy invented his symbol expressions, i.e., the manipulation of symbols without any number value, exactly for this reason.

OW: Yes, exactly, I just wanted to emphasize that. I think we can also relate this to something we discussed at the beginning, namely Herbert Simon's metaphor of different layers and different carriers of each layer consisting of elements held together by binding forces with different magnitudes of strength neutralizing each other.

To speak colloquially, if you compute an equation with unknowns, then these unknowns are called variables. Now the task is not the solution of the equation, but the equation is regarded as a description of a function yielding different values depending on what you assign to the variables, as mathematicians say. So an equation can be viewed as a formal description or a metaphor for the thought processes proceeding in a similar fashion, insofar as in this equation the lowest level consists of "atomic" variables. The latters' internal structure, however, is irrelevant. They just have to be of a certain type.

In mathematics, what you assign to x and y has to be numbers. But you can use whatever number you want. So you can assign complex numbers, integers, real numbers, and rational numbers – *but not anything else*. In computers this mapping is exact. There is the dynamics, e.g., that a variable is squared, and the two squares are summed up. But *what* is to be squared and *what* is to be summed up, you enter as a concrete number. You cannot enter a word, otherwise the machine will crap out or output an error. Now the important thing is that the relations are always the same, no matter at which level. Yet there is input besides numbers, which you can also assign to variables, e.g., letters or words. The freer you are in choosing these variable types, the more general the expression or function will be. As you see, we are coming closer to the *concept of prototype*, where at first it is not even certain of what type the variables are.

MS: But the big question remains: How do human organisms build up this prototype from attunements representing a situation by sensorimotor orientation and action readinesses?

OW: At any rate, by constructing the *prototype* you define what then becomes more and more concrete, until you reach a level corresponding to your task at hand, that is, corresponding to the orientation you want to reach in order to be able to work with it. On this level, things get rather concrete – even very concrete if you calculate with numbers.

MS: This is now a rough formal description of our experiences in introspection, where insight progresses from an *attunement* to a *seed*, and further on to *expansion* and *assembly*, i.e., from the general to the specific.

OW: Yes. Expressing this by a kind of equation is quite new to mathematics too. I don't think it's more than five hundred years old, when it looked much clumsier.

Besides, this is, just as the Turing machine, an idealized description of observations of what the mind does and then condensed to rules. I think, it has the same background, viz., what the human mind does all the time. Its main tool is this stage of expansion, because it always proceeds to the degree of concreteness, which can be afforded or achieved. There are, after all, many problems that we cannot even reduce to the adequate level of understanding because we simply lack the respective knowledge. But that is, of course, another question.

Recursion

MS: At the beginning of this conversation you addressed one of the central problems of AI. A physical symbol system provides the means to formalize any effective procedure, even recursive ones. Nevertheless it is certain that we do not yet have machines able to recognize and produce genuinely recursive procedures. It has not even been proved that this would be feasible by formal description. By using the term *genuine* recursion, which is *not* a technical term, I allude to your distinction between trivial and folding structures from your book on epistemology.[33] There, you define the creativity of human intelligence precisely as the ability to "fold" trivially repeatable structures, i.e., simple analogies, into generalizing procedures.[34] Generalizing problems and solutions affords to give regularities already discovered the form of modules, which then can be used multiple times according to their function. The computing traces, i.e., the spatiotemporal sequences the processes leave behind, are sometimes more important for folding than the result of the function. In these traces you can more easily recognize structures or loops, which you are then able to transfer to other data. Now, just these operational traces are invisible in parallel processing, e.g. in ANNs, because there they dissolve into distributed information.

OW: Yes, if engineers want to render their neural nets recursive, they face the problem of having to use one part of the net under different constraints multiple times. How to do that? The recursivity of artificial nets consists in the iterative "learning" process alone, i.e., in the approximation of a function. Yet, the execution of this function itself, mapping input to output, runs in parallel. Hence, it is not truly recursive. The process can be made recursive only by the intervention of an engineer analyzing and partitioning the function into sequences. Already in the 1990s, Geoffrey Hinton discussed this problem in his seminal paper.[35] He demonstrated that for every finite or fixed network there are problems, which the net will only solve, if parts of it are used multiple times. So by parallel processing alone these problems are not solvable. Furthermore, Hinton emphasized that the multiple use of network parts still remains without orientation, because its "role," that is, its operative function, to "search" for patterns and "copy them to the right," for instance, must be assigned at hierarchically different levels of the net.

In humans, however, a trivial recursion already begins when we perceive an analogy. So the concept of mathematical recursivity formalizes psychological similarity. Speaking of recursion, we mean analogies, which is actually the clearest meaning reaching back even to colloquial language. I've always said that an analogy of two strings is a Turing machine accepting or generating both strings. So this implies that a structure that has two strings in common is an analogy of these two strings. This, of course, is especially evident under changing constraints, when in a high-level programming language a particular module can be called by various other modules. In theory, Hinton proposed a "timesharing" of network parts. Yet, as far as I am informed, it has never been successfully implemented.

The problem of recursion in connectionist networks

At the same time, when Harnad attempted to ground his model of "symbolic" thought in "causal" connectionist processes, Geoffrey E. Hinton analyzed the general difficulties of mapping sequential, flexible, cross-level (i.e., recursive) processes onto connectionist networks. Before, these problems had been neglected in the discussion of neural networks inspired by physics or biology, as he wrote.

On the one hand, Hinton defends research on these networks against the objections of Jerry Fodor and Zenon Pylyshyn, who deemed them no more than a new edition of psychological associationism. Using the example of a specific network for the "family trees task," which was supposed to learn by back propagation the relations of two different family trees (twelve first names of persons and their kinship relations each, e.g., daughter, son, uncle, mother of etc.), Hinton showed by his content analyses of the optimized node weights that the network encoded much more than a lookup table mechanism associating the "explicitly" entered values and their connections. He showed that in this "trained" artificial network, the implicit isomorphism of the two family trees is used for the parsimony of processing. So it does not represent a mere association, but would have to be dubbed "intuitive" reasoning and could, therefore, be distinguished from the "rational" finding of regularities.

On the other hand, Hinton made clear that the fixed input-to-output mapping by such a network, i.e., by exclusively parallel processes, is by no means sufficient to solve more complex, hierarchically structured tasks. For every fixed network, new, unsolvable tasks can be constructed, e.g., tasks requiring the solution of subtasks, which in turn require the same processes to be applied to different types of data. Hinton concluded that the criterion for distinguishing between "intuitive" and "rational" reasoning is not seriality (the repetitive execution of network parts) but the sequential aspect pertaining to different data and levels.

Hinton suggested overcoming these limitations by "timesharing" (e.g., in visual word recognition). One part of the network is to be reused at different times with respect to its function (e.g., representing a letter pattern in each and every word). Hinton examined this reuse of network parts (or modules) first at one functional level (e.g., the level of letter recognition) and then as a full-fledged discrete-step ascent and descent across different levels of part-whole hierarchies. For the fans of "pure connectionism," his results were sobering. Reusing network parts across different levels does allow for the capturing of certain kinds of regularities, but only by resorting to sequential processes and, thereby, the loss of parallel processing.

Until this day, Hinton's analyses prove the ongoing difficulties of implementing sequential recursive processes in connectionist networks. His proposal to "timeshare" parallel processes across different layers remained theoretical. There has been no successful implementation so far. In this context, the later attempts by Alex Graves et al. to implement "neural Turing machines" should be mentioned.

Hinton, Geoffrey F , 1990. Mapping Part-Whole Hierarchies into Connectionist Networks. *Artificial Intelligence*, 46, 47–75.

Fodor, Jerry A., and Zenon W. Pylyshyn, 1988. Connectionism and Cognitive Architecture: A Critical Analysis. *Cognition*, 28/1–2, 3–71.

Graves, Alex, Greg Wayne, and Ivo Danihelka, 2014. Neural Turing Machines. *arXiv:1410.5401*.

MS

MS: Perhaps it is fair to say that an essential part of human intelligence consists not only in the discovery or recognition of patterns but also in the recognition and generalization of the procedures effectuating this feature. When it comes to generalizing the possible emergence of regularities by a method, it's not only the aforementioned development from the general to the concrete, but perhaps also from implicit, sensorimotor action to an explicit model. Does the process of assembly in human thought imprint into the over-determined and contradictive landscape of seeds an order leading to generalization and the construction of explicit procedures?

This question certainly is remotely connected to Hinton's attempts to train ANNs on family trees and then search for implicitly trained relations within these nets. But it was Hinton himself and not the network, who analyzed the implicitly computed weights of the units in the trained network. It was also he himself, who recognized the analogy that the network uses the same input-output structure for two different family trees, one with English and the other with Italian names. The recognition of over-determinacy of the network relating two phylogenetic trees may, in the broadest sense, be interpreted as the first step towards generalization or even to the recursive use of network parts. Only that in Hinton's case this creative achievement was not performed by a second ANN, but by Hinton himself. It would be interesting to investigate the relation between the apparently trivial or *brute force* search for regularities, on the one hand, and their true recursive generalization, on the other.

OW: Have you ever looked at how a Turing machine trivially writes down the multiplication table up to 100?

MS: Yes, to illustrate the difference in my classes, I even show the recursive multiplication M.TM from your textbook,[36] contrasting it to a trivial Turing machine computing a single number only.

OW: You can program a trivial Turing machine for the multiplication table up to 100, which of course writes it on the tape much faster than a recursive one. It reads the two numbers of the multiplication, i.e., the factors, digit by digit. For each digit there are branches until the correct place in the table, that is the correct product, is assigned an output. Trivial machines are very important, firstly as examples of primitive recursivity, because in fact they represent the zero level of recursivity enabling the general statement that this level is also recursive. Secondly, they are crucial, because the method of table lookup is the fastest implementation. Here again, we have a trade-off between memory and speed, because the trivial solution consumes a lot of memory. These are all things that need to be considered and certainly also play a role in our cognitive abilities.

MS: But then you define a very broad concept of recursivity instead of the usual one of calling one and the same module several times. I must also emphasize that the trivial machine is exclusively tailored to the application of the multiplication table only up to 100, whereas the recursive M.TM can in principle multiply any number by any other. The history of the invention of true recursion in multiplication would be relevant here. If I already have the trivial mechanism, how do I generalize it into a recursive multiplication machine? Equally relevant would be the question, why I am able to see what M.TM is doing, when watching its operations multiplying two numbers on the tape string? And why I am also able to see that it is doing exactly the same thing in two different places on the string? Why can I see this analogy instantly, while I have to fundamentally analyze an ANN to see it, as was the case in Hinton's example of the family tree?

OW: That's an interesting question. I didn't include the following point in my Turing machine book, but as a paradigm I introduced the multiplication machine you are talking about.[37] It has ten states and operates on a string of only two symbols, one and zero (and blank as separator). M.TM multiplies two blocks of ones, which it interprets, so to speak, as natural numbers in unary format, and outputs their product as another block of ones to the right side. After completing the multiplication it stops.

Now the basic idea was the following: I have M.TM with ten states. When observing the operations of M.TM on the string, everyone sees immediately that there are two cycles, which one can represent graphically as two circles. In fact the two are identical, but they occur twice in the table, i.e., in the program code. A run of M.TM consists of *three* cycles, of which *two* are actually identical.

MS: From a purely technical perspective the first factor is processed in exactly the same way as the second. It is also important that I recognize this on the basis of the trace of the run of the machine, even though the repetition occurs in two different areas of the string.

OW: Yes, exactly. My idea was to use one of these two parts of the program twice, which is the basic idea of recursion anyway. The important thing is that these two cycles are separately represented in the ten-state machine, that is, there are two different loops coded in the TM table. But both loops do exactly the same thing. The programming task I devised was how to avoid this and pack them into only one loop, which is then called twice. In order to achieve this you have to do quite amazing things: you have to outsource to the tape, i.e., to the string, by arranging extra compartments there. But because you have to arrange that in the code, it allows you to save only one state in the table, although one loop has four states. So the new M.TM' code still comprised nine states. But it now contained a module that could be called alternately for two different areas of the string. If the computation were more complicated ...

MS: ... then this ratio would become much more efficient and you would save many more states.

OW: If such a cycle does not comprise four states, but, say, hundred, then you could apply the same truncation method. At the same time, the truncation would become more and more potent, the more extensive and complicated the cycles are.

MS: So perceiving an analogy between the two cycles does not yet suffice to apply it in a recursive sense. The discovery alone is not enough. This is what I meant earlier. You must design or construct the machine as such recursively. If you want to apply a module analogously multiple times, then the machine has to "remember" where it is applying the module in its "role," as Hinton would say, the module has just performed. Has its isolated function been applied on the first factor or the second? That's what you mean by the additional "compartments," isn't it? You have to arrange for something we used to call an external memory: a symbol with marker function is written on the tape that identifies which factor is currently processed. This symbol is erased when a cycle is complete.

OW: Yes, yes, but that doesn't really amount to an external memory. Practically, it's an orientation as to which level the machine is currently working on. The machine itself doesn't know that. Machines such as this lack any coarse description or prototype of what they are currently computing. Only we as human beings are able to observe the machine's activity and then guess what it is doing. This is a kind of meaning production, which functions differently in humans than in shallow formalisms.

MS: If you ask me how I recognize a cycle of M.TM, I can tell you exactly which meaning I project onto it and what I see it repeating on the tape areas of the first and second factor. So I roughly grasp the content of a process: First, it "remembers" a symbol, "copies" this symbol, and then "carries" it to the other side across the blocks out of ones. Then it "drops" it in the result field as a "copy" and returns back, and so on. Of course, the machine does not *really* carry symbols across other symbols, nor does it *drop* a copy of a symbol anywhere! This meaning manifests itself only in my head when I recognize these procedures. Several seeds become conscious as I watch the machine's run, and they organize my orientation into a prototype of the observed sequence. This sequence, arranged sequentially according to content, helps me to interpret and recognize the concretely visible operations of the machine. The TM itself doesn't know any meaningful operations but is only executing state transitions. Of course, the Turing machine also doesn't know at which level it currently operates if this information is not implemented. And this implementation would have to be sequential. So this has very much in common with the problem mentioned by Hinton about how parts of a neural net are to be used as generalized method over multiple levels.

Stacks

OW: As far as orientation on different levels is concerned, in von Neumann computers this is implemented with a stack. In a Turing machine, you have to implement it in fact quite similarly. You have to construct some kind of stack. So I had to rebuild the M.TM into an M.TM', which then uses one module twice via the coordination of a stack. Certainly, the same principle is used today in ANNs as well. It is John von Neumann himself who is credited with this wonderful invention. Actually, stacks were already patented in 1957 under the name of the "cellar principle" by Friedrich L. Bauer and Klaus Samelson as well as described independently by Charles Hamblin in Australia at roughly the same time.

The *stack* or stack memory is an address list, as they say, functioning by the method of last in/first out. By "push" you put an object onto a stack, which in our example is the processed first factor of the multiplication, while the second factor is being processed with the same module, when called. By "pull" you then take the top object out of the stack again, e.g., if you want to go back to the first level after having processed the second factor. In more complex programs, of course, there are many more levels, so that stacking must be conceived of as a dynamic tree. If one module begins operation, then an address is added, and as soon as this module is processed, control is passed on or given back and the uppermost address is deleted, until ideally at the end the stack is again empty.

MS: You quote the stack as an example of a formalized aspect of orientation, which we also experience in thinking, namely to know what level we are at when operating with generalized methods at different levels.

OW: Yes, but I use the formalization of the stack method to compare them to the thought process. Well, since I suspect we've gone a bit too far with the technical aspect of the TM metaphor, I conclude by recommending everyone to think about how to implement such a stack as a Turing machine. Sometimes, you have deep insights based on finding solutions to even such simple tasks.

MS: One must not be discouraged by the banality of simple problems and solutions. For even in complex programs, these simple principles of modularization and of arranging heterarchies are inevitable. Most of all, they are certainly relevant for ordered thought. Even the most difficult problems of computability are based on such simple steps as you have shown in your textbook.

OW: We relate technical terms to introspection because we need clear formulations to delineate our thought experiences. If I want to gain insights into thinking, the computational metaphor – taken as an attempt to formalize living thought – is still a suitable method of comparison with the results of introspection, e.g.,

object (in the sense of object-oriented programming) <-> representation[38]

symbol, pointer, token, "index entry" <-> seed

concatenation <-> running environment, scaffold

tree structure <-> heterarchy

data structure <-> structure

bootstrapping <-> expansion (of seeds), assembly, scaffold, prototype

"pattern of activity" <-> structure

"distributed information" <-> parameters of cognitive dynamics

"subsymbolic" <-> tacit processes (readiness, attunement)

"designation" <-> meaning

"interpretation" <-> understanding

etc.

We need to supplement these concepts with some new concepts or formulations, and then summarize what has accumulated so far to build up an alternative theory of thought and intelligence.

---

1   Computational metaphor refers to all efforts from the 1940s onwards to represent processes analysed by cognitive, perceptual, or behavioral psychology – specifically human intelligence – by a universal descriptive computational framework (e.g., the universal Turing machine) or information processing (e.g., artificial neural networks). The premise is functional equivalence of man and machine. Understanding biological and psychological processes and structures on the basis of such functional metaphors or simulating their performance (on computers) gradually replaced the physical metaphors, e.g., of mental energies and forces and their causation, or of field theories.

2   Wiener, Oswald, 2018. compMet1 (Version 21 December 2018), unpublished.

3   Wiener, Oswald, Manuel Bonik, and Robert Hödicke, 1998. *Eine elementare Einführung in die Theorie der Turing-Maschinen*. Vienna, 10–27.

4   Wiener, Oswald, 2007. Über das „Sehen" im Traum: Zweiter Teil. *manuskripte*, 178, 170f.

5   Eder, Thomas, and Thomas Raab (eds.), 2015. *Selbstbeobachtung: Oswald Wieners Denkpsychologie*. Berlin.

6   Schwarz, Michael, 2015. Geometrie und Lernen: Aspekte des Operativen und Figurativen in Bezug zur Laufumgebung. Ibid., 165–189.

7   Wiener, Oswald, 2015. Glossar: Weiser. Ibid., 59–98.

8   In German "Implikation," "Irritation," and "*q*Bild," ibid., 64–65.

9   Piaget, Jean, 1923. La pensée symbolique et la pensée de l'enfant. *Archives de Psychologie*, 18, 273–304.

10   See "Cognitive Symbols: From Ontogeny to Their Actual Genesis. A Psychogenesis Based on James Mark Baldwin and Jean Piaget" by Michael Schwarz in this volume.

11   According to Oswald Wiener "a *structure* of a string is a Turing machine generating or accepting this string." Cf. Wiener, Oswald, 2015. Glossar: figurativ. In: Eder, Thomas, and Thomas Raab (eds.), *Selbstbeobachtung: Oswald Wieners Denkpsychologie*. Berlin, 100; id., 1988. Form and Content in Thinking Turing Machines. In: Herken, Rolf (ed.), *The Universal Turing Machine*. Oxford, 631–657; id., 1996. *Schriften zur Erkenntnistheorie*. Vienna, New York, 112–144.

12   Turing, Alan M., 1937. On Computable Numbers, with an Application to the Entscheidungsproblem. *Proceedings of the London Mathematical Society*, 42/1, 249–254.

13   Wiener, Oswald, Manuel Bonik, and Robert Hödicke, 1998. *Eine elementare Einführung in die Theorie der Turing-Maschinen*. Vienna, 121.

14   Newell, Allen, and Herbert A. Simon, 1976. Computer Science as Empirical Enquiry: Symbols and Search. *Communications of the ACM*, 19/3, 113–126.

15   See "Cognitive Symbols: From Ontogeny to Their Actual Genesis. A Psychogenesis Based on James Mark Baldwin and Jean Piaget" by Michael Schwarz in this volume.

16   Simon, Herbert A., 1969/1981. *The Sciences of the Artificial*. Cambridge, MA, London.

17   Wiener, Oswald, 1996. *Schriften zur Erkenntnistheorie*. Vienna, New York, 82.

18   Ibid., 83; id., 1984. Turings Test. *Kursbuch*, 75, 12–37.

19   Harnad, Stevan, 1990. The Symbol Grounding Problem. *Physica D*, 42, 335–346.

20   Wiener, Oswald, 2007. Über das "Sehen" im Traum: Zweiter Teil. *manuskripte*, 178, 168.

21   Ibid., 170f.

22   Wiener, Oswald, 2015. Glossar: figurativ. In: Eder, Thomas, and Thomas Raab (eds.), 2015. *Selbstbeobachtung: Oswald Wieners Denkpsychologie*. Berlin, 99–142.

23   Wiener, Oswald, 2015. Glossar: Weiser. Ibid., 59–98.

24   Hinton, Geoffrey E., 1990. Mapping Part-Whole Hierarchies into Connectionist Networks. *Artificial Intelligence*, 46, 47–75.

25   According to the experiments of Bluma Zeigarnik, unfinished tasks are kept in mind especially firmly. Zeigarnik, Bluma, 1927. On Finished and Unfinished Tasks. In: Ellis, Willis D. (ed.), *A Source Book of Gestalt Psychology*. New York 1938, 300–314. Cf. "Fantasy, Repression, and Motivation in an Ecological Model of Memory" by Thomas Raab in this volume.

26   Silberer, Herbert, 1909. Report on a Method of Eliciting and Observing Certain Symbolic Hallucination-Phenomena. In: Rapaport, David (ed.), 1965. *Organization and Pathology of Thought*. New York, 195–207.

27   Marcel, Anthony J., 1980. Conscious and Preconscious Recognition of Polysemous. Words: Locating the Selective Effects of Prior Verbal Context. In: Nickerson, Raymond S. (ed.), *Attention and Performance VIII*. Hillsdale, NJ, 435–457; id., 1983. Conscious and Unconscious Perception: Experiments on Visual Masking and Word Recognition. *Cognitive Psychology*, 15, 197–237. Cf. "Literature, Language, Thought: The Beginnings. A Conversation Between Oswald Wiener and Thomas Eder" in this volume, 65f.

28   Bühler, Karl, 1908. Tatsachen und Probleme zu einer Psychologie der Denkvorgänge: II. Über Gedankenzusammenhänge. *Archiv für die gesamte Psychologie*, 12, 1–23.

29   Piaget, Jean, 1923. La pensée symbolique et la pensée de l'enfant. *Archives de Psychologie*, 18, 273–304.

30   Newell, Allen, and Herbert A. Simon, 1976. Computer Science as Empirical Enquiry: Symbols and Search. *Communications of the ACM* 19/3, 126.

31   Wiener, Oswald, 1998. Wozu überhaupt Kunst? In: id. *Literarische Aufsätze*. Vienna, 21–41.

32   Wiener, Oswald, Manuel Bonik, and Robert Hödicke, 1998. *Eine elementare Einführung in die Theorie der Turing-Maschinen*. Vienna, 59–63.

33   Wiener, Oswald, 1996. *Schriften zur Erkenntnistheorie*. Vienna, New York.

34   Ibid., 237.

35   Hinton, Geoffrey E., 1990. Mapping Part-Whole Hierarchies into Connectionist Networks. *Artificial Intelligence*, 46, 47–75.

36   Wiener, Oswald, Manuel Bonik, and Robert Hödicke, 1998. *Eine elementare Einführung in die Theorie der Turing-Maschinen*. Vienna, 14–26.

37   Ibid.

38   Wiener, Oswald, 2007. Über das „Sehen" im Traum: Zweiter Teil. *manuskripte*, 178, 168.

Cybernetics and Ghosts[1]

In the No-Man's-Land between Science and Art

Oswald Wiener

Cybernetics

Once I began to waver whether or not I wanted to become a musician or a poet, the question of how, in what way, music and language exert their effects gradually became more important to me than these effects themselves – more important than my aesthetic emotions. How do we understand? What is the cause of the effect that Achleitner's "constellation" *baum bim* had on me?[2] So epistemology became more important to me than aesthetics.

What is a concept? How come that I know where I am *now* in this piece of music, and what it "means" what I hear? How do I lose the thread? What is meaning? Thus, I turned to philosophy and to psychology, but I realized, gradually, that they wouldn't provide satisfying answers to my questions. What I would need was not "conceptual work" but *mechanisms* – mechanisms that understand, and which I could observe and then learn to understand how they understand. It was the 1950s, and you could hear cybernetics coming. Finally, cybernetics would bring the answers ...

... not. Already in his famous 1950 essay Turing had written: "May not machines carry out something which ought to be described as thinking but which is very different from what a man does? This objection is a very strong one, but at least we can say that if, nevertheless, a machine can be constructed to play the imitation game satisfactorily, we need not be troubled by this objection" (Turing 1950: 435). So he had already realized that the coming development of "Artificial Intelligence" would not bother the exploration of human intelligence. Presumably, Turing *wanted* this development; but – in the Austrian backwoods fifteen years later and still unaware of his paper – I saw, how the use of computers indicated by him would block the way to a strong epistemology.[3] In 1984,[4] I still believed that Turing's behaviorist approach would not even lead to machines passing his own test. So thought I could spare any argument about his "objection" (although I should have noticed that he had placed it at the very beginning of his paper instead of in the context of his discussion of the objections he considered refutable; Turing 1950: 442ff.).

For then I could not imagine that the development of hardware would keep its speed till the twenty-first century. Today, we do have computers that are able to generate "all the possible combinations, whose number would frighten the imagination"[5] and to squeeze the Library of Babel into a sequence of a few letters forming one remaining sentence, which a human being is able to understand as a fitting bon mot. In 2011, a program called *Watson*[6] won three episodes of the television quiz game *Jeopardy!* against the two reigning champions of that series. Compared to the goals of today's projects, Watson was quite modestly equipped – only ninety *IBM Power 750 servers* with only sixteen terabytes of RAM, each server with only a 3.5 GHz 8-core processor, and each core only handling a maximum of four threads at a time.[7]

There is a trade-off between storage space and speed (as I wrote in the passage in footnote 3) because "deep" structures require less data but more time than "shallow" ones. With the immense growth of storage space and the incredible acceleration of processing speed, i.e., with decreasing processing costs per unit, Occam's razor itself becomes uneconomical, and remains, if at all, as a rule for mental exercise only. Today, processing speed exclusively serves the search of databases or generate-and-test[8] of flat formalisms. The abundance of storage space etc. renders any accommodation of structure unnecessary. Now "accommodation" only consists in collecting exceptional cases – thus a large, perhaps even huge, set of exceptions to a shallow rule replaces the deep rule (which would be troubled by any exception). Of course, a minimum of structure must exist. The goal is to find for each case that minimum which yields a universal machine in the given domain, so to speak.[9] This could largely be achieved by simple trial and error, if the development of computation is faster than the development of what is computed.[10]

At any rate, such programs show one thing clearly enough. As they are no longer dependent on the acquisition of structure, they achieve the goal set for them in quite different ways than human intelligence.[11] *Watson* computes words as bit strings – they do not mean anything. Controlled by a set of partially probabilistic[12] derivation rules and supported by its huge and ever-growing database, the program converts an input string interpreted by humans as a linguistic expression into an output string that humans understand as a sentence. This amounts to a perfect execution of Watson's (the behaviorist's) intrinsically Occamian concern to keep hidden variables as shallow as possible – "we denied the necessity of assuming imagery (...) for the reason that we can substitute for what it is supposed to do a mechanism which is exactly in line with what we have found to exist everywhere else, viz., an enormously developed system of language habits."[13]

For Watson and in *Watson*, thought is a mapping of word lists on word lists by a function with maximum extension and minimum intension. Its ideal is the lookup table.[14] In *Watson*'s case, the operations do not hide any puzzles. If it seems puzzling that they pass Turing's test, then the reason seems to be Turing's test itself. Watson, on the other hand, is puzzling enough (e.g., the reader has to guess why an excitation pattern in the speech apparatus so frequently and tediously transforms into chains of other excitation patterns of the same muscle group before the hand or the arm moves, etc.). Yet, unlike *Watson*, he functions quite differently than he is inferring from his own activity.

"[M]eaning is but a trick [of evolution] to overcome limitations of formal capacity; this insight extends to the guidance of formal manipulations content."[15] Well, *sense* and *meaning* are the ghosts of cybernetics. More generally, "subjective experiences" – "mental images," "figuring," "believing," "mind," and "consciousness" as such ... It seems ghostly that such words, which belong to colloquial language use alone, have now found their way back into science, and that for this very reason what is meant by them has begun to rumble once more. And it is no less ghostly that today's computer programs have been turned into explications of these words – now they "understand," "learn," "try out," "expect," "represent," and so on. In this respect, Turing was yet again right: Only a few will laugh (sadly) at the claim that today's machines are thinking machines.

Ghosts

"Content," "intuitions," "ideas," "propositions," and the like do not only haunt cybernetics (if this is the right name for today's applied computer science and its philosophy), they also play their tricks in physiology – *How Neurons Mean*[16] – and, of course, even more so in psychologizing philosophy. Isn't it a little spooky that the "view from within" wants to gain reputation by using crutches such as phenomenology and Franz Brentano? Or, that the countless new efforts to make sense of the word "consciousness" do not result in more than an interchange of words?[17] In any case, the devil must have his hand in it when someone tries to "visualize" "covert behavior" by fMRI scans, and at the same time excludes introspection unable to find such images as a diagnostic tool.[18]

For without introspection some crucial questions of psychophysiology will, I believe, remain unanswered:
– How do energy modulations in the environment impacting on the organism's sensory surface become parameters in the control of adaptive behavior?
– In what ways do people surrogate such impacts from their environment when thinking and imagining, and how are the stimuli integrated with these surrogates?
– What role does subjective experience play in the control of adaptive behavior? And most importantly:
– What is the physiological correlate of subjective experience?

The "cognitive revolution" of the fifties did not significantly change the status of these questions. As far as, for instance, the "contents of consciousness" are concerned (i.e., the second of my "all-important questions" above), Roger Sperry (1952: 295) declared: "The scope and diversity of opinion to be found in the current literature reflect our general confusion and almost complete lack of guiding principles." The decades since then have only increased this confusion insofar as we know less and less how to define it but at the same time try to clarify it with increasingly complex technical tools. Regarding the question of "neural correlates of conscious experience" – i.e., question four above – it was "really the 'brain' part of the mind-brain relation that most urgently needs clarification" (ibid.: 291f.). Thus, Sperry thought that physiology was to blame for the confusion. But should really neurobiology or neural engineering establish a "Theory of Representational Content"? I think that here we have two *different,* hitherto unsolved tasks: What is a mental apparatus able to grasp of its own workings, and how can it communicate with others about it? How are the introspectively established regularities realized in the CNS? Since Sperry did not take into account introspectively gained clues, it is not even clear what he actually meant by "subjective experience." To everyone seeking clarity, it becomes clear that here *psychology* has been erased from the picture.

Sperry's paradigm is the sensor→motor-transformation: "perception is basically an implicit preparation to respond" (ibid.: 302), it is "motor adjustment" (ibid. passim). So it is rather understandable that he, in 1952, kept a low profile concerning "imagery." But at the same time it is also regrettable, because in this direction, or so I believe, a breakthrough is possible. The internal representation of an object in the organism *is* its respective "readiness for adaptive response" (ibid.: 300), a specific readiness for action[19] – and there are strong arguments for such a motor-hypothesis of mental processes. However, it would have to be refined into an ideo-motor hypothesis, because any pure motor theory has difficulties with the "figurative aspect"[20] of thought. How can the fabric of my readinesses for action surrogate the behavior of an object I am prepared for?[21]

  –   What, then, would have to be explained? In the following I give an example from my fragmentary, selected, and edited introspection notes to pose the question of the phenomenal as well as to illustrate some functional aspects of imagery.

Seeds and running structures

While reflecting on an introspection report shared by T., I came across the following "content:"

A coordinate plane, first quadrant (top right); and a line segment t of constant length (hereafter also called "rod"); η as the end point of t sliding in the vertical y-axis, ξ as its other end point sliding in the horizontal x-axis.

I have already played with these ideas a few times in order to "see" which properties the "logic" of the object produces.[22] First, I try to elaborate on their phenomenal aspect from some relevant introspection episodes (i.e., for the time being I neglect the *meanings* of the "phenomena," namely their embedding within my orientation).

The quadrant of the coordinate plane appears as a seed, its origin in the lower left, its axes indeterminate –

indeterminate but constructible. An irritation, which was also already there, expands to a seed of the rod:

A front is shearing to the left [implication: across the quadrant – the coordinate axes have vanished], rearing clockwise. The center of rotation and attention is the area around ξ pushing towards the origin.

The phenomenal aspect is underdetermined: the "front" is a movement of something indeterminate but determinable, but during the process it is only an elongated zone wiping in the direction of its width in contrast to the assumed surface. The "wiper" is no proxy object, but a kind of change; the *dynamics* of the process is present. What is determined is the running environment: obviously, I am well oriented, but the running environment is neither *present*.[23] I only notice that "*this,* again ..." happens.

Present in the narrowest, i.e. in the decisive sense, are thus changes – changes of relations, of positions, of situations. Therefore, the present is not a point in time but lasts as long as I need to grasp the character of the ongoing change. The respective situation (running environment[24]) is constituted within the respective orientation. It manifests itself only indirectly, namely as the background controlling the changes.[25]

> New assembly, almost immediately. Now η upwards on the *y*-axis. The η-end of *t* is a steeply sloping elongated shadow or fringe unrecognizably connected to an obstruction half-right below outside the pan.

By the word "shadow," I appoint a deficit (something merely implied, a "defined lack" in Sartre 2004) to a "vague mental image" (Müller 1924).[26] How do I recognize what I imagine? I know *what* it is before it appears and, within limits, independent of *how* it appears.

Sometimes, I indeed notice that what "appears" is something different or has different features than what it was supposed to have. There is a transition from what is to be assembled to the new interpretation: a moment of uncertainty, of disorientation. An "association" has taken place, the beginning of assembly distorts, so to speak, the orientation and, thus, brings a new aspect into play (which is not always recognized as an aspect implied by the seed):

> My attention "slides" down at *t*, in the direction of that place where it snags. Through this "movement" *t* turns out to be a black rubber rope with a square profile, which from there is stretched against a pull towards *that there* [upper left].
> Following the direction of the opposite pull, I reach ξ, the dark end of the dark rope.

I did not notice but am able to remember the following: Meanwhile – or maybe only now, while I digress from the observing attitude – *t* slowly swings to the left, like a pendulum.

– The names of the objects – *t*, ξ, ... – only serve communication; during the observation of the episode "I knew" that *this* was *that* (the rod) and that *there* was "the other" end.
– Is this episode an artifact of introspection? Yes – because I experienced it when I intended to pay attention to the phenomenal aspect of the events. No – because something emerged that would have been produced even without this attention. Yet, it would have remained unnoticed and, therefore (see below), almost ineffective. I had noticed the rubber rope already in an early attempt and at times while trying to repeat the assembly. The seed originally implied an "expander" (an elastic luggage strap).[27]

I now turn to the functional aspects of imagery:

The movement of *t* satisfying the above instructions yields a curve – intuition tells this to everybody who imagines the movement under this aspect. Every single position of *t* is a tangent of this curve.[28]

– Intuition that *t*, when "swinging," slides along the curve while being fixed to a point that slides in it like ξ slides in the *x*-axis ("swinging:" turning the rod from position "*t* lies in the *x*-axis" to the position "*t* lies in the *y*-axis," or vice versa).
– Intuition that my right middle finger, resting in the middle of *t*, draws the curve.

The first intuition turns out to be correct, if I additionally allow the point of contact to shift in *t*. Notably, the second one is wrong: the center of *t* describes a quarter circle around the origin with the radius *t*/2.

... Various thought experiments by pursuing various intuitions. Attempts, for example, to determine the shape of the curve intuitively. Is it a quarter circle too? Or I "see" *t* as the base line of a triangle, as the fixed-length hypotenuse of a deformable but always right triangle, whose right angle (the angle of the coordinate axes at the origin) remains fixed, and whose variable legs lie in the axes. At the beginning of the upward movement the triangle is the line itself, namely the hypotenuse lying in the *x*-axis. Then it grows until it is half of a square cut diagonally by the hypotenuse. Then it shrinks back to the distance, now totally symmetrically in the *y*-axis. Seed of Thales's circle, or rather of Thales's circles, but they remain inconsequential for now. Yet, the intermediate results of all these variations become sub-structures of my "rod" running environment.

A "longer mind Game:" While *t* is swinging upwards from the *x*-axis I have the intuition of a *wave*. At the beginning, I was not really able to clarify it, i.e., to grasp the wave more clearly. Instead, intuition cum "logic:" a point moves from right to left on the rod swinging up. In front of this point the wave rises, behind this point it falls.

Following a vague impulse from this thought, I insert a perpendicular line, parallel to the *y*-axis and (quite "automatically:") at a distance from it, which is smaller than the length of *t*. How come? I assume that it arose from the repertoire of my geometrical routines, and that the then current running environment was favorable to this idea, to this association.

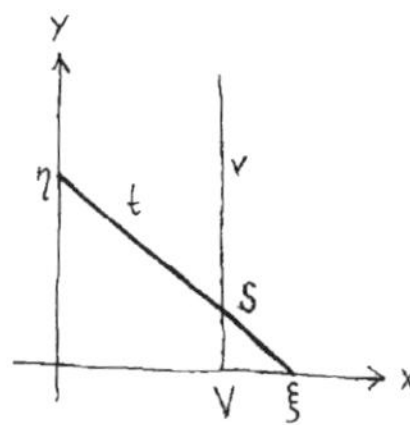

I observe the movement of the point *S* where *t* intersects this fixed line *v*. At the beginning *t* lies in the *x*-axis, and *S* lies in the base point *V* of *v*.

η starts to climb up the *y*-axis. The rotation of *t* in ξ slowly sliding to the left becomes clearer, seed of ξ, η now reduced to an irritation. Now *S*, *S* is given as a point on *t*, which, held by the merely implicit vertical *v*, slowly slides upwards on it.

A shift of aspect shows:

> S also "runs" along t in the direction of η – I get the feeling of scissors, wordless, only the movement of the scissors is present, the blades are merely implied by the position of v and t; an indeterminate object between the "blades" is pressed upward as they close.

Feeling: "Does not quite fit."
– the shear-movement had become a scissors-movement, which is to blame for the intuition that the distance from S to η decreases. An aspect grasping the relations more exactly, namely t becoming steeper particularly also between v and the y-axis would have resulted in the opposite intuition.[29] Later, the idea of scissors, albeit applied differently, will lead to new insights.[30]

t "gliding" over v is the guiding intuition for a more detailed exploration. My attention sticks to the movement of the intersection. Sometimes, I experience this movement as more or less continuous, sometimes as discontinuous transition from one position to the next. The "continuous" movement (apparently based solely on intuition) appears somewhat vague, as the intersection itself – a point?! – is not itself present. What is present is the upward movement of a place determined only roughly in terms of its size. I'd rather say: Present is the change of a seed of S, driven by a feeling of rotation represented by a tendency to supinate my right bent forearm. On the other hand, the single "snapshot" (intuition cum "logic") is equally vague. Actually, it consists only of jumps of attention to places, where the construction of a proxy subobject could possibly ensue.

I rotate t from the x-axis into the y-axis:

> η rises swiftly from the origin, ξ inertly follows the pull transmitted by t (in a sense t *is* this pull) moving in the (mere seed of the) x-axis. I attend to S; the seeds of t and v appear as line-fractions, but are only attended to as "forces" acting on S. S rises;

slower and slower; the fixation of the rotation in the axes decreases the pressure of the rod on S. For a moment η again becomes salient as pivot of the rotation, then suddenly a transition to wiping of t over v downward. It is impressive how t "is turning out of v" clockwise – S got stuck at the top (at the maximum), and the intersection of t and v drops down, briefly stalls in V and then accelerates bottomlessly.[31]

So the swinging rod affords the intersection to reach a maximum height above the x-axis. I imagine another perpendicular between v and the y-axis. Repeating the displacement of t I have the impression that the rod's highest point of intersection with the new perpendicular is higher than with the old one. I tend to think that these highest intersections are points of the envelope curve. And so forth.[32]

I try to sum up:

The descriptions of my introspections cannot satisfy any reasonably practiced and, therefore, skeptical introspector. I indicate my own concerns as follows:

Whenever I want to direct my attention to the sensory features of imagery, I fail due to the ephemerality of my "vague mental images." Since I don't find any "mental images" essentially comparable, e.g., to a sight or a sound, I conclude that we confuse the definiteness of our orientation with the clarity of stimuli. The reason is that for imagery the only analogy available is perception, because in the perceptual situation orientation is controlled by sensory influences of the environment,[33] and because we fail to realize that in perception orientation plays an almost equally dominant role as in imagery.

Then again colloquial language suggests a phenomenology of imagery, although it cannot describe what it simply posits as phenomenal by its own terms. Therefore, everyone who wants to describe it has to sidestep to the phenomenology of perception. Under these circumstances, the only legitimate manner of speaking is (as James would say) the "substantive" one, which is itself legitimate only as long as one refrains from psychological ambition and does not describe the sensory-phenomenal, the *quasi*-sensory/*quasi*-phenomenal as the trigger of ideas.[34]

In any case, it is clear that, in imagery as in perception, I attend to the phenomenal only if exactly this is the task (and then only with mixed and, in the case of imagery, very doubtful success). In such cases, the author later reads his description – like mine sketched above – differently than the reader, because he is oriented to the conditions of, e.g., the rod or the coordinate axes, etc. So the description is transparent to him or her.[35]

But neither do I pay attention to objects or to what would correspond to objects in imagery. I have already said it above: I pay attention to changes of the respective quite specific relations, and these relations are given and determined only as actions. Obviously, it depends on the specifics of these changes alone. The entities subject to the change are crucial only insofar as their changes are again mere changes of relations.

Such entities – James (1890, I: 243) calls them the "substantive parts" of the "stream of thought" – are not grasped by "sensorial imaginations of some sort, whose peculiarity is that they can be held before the mind for an indefinite time, and contemplated without changing" (!). For they are either seeds and so stand for "objects, with which one will occupy oneself if necessary," or an assembly ensues *immediately* and the seed comes to life as a s t r u c t u r e, which the subject experiences as a sequence of lawful changes and which s/he experiences only when operating them. "Some parts – the transitive parts – of our stream of thought cognize the relations rather than the things; but both the transitive and the substantive parts form one constant stream, with no discrete 'sensations' in it" (ibid.: 258). The "substantive parts" are insights into "things" insofar as they are seeds of structures of proxy objects; the expansion of the seed to the respective structure transforms the "substantive parts" into "transitive parts." The "conclusion" cannot be "a word or a phrase or a particular image" but a "practical attitude or a resolve" (ibid.: 260). "[T]he *meaning*, or, as we say, the topic of the thought" is nothing but a collection of more or less interlaced readinesses for action, i.e., a (germinating or running) structure.

For example, it is essential for the processes suggested above leading to the discovery of a procedure for computing envelope curves, that very specific intermediate results of running my *t*-and-*v*-mechanism, i.e., the positions of *S*, are "marked" by other sub-structures to yield a movement detached from the producing structure. That means they yield a separate structure. The new structure arises mainly by accommodation, adaptation, coupling etc. of already existing structures. It imitates the "movement" of *S* produced by the *t*-and-*v*-mechanism within my rearranged astroid heterarchy.

At first, the new structure almost always appears as a mere intuition ("association"), which must then be developed into a structure. Such intuitions accompany, in varying degrees of obtrusiveness, every move in orientation. Often, the intuition does not contain what I am looking for. But realizing, during the attempted assembly following the intuition, that it is wrong, increases my stock of useful structures too. Often the intuition can be corrected (like the middle finger above), and its expansion then leads to new aspects or insights.

Conclusion

When introspecting, even skeptically, one can hardly avoid experiencing the changes of one's orientation by imagery as changes of real objects, that is, of objects with intrinsic laws, which are not readily experienced as manifestations of one's own mental apparatus. One has few qualms about taking these workings of one part of orientation for the use of another part as *sensory* phenomena, but in doing so one should heed Shepard's remarks quoted in footnote 18.

Gaining knowledge of the nature, functionality, and biological implementation of these manifestations is one of the great desiderata of contemporary psychology. Can the "no-man's-land between science and art" shed some light on this area? In any case, the above fragments of introspections illuminate problems that only those will get to know who bother entering it. There s/he'll find a lot of questions. The ones already mentioned only pertain to a part of this territory:

-   Do the processes described have a functional core? In my descriptions the word "function" works as poorly as "phenomenon." In introspective explorations like those sketched above, problem-solving thought appears as the constructing, accommodating, parameterizing of structures, i.e., as the task-controlled changing of one component of current orientation under the influence of stimuli and of other components of this same orientation. Such introspections force us to conclude that accommodation cannot occur without "phenomena," that is, without stimulus configurations in perceiving or without "manifestations" of orientation in perceiving and in imagery. I simply would not have learned that S reaches a maximum on v, if I had not experienced it in the way described or in a "functionally equivalent" way. In any case, this relation has to be experienced as a specific spatio-temporal regularity, as an action determined by a certain background of action readinesses.[36] And I would not have been able to generalize my experience, if my attempts had taken place against a background too different from the one described.

That one part of orientation is beginning to have an effect on orientation at large can be compared to *broadcast*: Depending on the current orientation, such a broadcast updates several structures to different degrees and in different ways. I think that this "mechanism" (which is not a mechanism in the real sense, because "coincidences" contribute to its control) achieves what colloquial language means by "consciousness."[37]

-   If "mental images" do not function as images, and thought does not function by operating on images or on words, we have to ask ourselves: Function of *what*? If running structures are operations – where are the operands? Therefore, I refer back to the question: If operations are (spatio-temporal) *molds* of the operand – how can

such a "mold" of an object, its "negative," surrogate the object's
intrinsic laws?

Piaget (1951: 163) attempted an answer: "As we have seen, the image is
interiorized imitation, i.e., the positive of accommodation, which is
the negative of the imitated object. The image is therefore a schema
which has already been accommodated and is now used in present
assimilations, which are also interiorized, as 'signifier' for these 'signi-
fied.'"

I believe we should understand this the following way: Sensorimotor schemata differentiate by accommodations to the variable (but in
all its variability still regular) behavior of the objects, starting with slight
adaptations (*further ahead* ..., *more* ..., *slower* ...), parameterizations, then
anticipations of the object's behavior (reaching to where the object is
supposed to be) etc. If the organism is able explicate regularities within
these calibrations, i.e., render the control of its own behavior on the
object its proxy object, then the resulting structure represents the
intrinsic laws of the object, onto which the (preserved but now mod-
ified) sensorimotor schema fits.[38] Thus, the operands of the cognitive
operations are again structures.

Considerations such as these lead the introspector to the insight
that the real problems lie behind the "phenomena." The "phenomena"
are our metaphors for the dynamics of thought, whose peculiarity we
do not yet understand. Our cognitive apparatus does not store symbol
strings, which we might conceive of as images or as descriptions. The
structures my thinking already seems to have at its disposal are not
available as ready-made automata. So the heterarchy of my astroid, i.e.,
my astroid structure, must be reassembled every time "I think of the
astroid." What is obviously stored are "seeds," which, as construction
parameters, control the assembly of my astroid procedures, i.e., the
growth of suitable action readinesses within the respective orientation.

We do not yet know what it is that we are to take as the elements
of our cognitive structures. Is it the sensorimotor schemata?[39] What is
certain is that the flexibility of cognitive dynamics is based on the fact
that these elements are not hardwired to each other, but are held

together *ad hoc* and fall apart *post factum.* In other words, we do not yet know how the structures are implemented, of whose work we catch a glimpse in introspection. Introspection indicates that what colloquial language means by "mental image" is a seed, namely a readiness, a tendency.[40] And it also indicates that the nature of mental representations is to be sought in the direction professed by MacKay (footnote 19).

So from the perspective of my "no-man's-land," the situation looks like this:

Either I hallucinated what I tried to describe above; then I did not produce literature but bullshit. Or the mental must indeed be searched for at said physiological level of "broadcast," and the processes indicated in my introspective descriptions are indeed functional for such construction, accommodation, and adaption. In the latter case, we are forced to admit that neither contemporary psychology nor physiology, and much less the modeling of thought on computers, have even come close to elucidating these processes.

On the part of psychology, there is hardly anything to report concerning introspections: Philosophers deal with it, perhaps even demand the "view from within," which they themselves shun to share. There have been very few exceptions among the pioneers, but their introspective reports are far from sufficient too. Many of Brentano's doctrines, for example, suggest that he pursued his "self-perception" quite superficially.[41] From the schools of phenomenologists and neo-phenomenologists favorable to introspection, I have not yet witnessed one single empirical report.

How much today's physiology has to say about thought can be reviewed in works such as that of Parker et al. (2003). Modest is the psychologist who is satisfied with it. What, for instance, could today's imaging methods contribute to the elucidation of Anthony Marcel's crucial results (obtained without systematic introspection)?[42]

Indeed, I am convinced that new efforts based on introspection will reach far beyond the level of knowledge of the pioneers – since we, by our modest means, have already been able to take a few small steps.[43] More significant progress, however, can only be achieved through professionally organized research. Unfortunately, my experiences with research policy suggest that the potential of this approach will have to wait for a generation yet to come.

Appendix: Glossary, short version (details in Eder and Raab 2015)

A *structure* of a string is a Turing machine generating or accepting this string.

A *schema* is a biologically/epigenetically implemented structure.[44] From a didactic perspective the following idealization suggests itself: A fully developed "*schema of sensorimotor intelligence*" (Piaget) is (1) "automated," (2) controlled exclusively by sensory stimuli, and (3) shows itself exclusively by motor action.

A "*schema of conceptual intelligence*" is a heterarchy[45] of sensorimotor and conceptual schemata. The definition of the conceptual schema includes the fact that, as a heterarchy, sensorimotor schemata are able control each other without having to take a detour via the organism's environment.[46] To some degree, a conceptual schema can also become "automated," but in general it must be assembled on the fly, held together, and controlled by a "scaffold" of other schemata, i.e., by an adequate *running environment*.[47]

Intuition is the term for the activity of a sensorimotor schema when embedded in a conceptual schema, if this activity manifests itself as a seed.

The change of a structure is *registered*, if the run of the structure, before and after this change, can (possibly) be repeated in a way suitable for "broadcast." In general, such repetitions are surrogated with *seeds*.

Seeds are colloquially and misleadingly called "mental images" (or the like). A seed is the inchoate reconstruction of a conceptual schema. As

182

long as physiological explanations are missing, the best way to approach a definition of the term is by a physiologizing metaphor: A seed is a pilot excitation of varying strength providing components for scaffolding, which in any case already ensures Bühler's "structural determinations" ("Platzbestimmtheiten," Bühler 1907: 357ff., 1927: 116f.), namely the anchoring in relevant structures of the current orientation by providing the basis for an assembly.

Introspection indicates that these pilot excitations manifest themselves in quite different intensities. A seed can emerge as a "tachistoscopic" *intrusion*, or persevere as a mere *irritation* (the "meaning" of which is not *present* and becomes "broadcastable" only by *expansion*). Yet, it may also be expanded to the very structure seeded in the first place.[48]

The transition from the *expansion* of a seed to the *assembly* of a structure is continuous.

Action readinesses are pre-excited schemata whose excitations remain below the threshold necessary for a seed.[49]

The current overall arrangement of action readinesses is the organism's respective *orientation*.

Together with the findings of introspection, the fact that an "ordered thought process" is possible allows for the conclusion that heterarchies of action readinesses, as a background of implications, intervene in the control of thought processes (as "determining tendencies," Ach 1951).

References

Ach, Narziss, 1951 [1905]. Determining Tendencies, Awareness. In: Rapaport, David (ed.), *Organization and Pathology of Thought*. New York, 15–38.
Beth, Evert Willem, and Jean Piaget, 1961. *Épistémologie mathématique et psychologie / Essai sur les relations entre la logique formelle et la pensée réelle*. Paris.
Brentano, Franz, 1874. *Psychologie vom empirischen Standpunkte*. 2 vols., *Vom sinnlichen und noetischen Bewußtsein* (1928) as vol. 3, (I 1973, II 1971, III 1974). Hamburg.
Bühler, Karl, 1907. Tatsachen und Probleme zu einer Psychologie der Denkvorgänge I. Über Gedanken. *Archiv für die gesamte Psychologie*. 9, 297–365.
Bühler, Karl, 1927. *Die Krise der Psychologie*. Jena.

Calvino, Italo, 1986. Cybernetics and Ghosts. In: *The Uses of Literature*. San Diego, New York, London, 3–27.

Campbell, Murray, A. Joseph Hoane Jr., and Feng-hsiung Hsu, 2001. Deep Blue. http://sjeng.org/ftp/deepblue.pdf (14 March 2022).

Coltheart, Max, 2006a. What Has Functional Neuroimaging Told Us about the Mind (So Far)? *Cortex*, 42, 323–331.

Coltheart, Max, 2006b. Perhaps Functional Neuroimaging Has Not Told Us Anything about the Mind (So Far). *Cortex*, 42, 422–427.

Eder, Thomas, and Thomas Raab (eds.), 2015. *Selbstbeobachtung: Oswald Wieners Denkpsychologie*. Berlin.

Eliasmith, Chris, 2000. *How Neurons Mean: A Neurocomputational Theory of Representational Content*. Ph.D. Dissertation. St. Louis.

Ferrucci, David, Eric Brown, Jennifer Chu-Carroll, James Fan, David Gondek, Aditya A. Kalyanpur, Adam Lally, J. William Murdock, Eric Nyberg, John Prager, Nico Schlaefer, and Chris Welty, 2010. Building Watson: An Overview of the DeepQA Project. *AI Magazine*, 31/3, 59–79.

Guillery, R.W., and S. Murray Sherman, 2011. Branched Thalamic Afferents: What Are the Messages That They Relay to the Cortex? *Brain Research Reviews*, 66/0, 205–219.

Hadamard, Jacques, 1954 [1945]. *An Essay on The Psychology of Invention in the Mathematical Field*. New York.

Helmholtz, Hermann von, 1995 [1878]. The Facts of Perception. In: Cahan, David (ed.), *Hermann von Helmholtz: Science and Culture – Popular and Philosophical Essays*. Chicago and London, 342–380.

Hobson, J. Allan, 1994. *The Chemistry of Conscious States*. Boston.

Horikawa, Tomoyasu, Masako Tamaki, Yoichi Miyawaki, and Yukiyasu Kamitani, 2013a. Neural Decoding of Visual Imagery During Sleep. *Science*, 340, 639–642.

Horikawa, Tomoyasu, Masako Tamaki, Yoichi Miyawaki, and Yukiyasu Kamitani, 2013b. Supplementary Materials for Neural Decoding of Visual Imagery During Sleep; especially: www.science.org/doi/suppl/10.1126/science.1234330/suppl_file/1234330s1.mov and www.science.org/doi/suppl/10.1126/science.1234330/suppl_file/1234330s2.mov (22 March 2022).

James, William, 1890. *The Principles of Psychology*, Vols. I and II. New York 1950.

Lehrer, Jonah, 2008. Can a Thinking, Remembering, Decision-Making, Biologically Accurate Brain Be Built from a Supercomputer? *Seed Magazine* 3/4, http://shinyverse.org/al4ai/ extras/Seed-Out_of_the_Blue.pdf (11 February 2023).

Loftus, Geoffrey, 1985. Johannes Kepler's Computer Simulation of the Universe: Some Remarks about Theory in Psychology. *Behavior Research Methods, Instruments, & Computers*, 17/2, 149–156.

MacKay, Donald MacCrimmon, 1984. Mind Talk and Brain Talk. In: Gazzaniga, Michael S. (ed.), *Handbook of Cognitive Neuroscience*, 293–317.

Marcel, Anthony J., 1980. Conscious and Preconscious Recognition of Polysemous Words: Locating the Selective Effects of Prior Verbal Context. In: Nickerson, Raymond S. (ed.), *Attention and Performance* 8. Hillsdale, NJ, 435–457.

Marcel, Anthony J., 1983. Conscious and Unconscious Perception: Experiments on Visual Masking and Word Recognition. *Cognitive Psychology*, 15, 197–237.

Metzinger, Thomas (ed.), 2000. *Neural Correlates of Consciousness: Empirical and Conceptual Questions*. Cambridge.

Müller, Georg Elias, 1924. Über die undeutlichen Vorstellungbilder. In: id., *Zur Analyse der Gedächtnistätigkeit und des Vorstellungsverlaufs, III. Teil*. Second edition. Leipzig, 505–567.

Neumaier, Otto (ed.), 2015. *Grenzgänge zwischen Wissenschaft und Kunst*. Vienna, Münster.

Orden, Guy C. van, and Kenneth R. Paap, 1997. Functional Neuroimages Fail to Discover Pieces of Mind in the Parts of the Brain. *Philosophy of Science*, 64, Supplement: Proceedings of the 1996 Biennial Meeting of the Philosophy of Science Association, Part II: Symposium Papers (Dec. 1997), S85–S94.

Parker, Andrew, Andrew Derrington, and Colin Blakemore (eds.), 2003. *The Physiology of Cognitive Processes*. Oxford.

Piaget, Jean, 1951 [1945]. *Play, Dreams and Imitation in Childhood*. London.

Piaget, Jean, 1960 [1947]. *Psychology of Intelligence*. Paterson, NJ.

Poincaré, Henri, 1921. Mathematical Creation. In: id., *The Foundations of Science*, trans. by George B. Halsted. New York, Garrison, NY, 383-394.

Pötzl, Otto, 1928. *Die Aphasielehre vom Standpunkte der klinischen Psychiatrie*. Vol. 1: *Die optisch-agnostischen Störungen (Die verschiedenen Formen der Seelenblindheit)*. Vienna.

Rühm, Gerhard (ed.), 1985. *Die Wiener Gruppe: Achleitner, Artmann, Bayer, Rühm, Wiener*. Reinbek.

Ryle, Gilbert, 1963 [1949]. *The Concept of Mind*. London.

Sartre, Jean-Paul, 2004. *The Imaginary: A Phenomenological Psychology of the Imagination*. Translated by Jonathan Webber, London and New York.

Segal, Jakob, 1916. *Über das Vorstellen von Objekten und Situationen: Ein Beitrag zur Psychologie der Phantasie*. Stuttgart.

Shepard, Roger N., 1978. The Mental Image. *American Psychologist*, 33/2, 125–137.

Silberer, Herbert, 1909. Report on a Method of Eliciting and Observing Certain Symbolic Hallucination-Phenomena. In: Rapaport, David (ed.), *Organization and Pathology of Thought*. New York 1951, 195–207.

Skinner, Burrhus F., 1966. An Operant Analysis of Problem Solving. In: Kleinmuntz, Benjamin (ed.), *Problem Solving: Research, Method and Theory*. New York, 225–257.

Sperry, Roger W., 1952. Neurology, and the Mind-Brain Problem. *American Scientist*, 40/2, 291–312.

Stricker, Salomon, 1879. Studien über das Bewusstsein. In: id., 1883. *Vorlesungen über allgemeine und experimentelle Pathologie*. Vienna, 461-560.

Turing, Alan M., 1937. On Computable Numbers, with an Application to the Entscheidungsproblem. *Proceedings of the London Mathematical Society* Second Series, 42/1, 230–265.

Turing, Alan M., 1950. Computing Machinery and Intelligence. *Mind*, 59/236, 433–460.

Watson, John B., 1914. *Behavior: An Introduction to Comparative Psychology*. New York.

Wiener, Oswald, 1984. Turings Test. *Kursbuch*, 75, 12–37.

Wiener, Oswald, 1988. Form and Content in Thinking Turing Machines. In: Herken, Rolf (ed.), *The Universal Turing Machine: A Half-Century Survey*. New York, 631–657.

Wiener, Oswald, 1990. Kambrium der Künstlichen Intelligenz. In: Simon, Herbert A., *Die Wissenschaften vom Künstlichen*. Berlin, 175–228.

Wiener, Oswald, 2000. Materialien zu meinem Buch VORSTELLUNGEN. In: Lesák, František (ed.), *Ausschnitt 05*. Vienna.

Wiener, Oswald, 2013. *die verbesserung von mitteleuropa / roman*. Third edition. Salzburg.

1. The title "Cybernetics and Ghosts" is not mine, but was suggested by Otto Neumaier, the editor of the volume in which the essay originally appeared (Neumaier 2015: 173–196). He chose it in reference to the title of a lecture given by Italo Calvino in 1967 (cf. Calvino 1986).

2. Cf., e.g., Rühm (1985: 39).

3. Cf., for example, Wiener (2013: CXLIX): "if (...) koppernigk would have had a computer at his disposal, which could have easily multiplied or shifted the ptolemaic circles having become conspicuous, we would probably have a modern ptolemaic worldview and would nonetheless be tackling space travel," as well as further remarks passim. See also Loftus (1985).

4. Wiener (1984, the subtitle is not mine); see also Wiener (1988: 633) and Wiener (1990).

5. Poincaré (1921: 392).

6. Named after the founder of IBM; it could just as well have been named after the founder of behaviorism, see below.

7. See, for example, Ferrucci et al. (2010). During von Neumann's times, a computer with as many

tubes as the number of neurons in the human brain would have been as large as the Empire State Building, consumed the entire energy the Niagara River could supply, and would have needed the entire river for cooling. Now *The Blue Gene / Q System* at the *Lawrence Livermore National Laboratory* operates with 1.6 million processor cores and a memory capacity of 1.6 petabytes (1.6 * 1015 bytes). In 2005, the *Blue Gene / L System* was already running at 280 tera-FLOPS (280 * 1012 floating-point operations per second). The *Brain Activity Map Project* will engage about 300 petabytes per year. In a 2008 interview, Henry Markram claimed that his project is designed on the basis of half an exabyte of memory (0.5 * 1018). So the supercomputers of five years ago would occupy the area of a few American football fields. Markram estimated his project's electricity costs at three billion dollars per year (a typo? Cf. Lehrer 2008). Etc.

8   That is, generating and testing symbol combinations under respective constraints, which would amount to Poincaré's (op. cit.) calculations of the "subliminal self." Cf. also the operation of the chess program Deep Blue (e.g., Campbell et al. 2001).

9   The application of support vector machines (SVM) classifying all differences by the same method already points into this direction.

10   Of course, sooner or later this will lead to disaster ... but the, decision-making by human intelligence is unreliable too.

11   This statement also holds true, or so I believe, for all other contemporary attempts at mock intelligence, which are by far less successful.

12   Applying probability theory to psychology almost always carries the seed of sacrificing insight. Statistics and probability theory are the mathematical expression of behaviorism, the theorem of Bayes alone encapsulates its entire program: "When a response occurs and is reinforced {hit}, the probability that it will occur again in the presence of similar stimuli is increased" (Skinner 1966: 226).

13   Watson (1914: 324); his "language habits" are mysterious, as his introspection proves: "(...) glance for a moment at the complexity of habit systems with which we have to deal in daily life. (...) before me as I write is a calendar with 'Friday, January 9' upon its face. (...) The city bell rings 12 P.M.. I say aloud 'another day over, it's January 10!' I glance at the calendar and say aloud, 'tear off leaf.' Immediately the movement is executed. Two stimuli are present simultaneously, both of which act upon the same effectors, viz., the intra-organically aroused one (exercise of the throat muscles) and the one extra-organically aroused (i.e., by the spoken word).
(...) On the other hand, I may *think* the words 'Saturday, January 10, tear off leaf,' and the act will follow. (It is just at this point that the upholders of the image say that you can<not only think it by silent speech, but that you can also *imagine* the act and the movement will follow. Our contention is that in thought the words *must be uttered* silently before the habitual act arises.)
(...) if a suitable stimulus is at hand, the act of the hand and arm follows. Now this stimulus can have its origin in any receptor (or in any muscle, considering them now as receptors). We have found such a group of receptors to be the throat muscles themselves, i.e., the movement of these muscles, as the silent speaking of the word, will initiate the impulse which drives the muscles of the arms and hands. All such processes are at bottom really identical in nature" (Watson 1914: 332f., footnote).

14   "*Shallow*" table lookup: the function is a set of ordered pairs (question/answer); "deep" table lookup: the answer is computed (recursive tables = programs).

15   Wiener (1988: 646).

16   Eliasmith (2000).

17   Just as Brentano replaced the undefined term "psychic" by the undefined term "intentional," newer explanations replace "conscious" by the undefined term "aware;" cf., for instance, Hobson's "two theorems: (1) The mind is all the information in the brain. (2) Consciousness is the brain's awareness of some of that information" (Hobson 1994: 203).

18   Roger Shepard predicted such experiments:

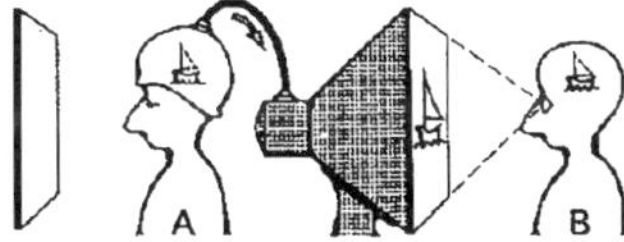

Device used for the externalization of a purely mental image (Shepard 1978: 128)

But he already warned: "our hypothetical device would [.] reconstruct an external like-ness of the object imagined, [but] this would not imply that the pattern of brain activity underlying the mental image had itself the shape of the external object" (ibid.), and "[n]ot only is it unnecessary to suppose that the brain process underlying a mental image is like some sort of picture, but in some situations it is unjustified to assume even that an exter-nally reconstructed picture can fully capture what is represented in that brain process" (ibid. 130).

The assumption that every time "I think of the same thing" a specific neural activity is more or less repeated seems evident today, but repeating an excitation pattern does not imply that the same *image* is activated. If a measuring instrument detects this pattern, we reach the strange conclusion that we now know "that I have thought something again," but still don't know *what* I have thought, and even less *how* thinking works.

Despite such concerns, Horikawa et al. (2013a, 2013b) did not refrain from "externalizing" some SVM classifications of their fMRI measurements on dreamers as image sequences – dream cinema in *Science* magazine.

19   MacKay (1984: 298) developed this notion one step further into the "notion of the internal representation of the external world, not by a model or analogue in the usual sense, but by a structure that embodies a matching state of conditional readiness for action."

20   Beth and Piaget (1961: 234).

21   Apparently, Sperry's ideas are irrelevant for today's neurophilosophy. In a book whose sub-ject as well as title could well be inspired by Sperry (Metzinger 2000), his name is mentioned only once (by Joëlle Proust on page 309), and only in connection with his concept of "*collat-eral discharge*" (which in turn, renamed *efference copy* by Guillery and Sherman [2011], could well include physiological arguments in favor of the [ideo-] motor hypothesis).

22   In this case, the "logic of the object" is the structure described by "coordinate plane, ..." Let-ting these structures run enables me to render the properties of the object explicit to myself.

23   Usually, my sense of orientation "seems rather a negative than a positive thing, being the mere absence of a shock, or sense of discord, between the terms of thought" (James 1890: 262f.). In my terminology it is the lack of an error signal.

24   "Working memory."

25   Addendum to footnote 23: sometimes also as an attunement.

26   "Our images are usually vague," wrote James (1890, II: 45), and he was not the first to say so; more detailed Hadamard (1954: 78) noted: "I see something like a formula, but by no means a legible one, as I should see it (being strongly long-sighted) if I had no eye-glasses on, with letters seeming more apparent (though still not legible) at the place which is supposed to be the important one."

27   The fantastic addition I describe here obviously has no elementary function. However, in retrospect I realize that it represents a condensation and/or a symbol and, thus, the seed of the following insight:

I cannot follow the movements of η and ξ simultaneously if I want to grasp local details (as, for example, comparing the distances covered by η or ξ in a given time). I am able to seed the implied simultaneity – in the present case by an irritation, or otherwise, for example, by motor or quasi-motor innervations. But the seed can only be expanded to a *structure*, and this structure is able to surrogate the relevant connection of the simultaneous events only by a *sequence* of operations.

Now, on the one hand, the increasing tension of the rubber string points to the "ballistic" movement of η outside the pan. On the other hand, it symbolizes (in a way reminiscent of Silberer) my own irritation. At the same time, however – and this is the main point –, it projects a virtual process – moving η, then going back in time to study the behavior of ξ while moving η – onto a physically possible process.

When I first had this experience, I did not know yet that the implied luggage strap type is called "expander." Otherwise, I might also refer to Freud's idea of the rebus – which is obvious anyway regarding the expressions of "con-nection" and "re-lation" (between η and ξ).

28   Intuition "tells" that, but it has yet to be proven.

29   I notice dream-like slips such as this so frequently that I believe they urgently deserve closer investigations (the "expander" commented above probably belongs to the same category). Are these normal intermediates of structural accommodation? "Splitting into partial qualities," "insufficient bundling of partial effects" (Pötzl 1928: 27).

30   Namely in the direction of the quarter circle of the middle finger, which I do not detail here.

31   The reader may ask him or herself how it is possible that s/he is able to understand this description.

32   If I wanted to know exactly what this curve is all about, I would have to do some more work on it, but the direction is now marked out. A little analysis tells me that I come to an exact description of the curve via the exact description of the rod and its movement; a formula for it can soon be found with the help of Pythagoras and the intercept theorem; swapping the independent variables brings in the "swinging;" the derivation of this function yields the maximum. By these operations I derive the formula of a curve, which, as I will soon find out, already has a name. It is an "astroid." And, by a series of generalizations, I further reach the harmonic oscillation and then the mechanics of the double slider mechanic – and who knows what!

My biggest yield is, of course, having found the general procedure for constructing an envelope curve (but, following what I said on the first pages of this paper, the reader should keep in mind that computers are able to compute the respective curve solely on the basis of the maximum principle, i.e., without any "insight" caused by finding a closed formula for the respective envelope). After all, this excursion has, among other things, brought me to a deeper understanding of how to parameterize curves, etc.

33   „Unconscious inferences," (Helmholtz 1995: 355) – "sense impressions change my orientation; now my orientation changes, therefore these are sense impressions ...;" "The visual character of my mental images seems less questionable, the less I pay attention to it" Wiener (2000: 79).

34   Sentences like "it grows until it is half of a square cut diagonally by the hypotenuse," although referring to experiences, leave the question of the phenomenal untouched.

Whoever wants to go beyond that should admit failure, as, e.g., "Subject XII [the author himself]: 'It was like some blurred seeing.' 'I would best compare it to the attempt of a blind man to see something, of which he knows where it is, and to look in that direction.' 'Seen extremely little. I was only aware of the compact environment. I did not move in empty space, but in the real store, although I saw very little of it. I could, however, indicate exactly the way I went" (Segal 1916: 433).

Ryle also hit the "phenomenological" ambition hard (but not fatally, since he could not show a viable alternative).

35   I have often tried to formulate this strangely indirect, i.e., exactly the seed-like, character of my "mental images" – "as if I were looking through it," "as if through a net," "looking over it," "next to it;" "as if I had just seen it," "as if it were lying next to me and I could look at it at any time."

36   "I am vaguely conscious of the fact that in the flow of words something attaches itself to the word-presentations, whereby they become more than mere word-presentations," wrote Stricker (1879: 41). By that he does not say much, but certainly something correct; amazing that he then continues: "But in active consciousness there is nevertheless only the word"! *"psychic overtone, suffusion, fringe"* is how James (1890, I: 258) specified Stricker's "self-consciousness" (= "potential knowledge") – "Since I have already used the metaphor of coal [for consciousness], I would like to add that it seems as if a large part of the coal depot is glowing without me hardly noticing it, but still it contributes to the general brightness, while only a small part of it actually shines" (Stricker 1879: 3).

37   "Coincidences" also encompass that an unprimed structure is triggered by the situation. As most of them seem to fade almost without any effect, I have the impression that most of these manifestations are consumed as control signals for reconstructions ("realizations," actualization of readinesses).

38   According to Piaget, this meta-accommodation (my term, *ad hoc*) becomes possible with the onset of "conceptual intelligence" (1960; also "representative intelligence," 1951: 161ff.) during the second year of human life.
The "image" is, of course, not a *sign* in the sense of a marking, but a s e e d or, if expanded, a structure, a *schema*, as Piaget himself indicated.

39   Cf. the short glossary appended above.

40   "Seed" is both a fortunate and an unfortunate term. At any rate, a seed is not a pointer in the sense of computer science, but t h e b e g i n n i n g o f a n a s s e m b l y .

41   Brentano (1874: 40f. and passim): "inner perception."

42   See, for example, Coltheart (2006a, 2006b, as well as the other papers in that same volume, and van Orden and Paap (1997) – thanks, Thomas Raab, for the references!

43   Eder and Raab (2015).

44   It does not take much introspection to understand that a structure is instantiated quite differently in an organism than, for example, in a computer. The concept of the Turing machine is just a "miroir" (of a specific, essential aspect) of the "pensée reélle" – "Logic is the mirror of thought, and not vice versa (...) we were led to this point of view by the study of the formation of operations in the child" (Piaget 1960: 27). I would translate "miroir" simply as "surface." In the same sense Piaget elsewhere spoke of a "decal" (*décalque*, Beth and Piaget 1961: 155).

45   A *heterarchy* is a hierarchy that can be rearranged (following respective laws).
The idea that "a conceptual schema is a heterarchy of schemata" does not lead to an infinite regress, because the elementary building blocks are "hard-wired" sensorimotor schemata (which can be "mirrored" as finite automata).

46   Conceptual schemata develop via *attunements* and affects.

47   Compared to the canonical Turing machine, the need for such scaffolding is an essential feature of "living thought."

48   Obviously, seeds are only expanded as far as the respective task requires. I often notice, for instance, that a completely undeveloped seed – "*This* [imageless] (is *also* involved)" – results in a radical rearrangement of current tendencies.

49   Such excitations are preconscious ("latently conscious," i.e., potentially expandable to a seed and beyond) or unconscious. A heterarchy of action readinesses can manifest itself, seed-like, as an ***attunement***.

Cognitive Symbols: From Ontogeny to Their Actual Genesis

A Psychogenesis Based on James Mark Baldwin and Jean Piaget

Michael Schwarz

In short, if experience appears to be one of the conditions necessary to the development of intelligence, study of the first stages of that development invalidates the empirical conception of experience.
– Jean Piaget (1936)

We know, for example, that an oyster is irritated by an object, when he turns a grain of sand into a pearl; but does his irritation, however keenly felt, give him awareness of an object?
– James Mark Baldwin (1906)

Introduction

By the term "cognitive symbol" I want to denote a complex, which in introspection can be related to the *experience of seed phenomena* (Wiener 2015a). The appearance of a seed manifests a specific aspect of a situation within current orientation. The expansion of a seed (by developing or clarifying the seeded aspect) enables the introspector to indicate its "meaning" or content as a mental potential. The latter is directed either to a thought or to the environment associated with *recognition or an initial understanding*. Here, I do not intend to introduce a new term, cognitive symbol, into the discussion, but only to free this discussion from both the historical burden and the ambiguity resulting from the rather broad notions of "(mental) image" or "symbol."

In his propaedeutic remarks on the concept of seed, Oswald Wiener (2015a: 86-88) wrote: "In particular, a physiological theory of thought will have to explain the relations between the two main facts of introspection: the 'appearance' of aspects or components of orientation produced by the respective thought process (the 'manifestations' of orientation by seeds) in relation to the constantly advancing assembly of the currently built structure and its running environment." Regarding the actual development of a thought, he added: "The frequent observations of the stalling of a running operation, of the repetition and modification of moves and sequences of moves even, suggest the conclusion that the working phase of the complex of schemas/running environment only develops *during operating.*"

These statements describe the dynamics of thought processes manifesting itself as cognitive symbols, their expansion and assembly into a running environment attuned to orientation, and as a "stalling" and sometimes leaping development. I believe that this actual-genetic process represents the struggle for *meaning*. It remains to be clarified whether or not this *meaning* necessarily expresses itself as the operations within the thought process or as relations of proxy objects of thought, and whether it must be experienced as a "mental image," felt as a "symbol," or is only *indirectly* determined by the orderliness of thinking ("structural determination").

Karl Bühler emphasized (1927: 12): "Thoughts are more and something else than the association of mental images." He also spoke of the generation of "coherence," i.e., of an "experiential unity" and the "aha experience," which occur, when we experience a meaningful complex. Moreover, he emphasized that despite their different research methods, especially the newer psychology of thought (he meant the Würzburg School) and psychoanalysis stand united in this respect. Furthermore, Bühler (ibid.: 16) underscored that Sigmund Freud found something decisive especially in his early work, "when he searched for meaning in the sphere of the apparently meaningless - in dreams, in the slips of everyday life, as well as in jokes playing with meaninglessness or with reversals of meaning."

So the crucial question remains what this "experience of meaning" consists of, how it comes about, and at what time during ontogeny we are allowed to define it as independent of practical action, i.e., as mental, cognitive symbol. Bühler himself had already pointed out that we over-simplify when we try to simply subsume meaning under the concepts of schema or of the structure of ordered thought. At times, the manifestation of seeds (aka cognitive symbols) is dominated by the orientation of learned sensorimotor schemas, as Wiener's introspections indicate in a replicable manner. This is the reason, I think, why he repeatedly spoke of dynamically controlled heterarchies of action readinesses. In the following, I would like to try to discuss whether it is perhaps a very specific kind of action readiness which makes for the basis of cognitive symbols and whose structure enables both thinking and the development of cognitive "internal models" as described by Wiener (2000: 18–23).

I would like to draw attention to a foundational concept that has attracted little attention, although to my knowledge it is not unknown. Yet, it has never been at the center of any argument and never played an adequate role, e.g., in the well-known imagery debate, which usually oscillates between the processing of mental images, on the one hand, and propositions generating meaning, on the other. I am talking about James Mark Baldwin's concept of *circular reaction* covering all conditions, which in ontogeny almost necessarily yield cognitive symbols. Jean Piaget also realized this connection of circular reaction and cognitive symbols, which I aim to make accessible in the following.

In his early writings around 1922, Piaget attempted to derive some aspects of the psychologically oft-undifferentiated notions of internal "symbols" or "images" from Sigmund Freud's notion of "symbolic thinking" in order to relate them to the child's pre-conceptual thought. He analyzed the ontogeny of pre-conceptual thinking in one of his key works, *La formation du symbole chez l'enfant* of 1945, by way of the *child's symbolic play* as well as of delayed and internalized *imitation*. In the following, I will try to trace some of Piaget's hypotheses and results on the development of the structure of these cognitive symbols.

At the origin of the genesis of human thought, imagery, and cognition, Piaget identified symbolic, but not yet socialized "syncretism" of ambiguous, i.e., over-determined proxy objects marked by displacements, condensations, and contradictions. For its egocentric nature, Eugen Bleuler (1912) called this syncretism "autistic thinking." Bleuler and also Piaget dated the *psychoanalytic concept of symbol* considerably later by pinpointing the time of the first occurrence of these "symbols" twenty months into child development. More importantly, they questioned their sensualistic origin assumed by Freud.

According to Piaget it can be shown that internalized pre-conceptual thinking begins with this cognitive, "symbolic" structure typical for humans, which in the child continuously develops from symbolic and imitative behavior. From then on, this primary thought on top of sensorimotor activity will always accompany purely practical action. In his early writings, Piaget showed that all the essential features of symbolic thought, which are so striking in the adult's dream "symbol," can already be detected in infantile pre-logical thought beginning with this most elementary form of imagery. He spoke about the "symbol" as "an embryo of a concept still charged with affectivity," the function of which consists in generalization. The role of symbolic thought is to be understood as a preform of logical thought and not as its opposite. On the basis of introspection reports (Eder and Raab 2015), these characterizations of Piaget also fit cognitive symbols (seed phenomena) not only in real-life thought, but also in problem-solving, where they emerge as effective preforms of a conscious insight.

I assume that these cognitive symbols carrying "meaning" in the adult's everyday life develop from the first intentional *attunements* – comparable to the pre-gestalts of actual genesis of Erich Wohlfahrt (1932). Yet, in the development of an insight (via seed phenomena) no sensory gestalts appear, but the premonition of a proxy object or, at any rate, a meaningful content is actualized. This content must not be analyzed as sensory data, because its origin lies in directed sensorimotor activity and not solely in perceptual mechanisms (e.g., in early vision). Yet such memories evoking meaning do not always refer back to childhood. Sometimes, they may also revive what only recently has been recognized. So not infrequently the "thought" experienced can only be interpreted according to its object content but not biographically. I would further claim that today's neuro-reductionist models neglect these cognitive symbols, which occasionally regroup an entire orientation and which reside at the essential foundations of all meaning and insight. Whether said models search for "symbolic representations" with "intrinsic meaning" (Harnad 1990) or whether they, as artificial neural networks do, perform bottom-up searches for "structures" for the visual "recognition" of "objects" (Schrimpf, DiCarlo et al. 2020) does not matter in this respect.

In Piaget's sense, one must indeed not forget that not only the "symbol" or "mental image," but already the *object* itself is an "epistemic category," whose structure emerges only gradually through action during child development, and that this structure of object permanence is itself one of the many conditions on the way to the development of cognitive symbols. I do not believe that at the biological level one should speak of object recognition at all. Even in the comparative ethology of the sea urchin (Jennings 1906), which, when shadowed at a certain speed from a certain direction, directs its spines in the direction of the supposed enemy, or of a spider whose prey pattern is activated when the web, which it sits in, is put into specific vibrations, notions of object recognition or object permanence are simply unnecessary for behavioral description. This stands in sharp contrast to fully developed human action, in which objects continue to exist, no matter how situations are changing. So Hans Volkelt (1912), too, emphasized with his concept of *complex quality* that if the spider is confronted with the "sight" of a fly in a vitally indifferent situation, it does not recognize it as such, i.e., as prey.

At this level of reactions directed to "external indicators," affective attunements presumably prevail, i.e., aversion or appetence of the respective coordinated activity. They yield specific effects in specific situations judged as pleasant or unpleasant, thereby also resulting in various intermediate forms of motivations. The child's awareness of a directed attunement, however, does not yet seem to be related to defined objects and certainly not to memories (symbols) representing them. Following Baldwin, it seems plausible to assume that even primitive *biological organisms* perform *directed* movements, even though Piaget locates true *intentionality* only at a later stage of development (means-end coordination). The life of a human infant also begins with a long phase of maturation (of the brain) and adaptation of sensorimotor action lasting at least four months. Only then does interest in objects awaken, and another approximately sixteen months later the child reaches the threshold to cognitive symbol use.

In the following, I attempt to project the actual-genetic process of reaching an insight, as we observe it in introspection as the transition from attunement, seeds (cognitive symbols), proxy object to a "model," onto some aspects to the developmental psychological hypotheses of James Mark Baldwin, which were later detailed out by Jean Piaget. I think there are a lot of indications that the course of experiencing and recognizing meaning in situations parallels the successively built up and structurally changing ontogenetic layers up to cognitive symbols. At least these parallels could help to improve our understanding of the latters' development.

Baldwin's hypothesis of "circular reaction"

After having published quite a few papers in the journals *Science*, *Nature*, and *Mind* during the early 1890s, in which he reported, among other things, on experiments with and observations on the learning behavior of his children, James Mark Baldwin in 1895 released his major work in developmental psychology, *Mental Development in the Child and the Race*. In this book he analyzed the developmental principles of the child's mind and also of biological organisms in general. He stated:

"We have – seen to proceed farther on our way – that there is one type of reaction, and only one, in which these two principles have a common application: *reactions whose issue tends to reinstate, in whole or part, the very stimulation that started the reaction.* Accommodation is there, in such a reaction, since the advantageous stimulation stands a better chance of repetition if the organism tends thus to get it; but since this repeated stimulus again stimulates to action, and action again follows there also is habit. So accommodation, *by the very reaction which accommodates,* hands over its gains immediately to the rule of habit. And this is the universal rule. How true, as a fact, this form of adaptation is!" (Baldwin 1895: 480).

In this description of his observations of learning new sensori-motor and, later, mental skills, Baldwin offers his principle of "circular reaction" (Baldwin 1898: 247), which he also termed "circular activity" (ibid.: 249) and, later in development, "child's imitation" (ibid.).

First of all it seems necessary to clarify Baldwin's hypothesis on the formation and adaptation of behavioral habits challenging the prevailing scientific theories of development of the 19th century. Nobody had reinterpreted the "fundament of all theories" to be applied to the development of all organisms, i.e., the stimulus-response mechanism, more profoundly than Baldwin.

His central criticism of biological and psychological research on the evolution of organisms concerned the assumption of a *passive habituation* of behavioral patterns instead of his conjecture that organisms are endowed with the *actively explorative habit formation* he had observed. If all theories before Baldwin based on experience, development, or evolution, whether they were traditionally empiricist (David Hume), psychologically associationist (Alexander Bain), reflexologist (Ivan Pavlov), or social Darwinist (Herbert Spencer), had one assumption in common, it was that they were all founded on the idea of a passive and spontaneously random repetition of behaviors occurring to the organism leading to the principle of habit selection by feedback.

Based on his own observations Baldwin rejected this *conditioning* of physical or causal relations of isolated material objects or, as in Bain, of associations formed by quantitative repetitions. The criticized traditional view of *adaptation* by imprinting objects onto the organism is still no less the basis of many of today's approaches, e.g., in research on "object recognition," even if the latters' more sophisticated mechanisms exhibit "active learning." Nonetheless, their function remains based on statistically acquired mappings and does not derive their concepts of "object" and "recognition" from the active sensorimotor interaction with the environment or *gestalt circle* (von

Weizsäcker 1940) postulating objects to play a role only much later in development and in a completely different way.

Actually, it only takes a few attentive observations of the facial expressions and the behavior of infants and toddlers while trying to grope something in order to gain and to practice these new actions in order to understand the innate aptitude for *active* habit formation described by Baldwin. It seems reasonable to assume that the organism is equipped with evolved organs and innate reflexes. But it seems also clear that during ontogeny there is then a transition to the active, affectively controlled acquisition of behaviors. I think that Piaget, and also Baldwin before him, believed that this transition begins as soon as the infant starts to actively apply the reflexes triggered by a stimulus, e.g., the sucking reflex, in order to re-experience their effects thereby starting to develop a sensorimotor schema. So the sucking schema is actuated and, at the same time, practiced. However, presumably as an early compensational action, the infant also sucks into the void without being stimulated. In addition, its own body posture is assimilated to this process of sucking.

This kind of active practice and extension of various reflex actions (grasping, looking, sucking, also vocalization and hearing) are at the center of an infant's interest in the first month after birth. Based on it Piaget introduced into his psychology his well-known concept of *active assimilation* as being reproductive, generalizing, and functional in recognition (Piaget 1963 [1936]: 42). He spoke of *accommodation* only when, beyond the reproduction and adaptation of innate behavioral patterns, new ones emerge as habits. Already Baldwin defined the capacity of *circular reaction* as a developmental process yielding new behavioral patterns directed towards the trigger stimulus so as to retrieve it by accommodative groping. Thus, the reflex schema can be integrated into a newly acquired schema. Baldwin generalized this learning process to every new sensorimotor habit, and even to the biological development of the simplest organisms. In any directed exploratory behavior these probing efforts are very evident. We always observe an effort to perform an action, the outcome of which is satisfying or disappointing, but also resignation or the successfully adapted skill that, through the probing cycles, transforms to a habit and, thus, to intentional and schematic action.

The *habit* of thumb-sucking, which is acquired quite early, offers a very clear example here. How does it come about in an infant? Perhaps only stimulated by one or a few purely random arm movements bringing the thumb into contact with the mouth, thereby unexpectedly triggering the sucking reflex, the *effect* of which pleases the child? How do kinesthetically and proprioceptively random actions finally result in a coordinated and intentional sensorimotor schema? Certainly not by very many equally random movements positively reinforced alone, as one would have to conclude from Bain or Spencer. This can easily be inferred from the behavior of the infant, whose emphatic desire and whose frequent effort to regain the same pleasurable effect, while at the same time it still clumsily attempts at learning to control its effectors we can easily observe. The schema accommodated by its repetitions finally becomes a completely new behavioral pattern, although before it didn't inhere in the sucking reflex or in the arm movement and certainly was not merely reinforced by passive exogenous selection. The new habit has been acquired actively and circularly.

Thus, *habits* develop only gradually through multiple active accommodative reactions in the form of a probing action-effect control, which then circularly extends a stimulus-response schema and, with this kind of adaptation, simultaneously yields a very different kind of energetic model.

Bio-energetic and psychological speculations

From a biological perspective, we could say that the positively evaluated effects mobilizing affective energy are a "surplus," which finds its *counterpart* in psychological pleasure. This energy not merely appraises and reinforces an accidental action after the fact, but rather becomes the impetus for activities that can lead to a systematic recovery of that same energy, which previously may have been achieved only accidentally. This different kind of energetic model serves as a *counterpart* for a very different kind of *psychological model* of hedonic consciousness of the *tendencies* and *attunements* of appetence and aversion, the *motivation* to *do the right thing*, the tension before success or failure (and disappointment) after missing the *positive effects* or escaping from the *negative effects* of the action. Or as Piaget (1954 [1937]: 229) said: "the complex of efforts, tension, expectation, desire, etc., is charged with efficacy." The model of passive or reactive movement is thus complemented by active, prospective adaptation. We arrive at directed learning, whose "goals" are initially set by organic structures preformed during biological adaptation or by reflexes and, later in development, also by interests in the *habits* developed and by the needs to act with them.

If we understand *habit*, just as Baldwin's contemporaries did, as a specific acquired motor response to a specific stimulus, then the sheer repetition of movements is certainly not the only thing an organism strives for. And yet the ordinary "Spencer-Bain theory" of habit formation by action repetition suggested that the evolution of behavioral adaptation can be explained by exogenous selection.

According to Baldwin, an *action schema* is not simply fixated by the first spontaneous movements, which happen to achieve a favorable effect. So it cannot be formed into a habit by "reinforcement" and frequent repetition. At the utmost, an incidentally achieved favorable effect creates the desire to achieve it once more, because the child must first learn to use, adapt, and organize its schematic methods to regain the desired effects, i.e., *endogenously* develop them by various attempts at accommodation. Additionally, these adaptations are only possible when using a framework of habits already formed. That is why Piaget would later claim that in the early stages of development no *accommodation* is possible without *assimilation. Acquired habits* very quickly go beyond reflex actions (milk-sucking, groping, etc.) by elaborating new movements or integrating new actions, some of which the child discovers on its own body, or by coordinating movements to yield a joint effect. Since new habits represent an improvement compared to the older ones, Baldwin called the developmental process *adaptation* by "*accommodation.*"

Futhermore, Baldwin assumed that his principle of an innate disposition for active habit formation resulted from Darwinian natural selection. Only organisms with the great advantage of circular adaptation would have prevailed. However, subscribing to habit formation as not being controlled by the environment does not mean that it is controlled by an "ego cogitans" (René Descartes, Maine de Biran), nor does it mean that one has to assume a *vitalistic* standpoint (Henri Bergson). In Baldwin's model, survival by active supply of the organs and, later, by the gradual buildup of intelligent behavior (not yet realized by the first habits) is solely implemented by a phylogenetically evolved organism and regulated by affects (attunements) and interaction with the environment.

Yet, if you fail to see this circular and directed activity while observing the early actions of organisms, your developmental theory will lack the necessary biological basis for intelligence. It will lack the effects of the organism on the environment, the feedbacks of which are necessary to accommodate behavior. Without this basis you will also be unable to derive later intelligent behavior with its experimentally practical character and thus to provide the groundwork for thought and active exploration. Consciousness of an interrelated proprioceptive-kinesthetic body system equipped with affects to be controlled, its effects on objects, and the coordinated handling of objects only appear at structural stages yet to be formed in the developing subject. All these stages must be tackled if we want to understand the emergence of cognitive symbols.

Meaning and purpose of actions

That is why it is important to go back to hypotheses about the conditions for the formation of initial habits in order to understand the foundations of thought and cognitive symbols. It seems clear that at this first stage of habit formation actions are organized rather according to a principle of trial and error. The systematic construction of procedures, i.e., of intelligent sensorimotor adaptations, are out of the question. Yet, in order to understand intelligent thought one usually does not hope to learn much by analyzing the formation of such simple habits. Based on Baldwin's hypothesis, however, the question of the genesis of this practical sense provokes at least two important points. Meanwhile, we shouldn't forget that this rudimentary sense also occurs in introspections of everyday thought as well as of problem-solving. Also, in thought not only some problem-relevant but also some cognitive symbols (seeds) extraneous to the problem derive their sense, and indeed sometimes their evident adequacy, from the meaning or purpose of sensorimotor action schemas (their orientation or readiness).

First, circular activity shows that even the simplest habits do not arise from the associative linking of arbitrary objects in the sense of classical association theories. Each and every activity is exclusively directed to effects – or, later, objects – satisfying a need. Thus, Piaget further argued that habits also do not arise through conditioning as long as the subject does not assimilate the "signals" as favoring an already existing schema (need). But if the activity refers only to very specific (though affectively generic) and not to arbitrary effects, it does not follow that these effects are not often obtained by chance or at least look arbitrary to the observer. The subject is not yet differentiated, so it is directed only to effects that serve to promote development. The "meaningful" effects are of interest to the subject simply because they circularly support the development of the genetically predisposed schemas of grasping, sucking, looking (which tracks movements), crying, and hearing, i.e., they "nourish" their own operation, as Piaget put it. Certain perceptual situations are subsumed under the purpose of activities, which in turn give them meaning or significance. Initially, sensory phenomena now become objects to suck, to grasp, or to follow with the gaze. Conversely, in order be useful, these activities have to adapt to the constraints of their objects and of the child's own body.

So the early knowledge of *causality*, of cause and effect, is not (yet) bound to experiences of physical properties but to the actions of the child. There is no consciousness of external objects yet, and thus no perception of mutually interacting things. I suspect that the infant experiences causality as the effort and the activity itself, impacting on phenomena and causing effects. One may perhaps even suggest – and Piaget (1954 [1937]: 351f.) does this in his tome on the structure of reality – that physical causality is not reflected in habits but that, on the contrary, the most elementary forms of causal relations are instantiated by the very function of *reproductive assimilation* (of circular actions). That would mean that the connection of action and effect is already implied in the action tendency (to re-achieve the effect by the action).

Although Piaget may agree with empiricism that these relations can only be established by probing experience, this agreement does not go so far as to call these relations ("connexions") at the beginning of development "rational" in any physicalist sense. If meaning does not, as is so often supposed, arise from the sensory domain, from sensations or from perceptual gestalts alone, it does result from interaction with the purposes of actions. If, for instance, the infant lying in a cradle experiences a *secondary circular reaction* by pulling a string to accidentally make a figure, which is attached to the roof of the cradle, swing and rattle, which in turn arouses its interest, it will immediately try to repeat the same action again. Piaget argued that, as soon as the relationship between action and effect has been consolidated by multiple actions, rudiments of analysis already become apparent in the infant, who immediately searches for the string after the figure has been reattached to the cradle roof.

At this stage, however, the connection established between the means (the string) and the end (moving the figure) is not yet "rational," since means and end are only a construction of the observer after the fact. The infant itself has not understood the relation. What looks arbitrary in the connection of action to the visually or auditorily triggered effect is of *interest* only from the third stage of sensorimotor development. And even then the trigger is not yet an objectified stimulus, i.e., not a *proxy object*. Therefore, at these early stages *purpose* in the sense of Karl Bühler (1927: 123) does not mean expediency or goal-directedness, since even a dog "barking at a locomotive" behaves purposefully.

I want to emphasize that the sense or meaning of sensory content is already instantiated by the first habits in the form of sensorimotor schemas. This meaning is thus carried by action into the appropriate sensory configuration. Ontogenetically, it is not only pre-logical and prior to any use of language, but also prior to thought and cognitive symbols and even prior to the consciousness of objects. But since this rudimentary *meaning* still plays a role in the adult's thought complexes, it is important for the theory of thought that the structure of thought and imagery is not conceived in complete isolation from it, even if it mostly goes unnoticed without controlled introspection and, even if not, is only realized by implication. Mind you, we do not yet speak about the *sense* of a biologically organic structure, of instincts and drives.

The *second* point pertains to the affectivity of meaning and purpose. Not only in his early works but also in his later one on equilibration of 1975, Piaget considered a synthesis between his genetic structuralism and psychological functionalism, as he dubbed the theory of Édouard Claparède and in some respects also Freudian psychoanalysis. The starting point of this synthesis are the concepts of *need* and *interest* as well as the different re-adaptations in the form of *regulations* to *compensate* for temporary *perturbations* of otherwise successful actions of assimilation schemas (leading to satisfaction). For according to Piaget (1985 [1975]: 68), the "functionalist perspective" is also based on the assumption that not only each action but also each cognitive activity is motivated by an underlying tendency to satisfy a need.

According to Piaget, every time the subject pursues the repetition of an effect but is temporarily hindered by a *perturbation*, what is required in addition to meaning is a *value aspect*, i.e., an *interest* motivating the *compensation* (the abolition) of this perturbation and the restoration of the original or of a new, differentiated balance. Even if all *regulations* are to be interpreted as reactions to *disturbances*, not every *perturbation* motivates to remedy the pending deficiencies. This can be seen, for example, when the child, even without achieving the desired effects, repeats actions several times, every time seeming to believe that it will do better the next time. Sometimes, it even gives up its efforts after a different perturbation takes place, or finds the perturbation itself so *interesting* that it directs its action towards it. So the strength of *interest* determines how strongly a pursuit is followed. Usually, an object is of *interest* as long as it can challenge and enhance habits in their adaptation, or, to put it simpler, as long as is remains within the range of what can be accommodated. From the second stage of development onward, value is attributed to objects because, while handling them, they stimulate activity (affordance). This, both Piaget (ibid.: 83) and Claparède argued, dynamizes interest because it "frees the subject's energies and incites action in the direction of the object" (ibid.: 68). This precisely parallels the Freudian concept of *cathexis* (investing an object with "psychic" energy), which Rapaport (1967) already highlighted in relation to the Piagetian value aspect of assimilation schemas.

The developmental function

What is crucial here is the distinction between two essentially different kinds of *perturbations* preventing the attainment of a desired effect of a sensorimotor action. Baldwin (1906: 49) already identified both of them in the child as "marked experiences: that of the absence of the satisfying, and that of the presence of the unsatisfying."

Piaget (1985 [1975]: 16) also speaks of "two large classes" of perturbations, the first class being due to negative feedback with respect to the adaptation of the schema (accommodation), i.e., to the compelling resistance that an object puts up against the testing attempts to form a habit (assimilation schema). However, not only external objects cause negative feedback, but also problems adapting the mutual interconnection (reciprocal accommodation) of subsystems (grasping, seeing, hearing) already formed by primary circular reactions but still isolated from each other. They can be mutually coordinated only after being formed by *secondary circular reactions.*

"Insofar as the subject becomes aware of perturbations of this sort, he experiences them as errors or failures," wrote Piaget (ibid.). In this context he also pointed to the frequent assumption that the *acquisition* of a *habit* is accompanied by a series of *positive feedback,* whereas obviously no *habit* is formed without testing actions leading to negative feedback. The case is again different when it comes to maintaining a habit by practicing and applying it. However, its formation always requires a greater effort, which every reader will have observed while learning sensorimotor skills.

The second class of perturbations Piaget (ibid.: 26) called *lacunae* because they leave needs unsatisfied. Here, too, *interest* plays a major role, and here, too, it must be emphasized that not every *lacuna* results in a *perturbation,* because this also depends on whether or not a schema has already been activated for assimilation. This is accompanied by positive feedback, while the lacuna is then caused by insufficient stimulation of the schema. That is, the *lacunae* refer to a missing object or to an unfavorable situation making an action difficult to perform. Later in development, the *lacunae* also include knowledge gaps when solving problems.

The entire cyclic process controlled by functional affects, however, also affords a second appraisal, namely as to whether the desired "goal" has been completely or at least partially achieved after the respective schemas have been regulated (to compensate for a perturbation). In simple sensorimotor activities, this "appraisal" expresses itself in recognition (recognitive assimilation) and, later in development, by the fact that "new relations have been grasped."

Incidentally, one could translate this functional aspect quite well into the *complex theory* of Otto Selz (1913/1922). He related *complex, schematic anticipation,* and *complex completion* (the effect) while applying a schema (the action) to a final *control* possibly leading to a *correction* (regulation). The complex corresponds to the mutual relation of an assimilation schema (purpose) and its sensory content (meaning). In his case, said value aspect could be supplemented by a complex quality (mood/attunement) and attributed to schematic anticipation, whose positive or negative cathexis decides on execution, reinforcement, or inhibition of the action. As early as 1922, Selz raised the question as to what extent his theory of *productive thinking* could be applied to sensorimotor behavior, i.e., how it could be applied "in its individual components to the intelligent behavior of the great apes as demonstrated by Wolfgang Köhler" (Selz 1922: 610–679) The latter succeeded in pinpointing many functional parallels in the sensorimotor behavior of primates capable of intelligent actions (coordination of means and ends, use of tools). Belonging to the tradition of the psychology of thought of the Würzburg School he was interested precisely in this functional and dynamic relationship in relation to human problem-solving. Only in passing did he also wonder about the nature of the first cognitive symbols enacted by the human *ordered thought process* and how *knowledge actualizations* develop ontogenetically from sensorimotor actions and what their relationship to the environment may be. I think it is the deep structure of successive layers of schemas that provides our mind with the faculty of representation and, thus, with a biologically special relationship to the environment and to other organisms. And I am convinced that shallow formal systems operating on arbitrary symbols will not be able to provide this deep structure to machines.

Structural development

In the changing structural *organization* of actions, i.e., in their developing relation to their effects, Piaget distinguished six sensorimotor stages building on each other before the cognitive symbol and symbolic thought emerges. Baldwin, however, identified only three essentially different relations toward the environment, each of which is reflected in a different meaning (in the sense of their implications). These relations are based on three essentially different manifestations of the circular reaction, which directs its actions once to signals and to indications, thereafter to objects, and finally to behavior analogous to the environment (in the imitative and symbolic sense). Baldwin (1895: 100–128) called these three stages *physiological, sensori-motor,* and *ideo-motor* "suggestion," respectively.

The first stage is purely kinesthetic. It finds its expression in the formation of habits regarding sensorily induced reactions in early childhood. Stimuli are triggered and habituated through purely kinesthetic action attempts progressively adapting the innate action schemas (sucking, grasping, seeing, making sounds, hearing). The developing and expanding cycle is directed to motor skills, to the spatiotemporal grasp of the environment and its moving objects. Thereby, awareness of different relations between the child's own and the perceived movements emerges, which can be understood as an extension of the reflex actions. But it does not yet create new associations outside the body.

The second stage pertains to sensorimotor development. The adapted and isolated habits of the first stage coordinate with each other in relation to usable things. The practical exercise of schemas results in a coordinated system of actions directed toward stable things and external situations. Interpersonal exchange also improves by two major advances, as the concept of object is formed and imitation behavior develops. The child now looks for or imitates the other person, even if that person has disappeared from the visual field. This is accompanied by a renewed turn toward kinesthesia and the child's own body, which, according to Baldwin, indicates the beginning of the third stage.

The third stage begins with *simple imitation*, through which already formed actions are related to those of another person. Later, this passes over to *persistent imitation* marked by new correspondences formed by the "overproduction" of actions. Here, one important extension is self-imitation, which begins with symbolic play.

These three essential organizations of circular activity, corroborated by Baldwin with observations on child development, formed the basis of Piaget's more detailed research. In the latter's three early major works he resumed the study of these stages in three different respects by applying his concepts of *assimilation*, *accommodation*, and *organization* of schemas.

Piaget's first major work was *The Origins of Intelligence in Children* (1936 in French). It focuses on the sensorimotor development as well as the *primary*, *secondary*, and *tertiary* forms of circular reaction, which he further classified into six developmental stages (detailed below). Through extensive observation and documentation of his own children's behavior Piaget was able to trace their development from the first reflexes to intentionality by the respective coordination of means and ends. The child then arrives at practical intelligence still lacking ideas and concepts. His second major work was *The Construction of Reality in the Child* (1937 in French), which "take[s] the point of view of awareness [of the child] and no longer only that of the observer" (1954 [1937]: xii). Now Piaget tackled the emergence of the concept of object, the spatial field, causality, and the temporal field. All of them are preconditions for examining the transition from sensorimotor to imaginative and intuitive thought as laid down in the last of the three related volumes, *Play, Dreams and in Childhood* (1945 in French). Ontogeny culminates in the formation of imitative and symbolic behavior and its internalization as schemas. Thus, the human organism arrives at effective forms of cognition that reach beyond the currently present situation and enable its anticipation. This is one of Piaget's few works in which he emphasized the necessity of cognitive symbols for imaginative and intuitive thought instead of their inadequacies, which, as he argued later, are supplemented and corrected by operational and logical thinking (1951 [1945]: 14).

So Piaget postulated six successive sensorimotor stages.

The first stage pertains to innate assimilation schemas, which Piaget introduced even before circular reactions. For him they are subject to pure practice and adaptation, e.g., the sucking schema adapts better from day to day. The reflexes are actuated spontaneously, and perturbations that occur at this stage are exclusively simple lacunae, e.g., "the need to suck might be momentarily unsatisfied because the breast is not available" (1985 [1975]: 69).

The second stage is characterized by the *primary circular reaction* yielding the first habits. It should be emphasized that at this stage, in contrast to the previous one, any integration of a reflex must be understood as a new element in a higher order schema (1950 [1947]: 100). Learning to grasp objects or to move them with the hand, tracking movements of things with the head, or even sucking the thumb accommodate the hand reflex, the ocular reflex, or the sucking reflex into a new schema, which in turn allows for new needs and satisfactions. Since during the many repetitions the schema is accommodated by practice, all phenomena experienced in the process are given meaning. By this the so-called "association" by conditioning becomes obvious: A recurrent stimulus (e.g., Pavlov's bell as a "signal") is given meaning by being included in that schema on which need and satisfaction depend. Without occasional satisfaction the conditional reflex vanishes and so no habit is formed. One major difference between this stage and the next is that here the regulations are still directed to the child's own body and not to changes that it triggers itself by acting on the environment.

Third stage: Further discrimination begins around the fourth month, when the newly acquired but still isolated *schemas* (first habits) are coordinated into a coherent system. Regulations by testing movements to look in the direction of a sound, for example, represent the earliest forms of *coordination* of vision and hearing (Piaget 1985 [1975]: 73). By bringing objects, which have been grasped outside the field of vision, to the mouth the same link is established between sucking and grasping. "The coordination of vision and prehension that occurs at about four or five months is the most important. The baby can take hold of what he sees, and can look in the direction of his hand when it is held so that it cannot move" (ibid.). This stage, presumably enabled by the maturation of neural connections, could be explained by the *lacunae* created, for instance, by an object only heard and not seen while otherwise seen and heard at the same time. In this case, the schema for seeing is co-activated, although the object is visually unavailable. Such perturbations mainly affect smaller spatiotemporal distances and are compensated by testing accommodation through moving to the opposite direction so that schema x (hearing) and schema y (seeing) are reconnected. According to Piaget (ibid.: 74) these additive schemas enable the coordination of new "multiplicative" schemas of the form xy with the property xy in addition to the property x or y.

This marks the beginning of the *secondary circular reaction*. By interacting with the environment, the interest now shifts to sensory phenomena and then to the behavior of objects or things, especially when the child produces desired effects by its own actions. In the example given above, a dangling figure moves accidentally as soon as the infant pulls on its string, and the induced effect stimulates repetition. Circularly developed abilities are transferable to new things and enable the recognition and, thus, discrimination of objects. So another form of *causality* comes to the fore, which results from the effect of the child's actions on objects. However, one must not over-interpret from the subject's standpoint. The things acted upon are not yet "permanent objects," nor is the pulled string a means to a goal. Since the coordination of actions cannot yet be separated from the properties of the object, awareness of a perturbation by objects is also impossible. In the example given, we even see a positive feedback resulting in the reinforcement of the repetition of the interesting phenomenon in order to let it persist. This kind of consciousness, however, does not yet distinguish subject from object. The visual scene is not yet subdivided into objects and, moreover, objects are also only gradually being distinguished from the stimuli emanating from the infant's own arms and hands. This can easily be observed, when the infant scares itself by its own movements in the visual field. Nevertheless, the transition to the next stage is prepared.

Fourth stage: From the eighth to the tenth month "the schemata constructed during the previous stage become susceptible of co-ordination among themselves, some serving as means and others setting a goal for action" (Piaget 1950 [1947]: 102). The skills of grasping or pushing, moving, or pulling things near, which have been learned at the previous stage, are now used, for example, to push away a pillow covering a coveted toy in order to get hold of it. General schemas characterized by adaptive connections are formed coordinating the end (reaching the toy) with the means (pushing things away). Yet in contrast to the third stage, the end is given before the means.

A new object can now be used to test whether it can be grasped, pushed, be sucked on, or whether it even makes a sound when shaken. This is because the child now tries to understand the object by using it. Thereby, the first kind of object permanence emerges, because now for the child an object continues to exist, even if hidden behind a screen, for example, and not least because the means to systematically move objects are available too. The consequence of this progress is that a visual situation can no longer be interpreted merely as a changing whole, but rather as an organization of separate objects, which the child is able to move against each other. Goals are no longer anticipated "rectilinear as in perception" (Piaget 1950 [1947]: 103) and unidirectional as in early circular reaction, but can now be perceived under different aspects. So the use of previously acquired schemas expands. The "utilization of earlier schemas begins to extend further in time" (ibid.), which is why at this stage Piaget already identifies the emergence of sensorimotor intelligence, although no *new* means are yet discovered.

At the next, the fifth stage, due to the *tertiary circular reaction* (ibid.: 104) *new means* emerge for the first time through trial and discovery – by "experiments to see" (1985 [1975]: 77). Now so-called *intentionality* is achieved, by which goals and means are coordinated through several intermediate links. The level of *sensorimotor intelligence* becomes capable of effective adaptation. Dealing with objects now leads to "individualized objects" having *substantial permanence*. Objects can now be searched for, even if they are not immediately present. Yet the child still cannot surrogate objects by cognitive symbols.

As Baldwin also emphasized, interpersonal relations play a particularly important role here, because the first substantial objects are persons. But these relations also initiate more complex imitation and an objectified causality, which is projected onto others by an "active principle." For example, the child moves another person's hand toward an object to bridge the distance to it or guides it to a box to have it opened. All of these advances are later continued at the stage of symbolic play. Now the child also discovers relationships between objects, as evidenced by the intentional use of a string or pad to pull objects nearer, or by the attempt to use a stick. Yet, this stage does not reach beyond randomly achieved effects yielding meaningful and circularly reinforced attempts at systematizing relationships. To reach a doll, for instance, the child first randomly pulls the cloth on which it sits in its direction, before it generalizes this schema of pulling over different kinds of underlays. The generalized schema already exists before the context (object *placed on* its support) can be understood and applied.

Finally, the sixth stage, "which occupies part of the second year (...) marks the completion of sensori-motor intelligence" (Piaget 1950 [1947]: 105). New means are no longer discovered exclusively through experimentation, but by "inventions by rapid internal co-ordination of processes now unknown to the subject" (ibid.). This process Piaget not only sees at work in Wolfgang Köhler's descriptions of a sudden restructuring in chimpanzees or in the "aha experiences" described by Karl Bühler, but also in the introspective feeling of a spontaneous practical insight. Children who had never had the opportunity to experiment with a stick until the age of one and a half can now occasionally understand the relationship of such a *tool* to a desired goal without previous testing experimentation as was necessary at the previous stage. Köhler also reported on experimental animals that "discovered the use of the stick, so to speak, by looking and without previous practice" (ibid.).

In order to understand the genesis of cognitive symbols, it is necessary to speak in more detail about this stage with both its great advances in imitation and its symbolic play now assuming a distinct structure. At this stage, Piaget already identified the anticipations of situations as *preconceptual*, since they come quite close to ordered imaginative thinking. Even though perception possibly plays a crucial role, Piaget does not believe that restructuring at this stage can be explained by perceptual gestalts alone, since they still belong to sensorimotor interpretation: "When the subject no longer acts when confronted with the data of a problem, and appears to be thinking instead, everything seems to indicate that he continues his attempts, but with implicit trials or internalised actions" (ibid.: 105f.). He reported that one of his children at the age of one and a half made various unsuccessful attempts to fish a chain out of an only slightly opened matchbox. Then, *pausing*, the child attentively looked at the small gap, seemingly considering the situation. At the same time, he showed a salient reaction by opening and closing his mouth several times. Immediately after this "reflection phase," the child unhesitatingly put his finger into the gap, this time widening it. So the practical execution of the "thought on opening/closing" was finally successful, and the child was able to take out the chain. I should not forget to mention that, as Piaget (1963 [1936]: 337f.) emphasized, the child did not know before how to open and close matchboxes. According to his interpretation, this sequence hints at motor *reflection* in the form of action imitation (1950 [1947]: 128f.). But what exactly does Piaget mean by imitation? To clarify this, one has to go back to Baldwin's circular reaction, which I will do in the section on imitation below.

Regarding Piaget's concept of successive developmental stages, which easily lends itself to misunderstandings, it should be noted that these stages merge into one another smoothly, of course. Yet each one cannot be dispensed with, since at each stage the acquisition of new schemas is directed toward new relationships and, therefore, involves new interests that lead to specific new abilities. Each previous stage also provides a repertoire of habitual schemas that are required for being coordinated into new schemas at the next stage. This principle is independent of the exact time of the schemas' formation, and also independent of the fact that the underlying schemas continue to be preserved, trained and eventually unfold. Crucially, the transition to the next stage must be explained in terms of regulations that integrate and reorganize the transgression from an already achieved equilibrium to a more comprehensive equilibrium. Thus, both Baldwin and Piaget conceived of development as a dynamic "spiral." The process of auto-regulation, which Piaget later called *equilibration*, aims at avoiding exclusive causation either by the environmental influence or by innate preformation.

Imitation and attention as the origin of cognitive symbols

So Piaget developed his concept of *imitation* from Baldwin's one, which the latter, for lack of a better term, quite self-critically used even at the biological level, namely as "organic imitation" (1895: 264). I think we have to understand this notion as autogenous imitation of the organism with an accommodative tendency and thus also as a circular process. In addition to these biological accommodation processes for the acquisition organic habits or instincts, Baldwin distinguished two crucial levels of *psychological* imitation that draw their great developmental potential mainly from interpersonal relations – with the exception, for instance, that a dog may begin to howl imitating a police siren by way of circular reaction. Already in this case, the behavior could be interpreted as *simple imitation*, since it refers to objects of which the dog is not aware. Simple imitation means that effects, which the organism perceives while already being able to produce them by itself, are repeated in order to make them last. But only when the subject perceives social counterparts and objects, and when the feeling of a causal relation between their own action and its effect has become objectified in order to transfer it to others, who then themselves become the source of the effect, is the subject finally able to relate their own productions to that of someone else. For up to this turn, imitation neither of social counterparts nor of objects is possible, but only imitation of the habitual effect.

Not least the development of imitation contributes to this turn. This is why Baldwin distinguished the *simple* from a more complex imitation, which he called *persistent imitation* (ibid.: 352f.) and which involves conscious "effort." He wondered: "how is the conscious person able to perform a *new movement* voluntarily and with attention?" (ibid.: 428). Baldwin concluded that in this case attention cannot, as in *simple* imitation, rely on memory, that is, on an "idea," or a "mental image" (ibid.: 429) signifying the movement in order to perform it with *intent*. Even if, in the first months of development, many useful activities developed from accidentally accommodated schemas with circular reaction contributing substantially to the number of such "happy coincidences," Baldwin stated, that "no one will deny that the 'hits' occur mainly through the child's *imitations* in cases of complex action" (ibid.). Here he alluded to speaking, singing, learning to write, or in general to everything that siblings, parents, or caregivers so often mutually imitate, i.e., accommodate and promote by imitative action (waving, clapping, gestures, facial expressions).

In these cases, attention is very much focused on the sensory effects (such as sounds) of the counterpart's movements. Meanwhile, adaptation takes place proprioceptively and kinesthetically by producing the same effects with one's own body. At the beginning of (simple) imitation, accidentally produced or habitual sounds are reproduced as soon as the counterpart repeats them. Hitting the pillow, shaking the head, or opening and closing the mouth are also repeated in this way. But imitation is always linked to the stages of sensorimotor development. Only from the third stage, when the grasping schema has already been developed and hand movements have become coordinated with visually perceived movements, can alternating imitations of hand movements of the counterpart occur. For only then can the visible movements of the other be assimilated to one's own motor schema.

But Baldwin's concept of *persistent imitation* also aimed at something else. In the case of a completely unfamiliar movement – when the child, for example, tries to imitate the extension or flexion of the index finger, which it has not yet habituated – the structure of imitation changes, according to Baldwin (ibid.: 356), from "monoideism" to "polyideism." That means nothing other than that the visible effect (the counterpart's hand and finger as a model) no longer coincides with the self-produced effect (the attempted imitation) either in the visual field or in the nervous system. So it is no longer possible to relate the familiar movement of the counterpart's hand to the effect of one's own habitual action. Instead, the visual effect produced by one's own body (the finger movement) must first be compared with that of the counterpart and then be corrected.

The child must thus actively relate to the imitated action. This is precisely what makes the imitation of unfamiliar movements the structural nucleus of any cognitive representation developed later! The world doubles, as it were, in the child's consciousness. Only now is it able to recreate an independent reality by analogy, i.e. to adapt to and, moreover, to construct the world attentively. This is perhaps already a precondition to internally represent the *lacuna* of an object, namely as an action readiness towards it. Yet, this proxy object is not sensory, as even Freud believed. It is not an image but rather a sensorimotor behavior directed to active copying (by bringing one's body into relation) having developed from accommodation.

Piaget (1951 [1945]: 52) described how this process of differentiation proceeds from a more general to an independent specific schema. One of his children observed interestedly how its father bent and straightened his index finger. First it tried to imitate this action by a parting gesture of arm and hand, then later by one hand alone, and finally, with evident effort, it moved its own index finger in a similar way. A comparison between the model and the elicited imitation by effortful accommodation is essential, although the latter may proceed in a variety of ways, e.g., by acting or trying out, and combining familiar or similar movements in order to adapt them. According to Baldwin, spontaneous movements may also be "overproduced," so that they can then be *persistently* compared and adapted to the model. Thus, what is necessary is "the development of a function of co-ordination" (Baldwin 1895: 453) of these overproduced movements. Here, Baldwin identified the reason for the focused *attention to persistent imitation*. For Piaget (1951 [1945]: 50f.), interest in new models, i.e., in persons and things that are no longer regarded as extensions of the subject's own activity, begins only at this forth stage. So here, for Piaget too, accommodation is established as an *independent function* alongside reproductive assimilation, although the latter does not cease.

Up to Piaget's third stage, adaptation qua imitation is nothing other than circular reaction (accommodation and assimilation in parallel). From the very beginning, circular reactions contain an aspect of imitation, since they first reproduce their own reflex movements, and then acquired habits (reproductive assimilation). Finally, they turn into reproductive recognition, which marks the beginning of *imitation* of effects produced by others (movements, sounds). This amounts to an "incorporation" into a familiar meaningful effect, because it can be reproduced by the subject's own actions and, thus, (reciprocally) result in satisfaction. At the fourth stage of development, when the permanence of substantial objects has been achieved, Piaget also believed that movements are now imitated by *indirect assimilation* via visible *indications*. The child knows these movements, but they are not visible on his own body, e.g., opening and closing the mouth, grasping the nose, or "infecting each other" when yawning. In addition to this mapping of familiar schemas onto seen movements, imitation of new phonetic and new visual models increases too. Only during the fifth stage does imitation then become more and more systematized.

Furthermore, Piaget (ibid.: 84) argued that accommodation plays a totally different role in imitation than in intelligent adaptation. In the latter, it only provides a proxy "negative" of object features during the use of the object. These features resist assimilation while operating with the proxy object, which could thus be dubbed the object's "mould." In the imitation of new outer models, on the other hand, accommodation by (persistent) imitation serves to construct "positives" (copies), i.e., "offprints" of such "negatives," which then allow a completely different understanding and anticipation of the object's behavior. This autonomy of imitation is detached from assimilation and the use of objects. It seems to yield imitation schemas on an entirely different level, now functioning as analogies (whether these can be localized in a different area of the nervous system is left open, because they still remain sensorimotor schemas).

From the sixth sensorimotor stage in which the coordination of schemas is gradually detached from direct perception, imitation gains three novel features (ibid.: 66). First, "complex new models" are imitated without any tentative trials first. For example, the child is able to pat itself on the shoulder with crossed arms and hands spontaneously when it sees the same action in an adult. Second, material things are increasingly imitated. For example, the child imitates the sound of a swinging window by swaying to the same rhythm and making similar sounds. At the same time, symbolic play intensifies. For example, a car's tail wag and its accelerating sound or a running and jumping cat are imitated. Third, Piaget distinguished a new *deferred imitation*. The first reproduction of a model's behavior now does not take place in its presence, but is delayed, sometimes even after a rather long absence. For example, the absent cousin is mimicked by "her staggering gait," whereby a past situation is actualized.

All this has to be kept in mind when Piaget speaks of *motor reflection* stemming from imitation and anticipating an action on or a behavior of an object, i.e., a situation. The matchbox already referred to, with its gap too narrow to take a chain out, is an excellent example, because it is only *after* the "representing" opening and closing of the mouth that the child is able to open it and take out the chain. This observation suggests a transition from imitation to the first cognitive symbol, even if the gesture carrying the meaning is still rudimentarily performed by the body and not yet fully internalized. It is not yet transformed into a *seed tending to possible action*. In short, it is not yet thought proper.

Cognitive symbols, syncretism, and egocentrism

Let us elucidate the matchbox anecdote in more detail in order to analyze the genesis of the cognitive symbol on the basis of the schema of opening and closing. First of all, we can state that through this gesture a specific aspect of the matchbox situation is recognized and anticipated. But what is "mentally" recognized so that the entire situation gets restructured? And what exactly is it that at the previous developmental stage could only be discovered in a practical way by sensorimotor experimentation on the box itself (by accidentally pulling the box open, for instance)? On seeing the box, the child now obviously recognizes that it could be opened and closed, namely *analogous* to the schema that is enacted by the mouth and that is connected to everything related to this specific aspect (the oral cavity, intake and outtake, etc.). The crucial difference is that the child now uses this schema as an "internal model," which now can intervene between stimulus and response. Thereby, the child's overall action readiness is restructured even before it acts on the object. For the first time, some "virtual" or pre-meditated enactment of meaning stands against or accompanies the practical action on the object. The oral gesture represents and anticipates a solution to the problem that the gap of the box is too narrow to take out the chain. According to Piaget, the "internal model" applied here very likely emerged before as a collateral imitative schema, that is, as an actively self-produced copy of what the child has before perceived in another human (the sight of opening and closing the mouth) and to which it now relates by analogy.

Moreover, there can be no doubt that the sight of a mouth opening has much in common with the sight of the gap in the box and acquires a corresponding meaning by being intertwined with the action. The example also shows that the bodily gesture of opening the mouth only "symbolically" represents the real action. For, in motor terms, it is completely different pulling the box open with the finger. Yet, beyond the opening-closing schema something essential is common to both actions, as there is also a deeper content delivered by the action's orientation (the cavity, being enlarged and made accessible, intake and outtake, etc.). So the analogy is condensed, and its orientation got shifted from the mouth to the box.

It is also easy to conceive of the process of internalizing of this gesture, if we compare it with the internalization of reading, which occurs later in development. In silent reading, the motor aspect of speaking is no longer executed but gets inhibited. Yet, if the gesture of opening the box is postponed and reproduced (remembered) only the next day in order to recall the situation (representation), it already amounts to a symbol. Together with the orientation towards the box, it now acts as a specific prototype representing one aspect of the lacuna (the non-existent box). So it has become a *cognitive symbol*. The seed of a sensorimotor schema that once arose from imitation now serves as a *proxy* of the object. Of course, what has been learned is not the schema of opening and closing the mouth but the use of this schema in the function of a representing (symbolic) and relating (imitating) prototype.

Arguably, positive prototypical (general) *proxies* can be constructed by imitation from all resistances of objects hindering assimilation that are observed attentively. Furthermore, the more generic the world of proxies still is, something develops that Piaget (1923: 104) called the *syncretism* of infantile thought. Its essential aspects had already been highlighted by the adults' dream analyses of Sigmund Freud, who already interpreted them as symbolic thought. These aspects are mainly the over-determination, displacement, and condensation of such symbols. In the example of the matchbox, the mouth gesture is over-determined, because it renders the action of another person an analogy of one's own action (*alter* and *ego*) as well as of the *proxy object* (matchbox). Depending on how you see it, displacement and condensation alternate, but in any case the connection is effective. It consists of the newly discovered analogy.

So the developing consciousness realizes that it is able to bridge lacunae not only by action but also by action readiness and mental shortcuts. The "gap" can thus be satisfyingly bridged by content and by one's own directed action. Therefore it is not surprising that at the sixth stage, behavior becomes egocentric again. The egocentrism, which the child had already overcome by practical action, now once more leads to a "turning away from reality," which, according to Bleuler (1965 [1912]: 400), even bears autistic traits and may replace, as it were, the entire world. Not least because of this feature, Freud discovered wish fulfillment as the most important aspect of dreams.

But to enable cognitive symbols (persistent), imitation would yet be way too heavily dependent on stimuli, i.e., to the presence of objects. The effort afforded by the objects would render imitation too inflexible if there were not another side to it, which has its origin not in accommodation, but in assimilation. It pushes the distance to objects so far that they can be interchanged almost arbitrarily.

Symbolic play

At the sixth sensorimotor stage, another specific behavior begins to take shape, which exceeds the motivation of motor play to form a skill just as (unpredictably) as the imitation of new models exceeds the use of objects. According to Piaget, this behavior develops from ritualized actions, the execution of which becomes more important than the objects themselves, on which they are executed (even though this was already in evidence from the fourth stage). So imitation of one's own actions develops.

The initial phase of this kind of imitative activity based on pure assimilation becomes evident when the child begins to act only to "make believe" (Piaget 1951 [1945]: 97). It is now able to perform a familiar action without its object. Thus, the child imitates itself. It performs the previous practice play of balancing on a board, but now without the board (ibid.: 120). Or it mimes lying down to sleep, or pretends to eat bread, symbolically represented by small stones on a plate represented by a leaf. Eating and sleeping themselves are by no means games, but merely mimicking these behaviors already belongs to the realm of symbolic play. Nonetheless, there is no doubt that this mimicry does not serve as a "pre-exercise" for better-adapted sensorimotor action, because for the most part it is performed only in outlines.

First, it is essential to this behavior that it relates action schemas to objects that are unsuitable for effective adaptation. Secondly, it is important that almost any object can be used to activate these symbolic schemas (ibid.: 97). As long as the child only imitates its own action, the relation to the object can only be inferred from a motive outside it – in contrast to a cat, for instance, playing with a ball of wool when it trains chasing prey. In my opinion, the interest of the child now centers around putting oneself into situations, which are not objectively present, whereby the action together with its orientation becomes the object. Piaget (ibid.: 121) called this the formation of "symbolic schemas," since they symbolically represent behaviors that were before only functionally performed in practice play.

In the second phase of symbolic play, even outside observers unmistakably see that play no longer serves sensorimotor training. Through "projection" children now begin to transfer those differentiations ("symbolic schemas" or prototypes), which they have reproduced on their bodies before, to "others," even to "things." The schemas are attributed to others: "The child will pretend to make objects other than himself eat, sleep or walk" (ibid.: 120). Furthermore, children imitate the sounds of crying, for instance, when they make a teddy bear, plush fox, or even a hat cry, or hold a box to the mouth of others after having used it to mime drinking and eating. Hence, we now arrive at a transition that makes symbolic behavior clearly discernible from sensorimotor practice.

This (effortless) imitation developing from assimilation executes "symbolic schemas" or prototypes of one's own actions. It thus becomes flexible and independent of the objects acted on, bypassing the difficulties of adapting to them. That is why this kind of play behavior is also accompanied by a *flow experience* ("Funktionslust" in Bühler 1927: 157). Soon imitations of others appear, albeit rudimentarily, to serve as cognitive symbols during play. The child, for example, pretends to read a newspaper or to make a phone call, as observed on others, or to sweep the floor symbolically with a piece of paper. By way of a corresponding projection, the child then makes a doll sweep the floor, read a newspaper, or make a phone call.

Finally, the last phase of symbolic play combines various episodic complexes, which can now be used to *anticipate* or to compensate for what has been experienced.

We may assume that these internalized complexes (orientations), held together by generic prototypes (of objects and facts), now enable a wealth of affective and effective proxies (analogies). As such they condition the first *representation* and, thereby, insight and the beginning of operational thought. To the extent that the child now strives to conform to reality rather than merely assimilate it during play, the cognitive symbol is increasingly transformed into internalized imagery. Piaget argued that at the same time imitation incorporates itself into intelligent or effective adaptation.

The cognitive symbol in adult thought and its actual genesis

The gradually growing system of meanings and proxy objects manifesting themselves as cognitive symbols (*seeds*) can be called episodic if the subject is able to additionally expand the contexts of the original situations. Quite often, we notice such over-determined complexes, i.e. displacements and condensations only in retrospect. I assume that the actualization of former orientation causes the fact that such episodes are accompanied by a wealth of seemingly sensory experiences, because any sensorimotor directed orientation necessarily implies sensory connections also. Yet, in order to experience them, the latter do not have to be re-stimulated, which is why we often erroneously speak of memory "*images*," mental or dream "*images*" (*emulation*).

Manifestations of seeds are purely *functional*, if only the prototypical, but deeply rooted aspect of their meaning unfolds. My introspection indicates that even in adult thought, new relations within situations and episodes can be noticed at any time. These connections subserve the thought process that follows or they may be used in the months or even years to come, when they actualize as entire complexes. Quite often, episodes from childhood or adolescence actualize again. It is not surprising that introspection is unable to trace the cognitive symbol of the adult back to its origins in the first imitative actions.

However, when I ask myself *how* a specific content was given to me (by way of what I call follow-up concretization), both introspection and closer examination of dream contents indicate that to a certain degree I am always able to expand and thereby explicate a syncretic structure, which seems implicit in the actualized orientation. Above all, syncretism becomes obvious when several cognitive symbols (*clutter*) and their over-determined contexts manifest themselves in orientation. Then the generic aspect of what has been grasped is not yet coordinated and greatly "exaggerates" the displacement of particular features. What is still missing is a structure eliminating unnecessary or contradictory elements. Nevertheless, I suspect that these rich implicit relations are responsible for any deeper meaning, sometimes even for the manifestation of an insight expressing itself in living thought as an "aha experience." Cognitive symbols always imply the intentional and representational content of meaningful situations, which are yet to be unfolded. Their orientation reaches far beyond any word or linguistic sign but can be related to any arbitrary sign if it can transport epistemic content in addition to its formal meaning. It is important to keep in mind that this newly enabled "semiotic function" (Piaget 1985 [1975]: 112) assigning meaning to any linguistic or arbitrary sign relations must have emerged from the as-if function abstracting from objects. The structure of setting something into relation and comparing an idea with "reality" originates from the (persistent) imitation of new models.

In my assessment, every "thought" begins as a reaction to a lacuna in orientation that developed into a perturbation (*irritation*). So it always begins with a seed phenomenon, whether in living everyday thinking, in problem-solving, or as a controlling constraint of perception and action. In my introspection, cognitive symbols are often accompanied by an attunement to a "pre-object." I experience a premonition seeding a certain direction, i.e., a quite general meaning. If I do not intend to dig deeper, I can then leave it at that and merely assimilate (*seed thinking*) as long as my orientation carries me on *in actu*.

It was Karl Bühler (1908) who already drew attention to some of these aspects. Let us recall his description of the "inter-thought relations," which do not pertain to the intrinsic content of thoughts, but accompany them and bind them to experiences. They include, e.g., the knowledge that the current thought belongs to the previous one, relates to another one in this or that way, or fits the entire complex or not. Only the totality of these "contents of consciousness" "warrants the unity of the thought process; it is the expression of the control, which the thinker himself exercises over what is going on in him. If they are completely absent, the thinker has lost his orientation; he stays with a single thought without knowing what it is actually supposed to accomplish at this point" (Bühler 1908: 5).

Bühler described two types of such inter-thought relations. The first type concerns experiential relations and the second object relations. According to Bühler, the latter make us aware of how "one thought is related to another by its content, whether they relate to each other as opposites or [...] whether they contradict each other" (1908: 7). I think that these descriptions also fit very well with the difference between *expansion* and *assembly* of cognitive symbols, because the character of the unfolding process of experiential relations to me seems similar to expansion, while the more object-related "rational" pondering is characteristic of *assembly*, which, according to my introspection, occurs later.

Early thinking, both infantile and understood as the first actual-genetic steps from expansion to assemblage, is over-determined and contradictory, but still without consciousness of these contradictions. This is precisely the reason that it is so rich in analogies. In my view, a seed must be expanded to its representational content only if the seeded superficial meaning is not sufficient to resolve an *irritation*. Having an introspective attitude, I very often register that the *over-determined* character of proxy objects only emerges after expanding this meaning. If attention remains mainly directed to the first thought content (prototype), then the cognitive symbols, appearing as unordered *clutter*, are calibrated against each other in an assembly without becoming proxy objects themselves. They are either rejected as inappropriate, reorganized, or embedded differently, namely into a developing context (*running environment*) that mutually supports the assembly process and becomes more and more specific.

Deriving cognitive symbols from their ontogeny, as I have tried to do here, shows that they do not originate directly from the purposeful *use* of objects. Instead, they are specific readinesses for action originating in imitation in order to repeat and represent the behavior of objects and persons by handling them in play. My introspection indicates that the orientation coming with imitation may stem from all possible life situations, of which one is indeed the use of objects. The first cognitive symbols already seem to preform more appropriate *cognitive representations* appearing later in development, as highlighted by Wiener (2015b: 102). According to him, the latter are *procedures* representing relevant intrinsic regularities of the object, on the one hand, and *procedures* operating on these regularities, on the other.

It was again Bühler (1907: 331) who already drew attention to the temporal aspect, which expresses itself in a "successive series of experiences or partial experiences" before yielding a "finished thought," which he called "experiential unit" and during an insight is accompanied by an "aha experience" (Bühler 1908: 18). It is this actual-genetic aspect that I am particularly concerned with here. It is further discussed in my conversation with Oswald Wiener (see "Pleomorphism in Thought and the Computational Metaphor" in this volume) under the headings of "bootstrapping" and "assembly."

The essential difference between adult and infantile thought or between adult thought and "symbolic thought" in dreams could well be the latters' lack of potential *assembly*, which is not yet developed in the two- to three-year-old child and regresses during sleep, respectively. If assembly *does not* use meanings and objects appearing as seeds for their "unity and purpose" or does not question them in retrospective analysis, they seem to be experienced like a "dream fragment." Hence, there seems to be no unconscious active censor at work producing the "dream images" as "symbols" for the purpose of self-deception (Freud). Cognitive symbols are rather over-determined preforms of thought, which refer to analogies and, thus, certainly to hitherto unnoticed affective problem contexts.

In adolescent thought, syncretism is gradually synthesized (cf. Freud's reality principle). This enables the subordination and classification of part and whole, the formation of heterarchies of action readinesses, and the resolution of contradictions. Thus, the ontogenetically developed structure of cognitive symbols could be both a preform and a condition for later operational and formal thought processes.

Concluding remarks on AI and the psychological basis of cognitive symbols

My account indicates that the affectively and effectively meaningful relations within and between *cognitive symbols* necessarily afford actual-genetic expansion and an assembly process. Hence, on the one hand, they cannot be derived from a coherent formal system of symbolic contents with fixed meanings, as linguistics and, to some extent, symbol-processing AI had envisaged. On the other hand, a proxy object in thought – e.g., an action readiness substituting for an object or a situation – also cannot easily be implemented by the distributed information of "newer" AI based on artificial neural networks (ANNs). To my knowledge, there is not even a plan to advance the development of such a competence.

Cognitive symbols and their content do not emerge from machine learning of images or other data transmitted in modal isolation, even if it is indeed impressive that ANNs are able to bring the first biological steps of, e.g., visual perception into a functionally coherent, and partly equivalent, scheme (Schrimpf, DiCarlo et al. 2020). However, by mere sensory "recognition" and classification of "objects," ANNs cannot produce cognitive symbols. This, nor can they provide the hoped-for "grounding" of "symbol processing" in computers. As Stevan Harnad et al. had pointed out, neural nets were designed to provide the causal basis for the higher order symbolic processing and the representation of objects. But a true causal interaction with the environment necessarily requires directed and actively executed and sensorimotor acts accommodating in real-time. So the conceptual separation of sensory processes and motor responses (reflex arc) must be viewed as an inadequate relic from the artificial laboratory conditions of early experimental psychology, which used fixation, i.e., the prevention of movement while "perceiving," which is nonetheless still used in experiments today.

A theory of perception, for instance, cannot ignore the "ecological" aspect (James J. Gibson) by disregarding motor activity in perceiving. It is the very concept of circular reaction that explains the actively directed feedback onto environmental phenomena and onto the behavior of objects, and, later, of relations between objects. Without this feedback, efficient adaptation (accommodation) of action schemas tuned to anticipate their objects simply isn't possible. Only these anticipatory (or meaningful) schemas developed by action enable new proxy schemas constructed as analogues to objects. Only they result in cognitive symbols, the embedding of which I also find missing, for example, in the so-called imagery debate. According to my hypothesis outlined here, cognitive symbols are "pictorial" (Stephen Kosslyn), i.e., figurative operations, only during very specific task performances. Their operands, however, are not "pictorial." Nor are cognitive symbols representations reducible to linguistic propositions (Zenon Pylyshyn), because their *meaning*, e.g., discovering that you can pull close an object standing on an underlay, has to be implicitly acquired and generalized by experimental action. This meaning exists as an action schema even before the context becomes (even partially) clear enough to be represented by a linguistic proposition.

The "symbol grounding" debate, i.e., the question of embedding or grounding artificial intelligence in the environment, whether sought after in order to understand human language (John Searle) or to manipulate formal systems of arbitrary symbols (Harnad 1990), is obviously missing the description of the structural basis of development, which I have tried elucidate here by referring to Piaget's sensorimotor stages. Introspection of the actual genesis of a thought at least rudimentarily indicates such a basis. In order to be grounded in the environment, not only symbol systems and language would require the feature of human understanding and negotiating meaning. This foundation is also fatally missing in artificial neural networks currently serving as universally successful "mock intelligence" (see the essay by Oswald Wiener "Cybernetics and Ghosts" in this volume). ANNs lack this foundation, even if they are able to classify sensory objects, because until now they too remain totally isolated from the structural development outlined above. ANNs operate without any sensorimotor meaning, without proxy objects, without any possibility to set themselves in relation to the environment, and ultimately without models of the environment. I must call this lack fatal, because, in contrast to sensorimotor operations, trained networks achieve their goals, while at the same time rendering the computing process inaccessible to interpretation.

A living being is grounded already at an early sensorimotor stage, because within its ecological niche it is balanced between adaptation and habit as well as between need, interest, and satisfaction. According to the hypothesis presented here, the essential basis of establishing and promoting this equilibrium is, at least initially, circular reaction alone. Yet, we can observe that during the entire process of equilibration, the ongoing equilibrium is overstepped at several stages (at least six times during infantile development). Each time it gets oriented towards new relationships and new interests. Each time a new equilibrium is found until ultimately, at a later stage in human development, the use of cognitive symbols emerges.

That was my central question: At what point in ontogeny do cognitive symbols and, therefore, the use of language and arbitrary sign associations become possible? My answer was not complete but, in short, they become possible by the interaction of imitative schemas and their internalized use as an object surrogate, which are brought into a schematic analogy with the environment, the question of symbol grounding is tentatively resolved. Our for the most part covertly calibrated orientation enable cognitive symbols to remain bound to the entire sensorimotor development and its meaning. While the arbitrary symbols of symbol systems gain their operative meaning by active reproduction, human languages establish a hierarchy of symbols, which have to be referred to the meaning of the cognitive symbols and are, thus, grounded actively by new assemblies to be understood. So the general question of grounding formal systems, languages, or even artificial neural networks must be answered clearly: So far no formal system has ever been grounded or, rather, able to ground itself by being integrated into an organism, which has undergone the structural genesis leading to cognitive symbols.

I believe that this structural development of cognitive symbols, which begins as a very specific action readiness relating to the environment and ends with the anticipation of situations by constructing heterarchies of action readinesses (assembly), seems to go far beyond what J. J. Gibson would have seen as the recognition of situations. It seems to end up in imaginative processes, which Wiener (2000: 18–23) dubbed dynamic "internal models of the external world." So a coherent biological theory of our endowment for active habit formation, i.e., the circularly reproducing assimilation with its accommodations, initiating this entire ontogenetic development, would stand as a major scientific breakthrough.

References
The page numbers in the text refer to the English translations.

Baldwin, James Mark, 1895. *Mental Development in the Child and the Race: Methods and Processes.* New York.
Baldwin, James Mark, 1906. *Thought and Things: A Study of the Development and Meaning of Thought or Genetic Logic.* Vol. I: Functional Logic, or Genetic Theory of Knowledge. London.
Bühler, Karl, 1907. Tatsachen und Probleme zu einer Psychologie der Denkvorgänge: I. Über Gedanken. *Archiv für die gesamte Psychologie*, 9, 297–365.
Bühler, Karl, 1908. Tatsachen und Probleme zu einer Psychologie der Denkvorgänge: II. Über Gedankenzusammenhänge. *Archiv für die gesamte Psychologie*, 12, 1–23.
Bühler, Karl, 1927. *Die Krise der Psychologie.* Frankfurt am Main.
Bleuler, Eugen, 1912. Autistic Thinking. In: Rapaport, David (ed.), 1965. *Organization and Pathology of Thought.* New York, London, 399–438.
Eder, Thomas, and Thomas Raab (eds.), 2015. *Selbstbeobachtung: Oswald Wieners Denkpsychologie.* Berlin.
Harnad, Stevan, 1990. The Symbol Grounding Problem. *Physica D*, 42, 335–346.
Jennings, Herbert Spencer, 1906. *Behavior of the Lower Organisms.* New York.
Köhler, Wolfgang, 1925. *The Mentality of Apes.* London, New York.
Piaget, Jean, 1923. La pensée symbolique et la pensée de l'enfant. *Archives de Psychologie*, 18, 273–304.
Piaget, Jean, 1936. *La naissance de l'intelligence chez l'enfant.* Neuchâtel (Engl.: *The Origins of Intelligence in Children.* New York 1963).
Piaget, Jean, 1937. *La construction du réel chez l'enfant.* Neuchâtel (Engl.: *The Construction of Reality in the Child.* New York 1954).
Piaget, Jean, 1945. *La formation du symbole chez l'enfant: Imitation, jeu et rêve – Image et représentation.* Neuchâtel, Paris (Engl.: *Play, Dreams and Imitation in Childhood.* London 1951).

Piaget, Jean, 1947. *La psychologie de l'intelligence*. Paris (Engl.: *The Psychology of Intelligence*. London 1950).

Piaget, Jean, 1975. *L'équilibration des structures cognitives: Problème central du développement*. Paris (Engl.: *The Equilibration of Cognitive Structures: The Central Problem of Intellectual Development*. Chicago, London 1985).

Rapaport, David, 1959. The Theory of Attention Cathexis. In: Gill, Merton M. (ed.), 1967. *The Collected Papers of David Rapaport*. New York, London, 778–794.

Schrimpf, Martin, Jonas Kubilius, Michael J. Lee, N. Apurva Ratan Murty, Robert Ajemian, and James J. DiCarlo, 2020. Integrative Benchmarking to Advance Neurally Mechanistic Models of Human Intelligence. *Neuron*, 108/3, 413–423.

Searle, John R., 1980. Minds, Brains, and Programs. *The Behavioral and Brain Sciences*, 3, 417–457.

Selz, Otto, 1913. *Über die Gesetze des geordneten Denkverlaufs: Eine experimentelle Untersuchung*. Stuttgart.

Selz, Otto, 1922. *Zur Psychologie des produktiven Denkens und des Irrtums: Eine experimentelle Untersuchung*. Bonn.

Volkelt, Hans, 1912. *Über die Vorstellungen der Tiere: Ein Beitrag zur Entwicklungspsychologie*. Leipzig.

Weizsäcker, Viktor von, 1940. *Der Gestaltkreis: Theorie der Einheit von Wahrnehmung und Bewegungen*. Leipzig.

Wiener, Oswald, 2015a. Glossar: Weiser. In: Eder, Thomas, and Thomas Raab (eds.), *Selbstbeobachtung: Oswald Wieners Denkpsychologie*. Berlin, 59–98.

Wiener, Oswald, 2015b. Glossar: figurativ. In: Eder, Thomas, and Thomas Raab (eds.), *Selbstbeobachtung: Oswald Wieners Denkpsychologie*. Berlin, 99–141.

Wiener, Oswald, 2000. *Materialien zu meinem Buch VORSTELLUNGEN*. In: Lesák, František (ed.), *AUSSCHNITT 05*. Vienna, 1–120.

Wohlfahrt, Erich, 1932. *Der Auffassungsvorgang an kleinen Gestalten: Ein Beitrag zur Psychologie des Vorgestalterlebnisses*. Leipzig.

Reciting "Timidity"

Remarks on the Memorization of Speech Events Using the Example of an Ode by Friedrich Hölderlin

Thomas Eder

0 General premises

As a literary scholar I feel split. Apart from philology, I also pursue questions of the psychology of thought. How do we understand language? What do rote memorization and recitation of speech events mean and what is their phenomenal side? How does memory and recollection work? So in order to introspect, I regularly choose difficult poems as tasks, e.g., poems by Paul Celan or Friedrich Hölderlin. I have, for instance, memorized Friedrich Hölderlin's ode "Timidity" (German title: "Blödigkeit"), occasionally reciting it to myself aloud, but mostly silently. Some asides: What does "reciting silently" mean? Whispering it? Or articulating it subvocally? Or imagining it *quasi*-loudly, i.e., *quasi*-sensorily? But then, what does "*quasi*-sensory" mean, or even "to imagine"?

In order to approach such questions, in the following I summarize and selectively detail introspections as they occurred during a multitude of recitation trials. In most of them, I recited the poem inwardly, sometimes only partially and sometimes almost involuntarily. My introspective procedure may be viewed as an extreme approach to the esthetic of reception, yet with the additional intricacy that I served not only as the subject of the experiment, but also took the protocols of my phenomenal experiences while reciting the poems. I do acknowledge all the well-known difficulties and doubts concerning introspection (e.g., Watson 1920, Lashley 1923, Nisbett and Wilson 1977, Russo et al. 1989, Massen and Bredekamp 2005, Hurlburt and Schwitzgebel 2007) and disclose the following empirical premise. The more familiar a sentence or text is, the easier it is to understand, but the less we gain any introspective access to the cognitive processes of understanding it and, therefore, to conscious parts of language comprehension. So already Karl Bühler, for example, stated in 1909:

"How does a (composite) thought build up in the consciousness of the listener? In the case of simple or familiar sentences even the most experienced subjects cannot provide any information about it. On hearing the sentence, its sense seems to be readily apprehended, and introspection is unable to state any event at all. This only changes when comprehension is disturbed or hampered. Then the subject is often able to notice that after hearing the words their meaning takes a while to become conscious. Sometimes, understanding comes slowly, sometimes suddenly and with an inner jolt. The subjects then often exclaim loudly or softly 'Aha!' The meaning surprises them [...]" (Bühler 1909: 116f.).

Translated into Oswald Wiener's terminology, this would mean: Language understanding or, more generally, seed phenomena triggered by words are only indirectly accessible to introspection by way of error signals possibly triggering *q(uasi)*-visual intrusions.

"Introspection is unable to probe the mechanisms converting linguistic input into structures (structural components) and assembling them into the pre-existing structure of readinesses. These mechanisms can at best be introspected indirectly by way of error signals or, sometimes, 'attunements.' However, introspection enables the registration of some effects of these processes on higher levels, to which, for example, efforts at eliminating a contradiction discovered by underlying mechanisms filter through" (Wiener, personal correspondence).

So the processes leading to the translation of linguistic input into other layers of thought are usually not accessible to introspection. However, one cannot deny that as soon comprehension is impeded – when, for instance, linguistic input creates irritations by ambiguity – we are forced to interrupt smooth automated comprehension and start task-driven assemblies triggered by the speech events (cf. Eder 2015).

In contrast to previous reading research (Afflerbach 2000, Afflerbach and Pressley 1995), which proceeded by recording and transcribing so-called "think-aloud protocols" by test subjects, which the experimenters then subjected to protocol analysis (Ericsson and Simon 1980, 1993), I did not make exact protocols of every single recitation.

I refrain from doing so because I doubt several assumptions fundamental for this procedure. Among other things, I question that such language protocols are able to reflect what is going on in and what is relevant for the thought process involved, or that the analysis of such protocols by the experimenters, who usually "code & count" words and thus face difficulties comparable to those of their subjects reading the text, could possibly be productive. Above all, the required "thinking aloud" as simultaneously as possible only addresses immediate (usually singular as well as first) readings. Aside from problems of the interaction between test subjects and experimenters, this seems especially unsuitable for literary texts.

So far current research on the phenomenal processes of language comprehension during reading (which despite all differences is comparable to the silent recitation of poetry) seems to have yielded rather meager results: "the experimental literature on reading has told us a lot about the cognitive architecture recruited for reading but very little about the conscious experiences that people have while reading" (Moore and Schwitzgebel 2018: 58). This clearly indicates the need to reassess and renew the agenda of research on reading, as well as to reconceptualize the relation between protocol analysis and introspection. Therefore, I tried to pursue a somewhat intermediate course between the philologist's approach focused on textual interpretation, applying extra-textual tools as well as the methods of his discipline, on the one hand, and the description and reflection of my introspections while attempting to understand a poem with the goal of gaining insights into the thought process itself, on the other. Unlike the initial and spontaneous processing of text studied in most experimental designs reported in psychological literature on language comprehension, I was interested in the philologist's reading practice – in *my* thoughts while trying to understand a complex text, in the repeated and sometimes retrospective observations of my thought processes, in moments and experiences when something suddenly changed my understanding of the text fundamentally.

So I will largely refrain from a comprehensive treatment of Hölderlin's poem, which would have to include a philologically acceptable interpretation. Instead, I aim to describe a detailed problem, which also seems interesting from a psychological perspective. I would like to specify a few questions that seem urgent to me on the basis of my experiences and difficulties in memorizing, retaining, and reciting one or two stanzas/verses of the ode. A particular focus will be placed on the phenomenon of ambiguity, because I agree with Tobias Christ's findings on the "Night Songs" that for Hölderlin's late poetry the following applies:

"The fact that Hölderlin's texts are structured at certain (usually central) points in such a way that they allow several readings at the same time (overdetermination) or downright omit semantic and logical connections (underdetermination) implies that in the process of reading the conventional linear orientation toward the unambiguous extraction of meaning, which assumes that one sentence corresponds to one statement, has to be abandoned. Instead, Hölderlin's late texts call for a non-linear multiple reading with the complementary help of interpretation, that is, for a hermeneutic reading resulting in a plural constitution of meaning, insofar as the linking of sentence elements and text sequences is not unambiguously predetermined, but rather the text either offers the reader several variants of reading or contains only insufficient or even no determining signals" (Christ 2020: 437).

On my memorization trials

There exists a vast literature on the question of language memorization. Since Ebbinghaus's famous experiments on memorizing meaningless syllables (Ebbinghaus 1885), psychological testing methods have been regularly applied to the problem of language memorization leading to the development of extremely elegant and informative test designs (Neisser 1978a, 1978b, 1988, 1996, Dickson et al. 1988, Kintsch 1975, Graesser and Mandler 1975, Barclay 1973, Bever 1970, Asch et al. 1960, Bartlett 1932).

As a literary scholar, however, I am concerned with a phenomenon which arguably has to be individually and pre-scientifically experienced first. It seems probable that the disciplines mentioned would have to invent methods and experiments in order to investigate my conjectures by explorative studies and, then, by proper scientific experiments according to their standards. Nevertheless, I consider it difficult to operationalize my introspections for experimental purposes, because they are based on my very individual knowledge and perhaps even idiosyncrasy. This, I admit, is a well-known objection against introspection as a psychological method.

1 Friedrich Hölderlin: "Blödigkeit" ("Timidity")

Blödigkeit

Sind denn dir nicht bekannt viele Lebendigen?
Geht auf Wahrem dein Fuß nicht, wie auf Teppichen?
Drum, mein Genius! tritt nur
Baar ins Leben, und sorge nicht!

Was geschiehet, es sei alles gelegen dir!
Sei zur Freude gereimt, oder was könnte denn
Dich belaidigen, Herz, was
Da begegnen, wohin du sollst?

Denn, seit Himmlischen gleich Menschen, ein einsam Wild
Und die Himmlischen selbst führet, der Einkehr zu,
Der Gesang und der Fürsten
Chor, nach Arten, so waren auch

Wir, die Zungen des Volks gerne bei Lebenden,
Wo sich vieles gesellt, freudig und jedem gleich,
Jedem offen, so ist ja
Unser Vater, des Himmels Gott,

Der den denkenden Tag Armen und Reichen gönnt,
Der, zur Wende der Zeit, uns die Entschlafenden
Aufgerichtet an goldnen
Gängelbanden, wie Kinder, hält.

Gut auch sind und geschikt einem zu etwas wir,
Wenn wir kommen, mit Kunst, und von den Himmlischen
Einen bringen. Doch selber
Bringen schikliche Hände wir.

(Hölderlin 1984, 699f.)

Timidness [Timidity]

Of the living are not many well-known to you?
On the truth don't your feet walk as they would on rugs?
Boldly, therefore, my genius,
Step right into the thick of life!

All that happens there be welcome, a boon to you!
Be disposed to feel joy, or is there anything
That could harm you there, heart, that
Could affront you, where you must go?

For since gods grew like men, lonely as woodland beasts,
And since, each in its way, song and the princely choir
Brought the Heavenly in person
Back to earth, so we too, the tongues

Of the people, have liked living men's company,
Where all kinds are conjoined, equal and open to
Everyone, full of joy – for
So our Father is, Heaven's God,

Who to rich men and poor offers the thinking day,
At the turning of Time holds us, the sleepy ones,
Upright still with his golden
Leading-strings, as one holds a child.

Someone, some way, we too serve, are of use, are sent
When we come, with our art, and of the heavenly powers
Bring one with us. But fitting,
Skilful hands we ourselves provide.

(Translated by Michael Hamburger)

It took me some time to properly understand the syntactic structure of the poem – perhaps I never did, or never even could, because the poem might be syntactically ambiguous, irresolvably ambiguous at its core even (cf. Christ 2020: 437). Since I often made errors while trying to resolve this syntactic complexity, I will focus particularly on error signals. Following Oswald Wiener's theory, I believe that the respective passages led to a partial loss of orientation. This partial loss of orientation manifests itself, I assume, in error signals accompanying it.

At first, I was hardly able to reproduce what I had tried to learn by heart because I had difficulties remembering and recalling the sound and letter sequence. So I defined markers following the commas in order to segment what was to be remembered. This provided a rhythmic-metrical framework, which for the moment rather followed the verse boundaries as well as prosodic and metrical constraints. From a philological, or rather declamatory point of view (cf. Meyer-Kalkus 2019), this may have been unwise.

There are cases of memory and recall, which strictly depend on whether or not verbatim reproduction succeeds. So Schiller's "Die Bürgschaft" ("The Pledge"), Goethe's "Erlkönig" ("Erlking"), or the beginning of the first paragraph of the Austrian federal constitution are either remembered and reproduced word by word or they are not reproduced at all (cf. Rubin 1982 [1977]). Without any doubt, the poem of Hölderlin's I chose belongs to this category. Whether or not I succeed in memorizing and silently reciting it, depends on whether I am able to remember and silently or loudly reproduce it exactly word by word. Nevertheless, among many other features that I will not discuss here, my introspections suggest a phenomenon that I consider worth sharing and discussing in light of the existing research literature on memory of speech events:

I gained the impression that, although I was able to recite simple passages that I understood correctly in terms of their meaning and approximate wording, I nevertheless erred in their *exact* wording. At times, I misreproduced some words, that is, I used synonyms instead of the actual words and, above all, I often misreproduced their order. This happened *less often* with passages that appeared rather opaque or syntactically difficult to me. I *either* could not recite them at all (and halted) *or* was indeed able to recite them verbatim and syntactically correctly. As far as the reason for this seeming paradox is concerned, my best guess is that I tend to memorize these passages according to "formal" criteria. Of course I would have to define what I mean by "formal," which I will try to do below. On the one hand, my observations convinced me that I was able to memorize the passages difficult to understand word by word (although some of them I still don't understand) and also to retain them over long periods of time while I wasn't reciting the poem at all. Yet, on the other hand, I often found myself unable to recite verbatim those passages I understood well and hence found easy to memorize. In these cases, I could only reproduce the content (in approximate words) and not the words in their exact order. It seemed as if I had somehow condensed what was easy to understand (cf. infra), that is, I had memorized the words' meaning, and therefore did not have to pay so much attention to the exact wording. Conversely, I seemed to have memorized the hard-to-understand passages differently, namely in a verbatim and accurate fashion. Nevertheless, I kept trying to understand these passages and after having repeated them many times, I succeeded at least partially. I believe that, in this regard, the distinction between "rote memory" versus "meaningful learning" (Neisser 1978a, Rubin 1982 [1977]) could be productively applied to the question of verbatim memorization, but perhaps even more so to the aspect of memorization over longer periods of time, which should possibly be distinguished from simple rote learning (Rubin 1982 [1977]). Presumably, memorization and remembering over long periods of time are to be distinguished in particular from retention after only one single exposure for a very short time, as it is mostly studied in psychological experiments.

The following observation by Wiener seems to be instructive for an explanation of the fact that "short internal sound sequences (such as spoken ones) can be 'automatically' reproduced over a long time." It resulted from his attempt at introspecting and reporting experiences in the course of an extended trial "to clarify a theorem of elementary combinatorics: 'The number of permutations of n elements is given by the expression $n!$'" (Wiener 1996: 301). The observation reads: "Far more useful than *quasi*-visual-images were acoustic images (frequently accompanied by quasi-movements of the speech apparatus).[1] Naming a permutation such as 'be-a-de-see' contributed a lot to the stabilization of thought. Obviously, this is not language in the proper sense, but rather the use of the curious fact that 'sensory memory' (the short perseveration of a sensory impression after the stimulus ends) holds longer in the auditive mode than in the visual mode, which seems to have a parallel in the 'inner sensorium' (not yet clearly understood). Perhaps even more often, one exploits the fact that short internal sound sequences (such as spoken ones) can be 'automatically' reproduced over a long time without disturbing conscious thinking about other things. Of course, the name 'be-a-de-see' for one single permutation does not help the dynamic processes of manipulating its elements. Its role is to fixate only one phase of the process. If I, for instance, lose sight of individual elements, or the entire construction collapses because of a slight distraction, which occurs quite regularly, the name might still be present, so that I am able to use it to reconstruct the situation without being thrown back to the beginning. Such quasi-movements of the speech apparatus as well as their quasi-acoustic perception become conscious at the fringe, so to speak. Generally, I attend to the dynamics of the events much more than to the quasi-sensory impressions of which the linguistic ones are least salient. It is as if I would hear them 'resounding' in passing like a kind of auxiliary bookkeeping, until they are finally needed for reconstruction" (Wiener 1996: 302f.). Of course, it is relevant to my problem that I do not use "internal sound sequences" to support another task but that learning, memorizing, and reproduction of the sound sequences is the first part of my task. The second part is that of understanding these sound sequences in the sense of interpreting Hölderlin's poem.

After a brief report on the ambiguities involved I will try to detail my experiences while memorizing the following part of the third stanza of the ode and to contextualize them in the psychological literature on the memorization of speech events:

Denn, seit Himmlischen gleich Menschen, ein einsam Wild
Und die Himmlischen selbst führet, der Einkehr zu,
Der Gesang und der Fürsten
Chor, nach Arten,

For, since song and the choir of princes
Lead human beings, like the heavenly, lonely as wild game,
And the heavenly themselves, each in its own way,
Towards *Einkehr* ...[2]

Jochen Schmidt syntactically normalized this text passage, which is characterized by so-called "harte Fügung" (Hellingrath 1911: 4f., "hard jointure, or *harmoníē austērá* between the elements"), to:

"In normal jointure: 'For since the song leads the people, who were like the heavenly ones a lonely game, to the contemplation' [Denn seit der Gesang die Menschen, die gleich den Himmlischen ein einsam Wild waren, der Einkehr zuführt]" (Schmidt 2019: 826).

Without doubt, Schmidt is partly right. But here I am not concerned with philological adequacy and correctness. For psychologically speaking, his clear simplification has a major disadvantage because it radically changes both form and content of the original while offering a single (albeit plausible) interpretation. All other aspects of the original are omitted.

In every recitation trial I feel relief as soon as I reach the transition from stanza 3 to stanza 4 for there I seem to have reached the safe haven of syntactic unambiguity:

"so waren auch // Wir, die Zungen des Volks gerne bei Lebenden" ("so, too, were // We, the tongues of the people, gladly among the living" [Corngold/Mergenthaler translation]).

Before this passage I used to get lost in the thicket of ambiguities of the third stanza, trying to relate the individual text segments to each other – partly due to cognitive capacity limits (MacDonald et al. 1992), partly due to the urge to form syntactic connections. As Fuhrhop and Schreiber (2019) said in a syntactic analysis of another, very famous poem of Hölderlin's ("Hälfte des Lebens" – "Half of Life"), which was published together with the ode "Blödigkeit" in a cycle that in a letter Hölderlin had called "Nachtgesänge" ("Night Songs") appearing for the Michaelmas Fair at the end of September 1804 under the title "Gedichte" ("Poems") in a pocket book at the Frankfurt publisher Friedrich Wilmans predated to the year 1805 (cf. Christ 2020: 6):

"The potential effect of this method can be defined thus: The later the position of the second finite verb ('tunkt'), the longer the reader or hearer is able to follow the strategy to both syntactically and semantically associate the apprehended word material with the first structure ('hänget' in verse 1), i.e., to the left or upwards" (Fuhrhop and Schreiber 2019: 93).

Did I proceed in stanza 3 just like in processing (parsing) so-called garden-path sentences (Sanz et al. 2013, Bever 1972)? Perhaps I followed an implicit hypothesis on the syntactic relations of the sentence until a specific word triggered a different implicit hypothesis about its grammatical construction. The oft-quoted example for this type of sentence is "The horse raced past the barn fell." Until the reader or hearer reaches the word "fell" he or she perceives the word "raced" as the main verb in simple past tense. Only when "fell" emerges are they forced to understand it as the main verb in simple past, while "raced" is being used as a passive participle opening a reduced relative clause; "horse" is the direct object of the subordinate clause (cf. Bever 1972).

I do not intend to present a list of readings and grammatical-syntactical assignments of this passage of Hölderlin's, some of which are more plausible than others, some requiring more effort and can only be implied from the verses by force, so to speak. Instead, I shall cite the extensive presentation of dynamic alternatives of interpretation, which Tobias Christ plausibly elaborated:

"In the passage, the inverted elliptical formulation 'seit Himmlischen gleich Menschen' is irritating at first, because at the syntactic position of the subject expected in normal usage the object of comparison ('Himmlischen') stands in, which can only be recognized as such by the little distinctive dative ending -n. The first – semantically ambiguous – interpretation thus is: 'seit den Himmlischen die Menschen gleich [sind],' meaning (1) that humans are essentially equal to the gods, as well as (2) humans are indifferent to the gods. However, depending on where the reader adds the missing verb, yet another meaning ensues. As the verb is absent, 'ein einsam Wild' can, on the one hand, be read as an apposition to 'Menschen.' This reading is supported by the temporal preposition 'seit' which is only now endowed with proper meaning: 'Seit den Himmlischen die Menschen gleichgültig [sind], [sind diese] ein einsam Wild' {'Since for the celestials people [are] indifferent, [they are] lonely game'}. On the other hand, it can also be understood as a predicate noun in an implausible but possible construction: 'Denn seit, Himmlischen gleich, Menschen ein einsam Wild [sind]' {'For since, like the celestials, people [are] lonely game'}. Both of these interpretations, however, have to be corrected when reading on. For now, with the inclusion of the next verse, 'ein einsam

Wild' itself appears as the subject of the sentence because of the following congruent verb 'führet', that is, 'ein einsam Wild [...] führet, der Einkehr zu.' This momentary suggestion is destroyed only because it (again only apparently?) belongs to a list ('ein einsam Wild und die Himmlischen') as well as due to the continuation of the sentence. Now, contrariwise, 'ein einsam Wild' appears together with 'die Himmlischen' as the object to the subject at the end of the sentence ('Der Gesang und der Fürsten / Chor'). Depending on the interpretation of verse 9, however, it remains unclear whether 'ein einsam Wild / Und die Himmlischen' belong together as a list, or rather a new clause begins at verse break. If we take semantic integration as a benchmark for syntactic integration, it seems more plausible to assume these are two sentences, because then the preposition 'seit' would make sense. Now ambiguity dissolves, and we are able to meaningfully integrate the sentence by reconstructing the obscured references: 'Seit den Himmlischen die Menschen gleich (und diese jenen gleichgültig) [sind], [sind sie, die Menschen] ein einsam Wild, und der Gesang und der Chor der Fürsten führet nach Arten (auf unterschiedliche Weise und nach dem Unterschied ihrer Art) die Himmlischen selbst der Einkehr zu' {,Since people are equal to the celestials (and these indifferent to those), they [the people] are lonely game, and the song and the chorus of the princes in different ways lead the celestial men themselves to retreat.'} – Reinforced by these hard syntactic jointures, the grammatical function of the clauses becomes momentarily destabilized, ambiguous, making reading a process of progressive revision and correction that not only simulates reflection on language, but also stimulates it. The method of syntactic condensation yields instantaneous, unstable, and multiple references as well as poly-functional clauses. Structurally similar to zeugma, two clauses or parts of clauses share one and the same member, which is not written twice (here 'ein einsam Wild' simultaneously functions as a predicate noun and as a direct object). This double-referential construction is called apokoinu (ἀπὸ κοινοῦ = 'of the common') and is a stylistic device frequently encountered in Hölderlin's later poetry. It results in a kind of 'tipping effect,' that is, an almost 'seamless' syntactic transition between different units of meaning" (Christ 2020: 382ff.).

Yet, in contrast to Christ, I do not presuppose a disambiguation of potentially polysemous constructions. His analysis is based on the premise: "In the form presented here the apokoinu constructions might effect an irritation but no ambiguity; in this case, the double reference of the syntactic hinge does not yield semantic ambiguity of any part of the sentence, to which it is referring; instead it produces the same definite meaning for any of them" (Christ 2020: 385).

Instead, I assume that in Hölderlin's apokoinu and other syntactically ambiguous constructions (inversion, hyperbaton, anaculothon, ellipse, hard jointure, zeugma, among others) verse parts have two or more inconsistent positions at the same time. This is hard (or almost impossible) to grasp but may be partly responsible for the esthetic effect of poems such as "Timidity."

Ultimately, the syntactic ambiguity of such poems can be traced back to our expectations concerning poetic language, which I for my part often feel and which since modernism have become quite normal, if not for all readers. It is the expectation of parsimonious ambiguity.

In contrast to garden-path sentences, which only temporarily effect ambiguity, Hölderlin's staggering poetic verses show a permanent and irresolvable syntactic ambiguity also affecting the semantic level. Their multiple-aspect images elicited by syntactic ambiguity as well as their oscillation between main and subordinate clauses simply make me happy.

2 Aspects of memorizing Friedrich Hölderlin's "Timidity"

Put bluntly, the thesis derived from my collected introspections on memorizing, recalling, and reciting the ode "Timidity" is:

I am forced to rote memorize the syntactically ambiguous passages (like those in stanza 3), because the contextual ambiguity of the words' meanings overstrain my cognitive capacity and because there is possibly no ultimate resolution of their ambiguities. So I have to stubbornly learn them by heart, perhaps exclusively paying attention to the formal sequential arrangement of the words. To some extent I proceed as if I was dealing with (maximally) meaningless, (maximally) formal symbols. (Another caveat: on the impossibility of purely formal, completely meaningless operations, see infra).

With most of the other passages of the poem I proceed differently, particularly with stanzas 1 and 2 as well as with the transition between stanzas 3 and 4 from the verse/sentence "so waren auch // Wir, die Zungen des Volks gerne bei Lebenden." Here, I rather memorize the core meaning or gist. When reciting the poem, however, I sometimes make mistakes concerning the exact wording, although I usually remain certain of the intended content – even if only as far as I understand it at that point. Of course, an appropriate semantic interpretation of a poem like this, even of its supposedly simple passages, could be much more complex than I practically assume.

Yet, the syntactically complex, ambiguous passages of stanza 3 I mostly recite mindlessly without at the same time being able to understand their meaning. Initially, I maybe even proceed by parroting like a true psittacist using language thoughtlessly. Perhaps I like to employ "tout nû des caractères, comme il arrive à ceux qui calculent en Algebre sans envisager que de temps en temps les figures Geometriques dont il s'agit et les mots font ordinairement le même effect en cela que les caracteres d'Arithmetique ou d'Algebre. On raisonne souvent en paroles, sans avoir presque l'objet même dans l'esprit" (Leibniz 1882: 171).[3] Only during later trials do I strive to understand the words of this part of stanza 3 already learnt by heart by trying to assign meaning to them and considering syntactic alternatives.

Even if the distinction is only gradual and certainly not diametrically opposed: While reciting the text it seems that I somehow approach it (as a speech event) from two angles. The first is the angle of content, which I have memorized and which I recite verbatim, as far as possible, following the metrical, rhythmic, and strophic constraints. Nevertheless, slight mistakes – deviations from the exact wording – occur quite frequently. The second angle pertains to the rote-memorized wording of said passage of stanza 3, which I am almost always able to chatter verbatim, although initially without any or only little understanding. Similarly, the first verse of the last stanza ("Gut auch sind und geschikt einem zu etwas wir") is "ingrained" into me verbatim. Initially, I chattered this sentence too and had to try to understand it anew during each end every recitation trial. Yet, compared to other verses this one appears more complex and difficult. Moreover, my ability to recite such semantically difficult verses word by word remains intact for considerably longer than is the case with the other passages of the poem that are easier to understand.

Remembering form versus remembering content
In psychological research the question of discerning "meaningful" and "formal" "representation" has been discussed broadly (in spite of problems of definition). Anderson and Paulson (1977), for instance, distinguish between "verbatim information representation" and "gist representation" and ask what is special about the verbatim memorization and reproduction of speech events. According to them, data from reaction-time experiments suggest that two different kinds of information about a sentence presented are "stored:" "verbatim information about a sentence's exact wording and gist information about a sentence's meaning. These two kinds of information appear to have different retention characteristics with the verbatim information being less durable" (Anderson and Paulson 1977: 439).

For these authors, "verbatim memory" means keeping in mind the exact word-by-word sequence of a sentence. They assume that instantly after the presentation of a sentence, "verbatim memory" is stronger and more likely. The more time passes between presentation and reproduction, the more the difference between "verbatim memory" and "gist memory" attenuates, until finally "gist memory" proves more durable and stable, whereas "verbatim memory" decreases:

"It appears that gist is better retained than verbatim information. Evidence for this assertion is the fact that subjects show virtually no loss in their ability to make accurate gist judgments but do lose ability to make judgments about word order" (Anderson and Paulson 1977: 441).

As already indicated, my experiences are contrary. Especially when longer periods (weeks or even months) have passed before I again recite the poem, the literally memorized passages (of stanza 3 and the beginning of the last stanza) come without any problems or errors, while those passages I believe to remember in terms of their content sometimes come incorrectly. This chiefly pertains to function words (prepositions, conjunctions, pronouns, ...) as well as to the words' exact sequence. Of course, I could have decided to deal with the two problematic passages (parts of stanza 3, first verse of the last stanza) more intensely and more often than with the others, because they are more difficult to memorize. Verbatim retention would then be a mere function of my engagement. Furthermore, differences of task and of the "test designs" between my rote memorization and the experiments of Anderson and Paulson could be responsible for our conflicting interpretations. The two scholars confronted their test subjects with sentences, which they were told to retain. After various intervals they then confronted them with so-called test sentences, which they had to judge according to their relation to the retained sentences (equal sentence or not). The shorter the interval between the two presentations, the more successful the subjects performed concerning verbatim similarity instead of mere similarity of meaning. The longer the time passed, the relation reversed. By contrast, my task consisted in memorization and reproduction of relatively complex speech events (Hölderlin's poem). It was thus not directed at recognition but verbatim reproduction.[4]

The relevant theoretical discussion brought forth different kinds of explanations. In particular it distinguished between a so-called propositional and a so-called perceptual mode of representation (e.g., Anderson 1974, Anderson and Paulson 1977, Keenan 1975, Kintsch

1975), which I do not want to detail here. In line with Ulric Neisser and the theory of Oswald Wiener, I rather assume that remembering and reproduction are not based on any static "engrams" or "memory traces" at all, but on the dynamic, generic, and schematic reconstruction of habitually repeated experiences. Human memory cannot function like storage in a computer: "What is remembered [...] is an underlying structure that has become manifest on several different specific occasions. [...] [T]hose occasions themselves may not be recalled at all. Generic memories can persist even when the individual episodes that gave rise to them have been entirely forgotten" (Neisser 1988: 360). This is the reason why rote memorization of speech events cannot easily be explained by the practice and theory of the method of loci, which have been well known since ancient times. This method consists in mentally associating unconnected words with salient landmarks along an imagined topographic path, e.g., in a well-known building or landscape (ibid.: 369). These loci then facilitate recall and reproduction of the associated items. Yet, I for my part experience the dynamic of (silent) recitation as if I wandered on a path through a *generic* landscape containing turns, behind which I expect something I cannot yet see, but know that it must appear. This experience I metaphorically describe as "wandering" cannot be precisely compared to a movement through space and time along predefined landmarks. Nonetheless, I feel that I do erect new "landmarks" with each and every word I recite loudly or silently. But I really cannot connect them as smoothly as it seems to be the case with normal everyday speech acts (cf. Eder 2015). Through my landscape of superposed meanings I rather move by following the attunements the poem "Timidity" unfolds in me. Still the question remains why I am able to rote memorize and reproduce difficult passages.

Certainly, the rhythmic-metric structure of Asclepiad odes not only plays a great role for remembering and reciting, but also for resolving the meanings invested in it. This becomes apparent through the metrically required break/dihaeresis (Groddeck 2020: 161f.) after "gleich" in the verse "Denn, seit Himmlischen gleich | Menschen, ein einsam Wild." The break does not have to be marked by a comma but is nevertheless crucial for syntactic attribution, which I cannot describe in greater detail here. Additionally, there are studies confirming that memorization and reproduction over long periods are markedly facilitated by rhythmic-metric structure: "Where a rhythmic structure is available, subjects can make use of this structure to begin remembering the chain again after a unit is forgotten" (Rubin 1982 [1977]: 309). However, Rubin declines to deal with the "meaning" of the linguistic entities involved, probably because he fears possible complications of his theory.

In the following, I want to briefly return to my efforts to achieve a meaningful understanding of the syntactically difficult passage of the third stanza from a theoretical perspective. It is often assumed that in order to understand language, the exact wording is less important than understanding the meaning: "When language is comprehended, it seems that the meaning of what was heard or read is remembered to some extent, but unless special attention is given to the style or other characteristics of the words, the exact wording is forgotten. This phenomenon can be viewed in the framework of a model of comprehension derived from linguistic theory [e.g., Chomsky 1965]" (Sachs 1967: 437).

3 Aspects from the psychology of thought

Here, I cannot deal with all the very different aspects of my efforts at understanding said part of stanza 3, which also encompass philological aspects of Hölderlin's work. Instead, I want to interpret the already mentioned phenomenon of retaining several syntactic possibilities while simultaneously reciting and trying to understand stanza 3 by the theory of Oswald Wiener, leading to further open research questions.

The dispute between proponents of the hypothesis that syntactically ambiguous sentences are serially processed (e.g., Meng and

Bader 2000), and proponents of the idea that they are processed in parallel, also extends to the psychological, psycholinguistic, and neuropsychological literature: "Does the parser compute syntactic representations serially or in parallel? The results of the present study provide a rather clear answer in favor of parallel computation" (Hickock 1993: 249). At stake here is the architecture of parsers, i.e., the processes involved in handling syntactically ambiguous sentences: "The serial architecture proposes that the parser builds just one syntactic analysis without keeping track of any possible alternative interpretations when syntactic ambiguities arise (serial parser). The alternative parallel architecture assumes that the parser computes all possible alternative interpretations on-line, and eventually, ranks alternatives into more or less preferred syntactic analyses (parallel parser)" (Hopf et al. 2003: 173f.).[5]

Wiener seems to subscribe to the seriality of understanding when it comes to processing speech events: "introspection shows that discrete signs function in communication because the referring proxy objects are discrete, as their behavior is experienced as a sequence of stations" (Wiener 2017: 4). In contrast to automata theory, however, the mind does not necessarily pass from one sign to its immediately neighboring one. There is also the possibility of "short-circuiting sequences, namely, to pass from a given state or symbol immediately to a non-neighboring one" (Wiener 2017: 5). This increases possible complexity: "In general, [...] the formally linear string, i.e., the program, describes procedures that can recursively 'call' other procedures as their subroutines, that is, a non-linear system of procedures organized over several levels [...]. Attentive problem solvers experience this as an occasional tying down or, on the contrary, tying in of deeper levels, as short-circuiting of procedures by using placeholders (variables: 'seeds'), and in an important class of cases as working with procedures, which are not available at all" (Wiener 2017: 5f.).

Anthony J. Marcel (1980, 1983) was able to show that, at least in everyday language, polysemous words with semantic ambiguity are disambiguated serially by gradually being built into a wider context (the subject's orientation). This process proceeds from preconscious identification to the conscious perception of meaning. While assuming this process for everyday language seems adequate, one of the peculiarities of understanding literary texts appears to be that ambiguities have to be kept unresolved. The feeling of simultaneous ambiguity enabled by the enduring "activation" of word meanings is not only crucial but sometimes also intended by the authors of literary texts themselves. Marcel (ibid.) conjectures that the multiple activations a potentially polysemous word may evoke in the preconscious phase of understanding are then inhibited by the orientation of the comprehender, as soon as the word and its meaning are consciously perceived. Yet, my introspections while understanding poetry suggest that I deliberately set myself the task to suspend this inhibition even in said phase of conscious perception, and in retrospect regularly succeed in doing so (cf. Eder 2015). In the case of Hölderlin's poem, I attempt this suspension not only for potentially polysemous words (homonyms and synonyms) but also at the level of linguistic structure, when the individual clauses could be connected in different ways, as exemplified in said section of stanza 3.

Let me try to look at some aspects of my Hölderlin introspection through the lens of Wiener's theory. The basis of this theory is the definition of structure: "A structure of a string is a Turing machine generating or accepting the string" (Wiener 2015b: 100). Although this definition is clear-cut in terms of automata theory, it is less clear how it applies to the psychology of thought. So it requires some effort to project results of introspection belonging to the latter onto the epistemological foundation of automata theory. For we (as human organisms) seem to confer structure to a string by assimilating it to our entire orientation, which stands in sharp contrast to the functionality of necessarily clearly delimited automata. Specifically, I am concerned here with the question of how strings, which the individual verses in Hölderlin's poem are, and my introspective experiences while trying to understand them can be described more closely in this light. Thereby perhaps further questions can be raised.

In his 1998 essay "'Cliché' as a condition of intellectual and esthetic creativity" Wiener – still a philosopher of automata theory then – drew on Piaget's notion of schema by tentatively defining it as a special-purpose automaton: "Each state [of a schema] filters the entire range of effective environmental influences into a finite number of many well-defined types of influences ('symbols'): the schema 'recognizes' the presence of a specific symbol by shifting into a specific sequel state determined by the schema's design. So the 'schema itself decides' whether a symbol is present and of what kind, if any, it is. We can interpret a symbol as a (local, current) state of the environment acting on a current state of the schema" (Wiener 1998: 115).

In the following, I refer to the sentences/verses of Hölderlin's poem as strings; if a sentence/verse lends itself to two (or more) interpretations, I refer to these interpretations as two (or more) different schemas/structures. Regarding my experiences while trying to understand the syntactically ambiguous stanza 3, this would tentatively imply that one and the same string ("Denn seit Himmlischen...") has two (or more) different structures, that is, two (or more) different schemas assimilate one and the same string at the same time. Apparently two (or more) Turing machines are somehow "connected" "if they are able to both generate (or accept) the same string" (Wiener 2015a: 1). This is what Wiener in the said essay called an "association:"

"If we use the term 'analogy' with respect to two different sign sequences being accepted by one and the same schema, we mean the insight that two strings have one structure in common. If we use the term 'association' with respect to two different schemas assimilating the same sign sequence, we mean the insight that one string has two different structures. In particular, these insights become 'conscious' in construction environments, that is, in environments having already selected and durably prepared specific schemas as conditional factors for a 'multiple determination.' These factors obviously serve the selection in goal-directed thought" (Wiener 1998: 124).

Yet in retrospect, Wiener (2015a), by now immersed in the psychology of thought, specified: "In my *epistemology* either a string is such a bridge between two structures [this could be the case in my multiple understanding of the Hölderlin stanza = "association"], or a structure is the bridge between two strings [= "analogy"]. From the perspective of the *psychology of thought* I must add: There are no strings in the mental realm, not even as an exception. Strictly speaking, which seems necessary, it follows that in humans there cannot be such a thing as pure rote learning of meaningless items. Just remember our pilot study for memorizing a meaningless letter sequence [cf. Ebbinghaus's meaningless syllables]: the trivial structure immediately sprouts in all possible directions" (Wiener 2015a: 2).

Thus, also for the realm of a natural language and language comprehension, we have to conclude: humans are unable to execute purely formal, completely meaningless operations, because unlike computers they cannot operate on "meaningless symbols." On the one hand, *intuitions* are thus unavoidable even when dealing with (seemingly totally meaningless) formalisms (cf. Eder 2015). And yet, on the other hand, this is precisely what has to be explained about memorizing, retaining, and then reciting sentences, and perhaps about human language comprehension as a whole: that sentences, which in Wiener's epistemology are strictly polarized as symbol strings, can be learned by heart and understood by acquiring the psychological quality of being understood as structures. So even the formal operations of memorizing may turn out to be structures, which in turn are possibly associated and used as analogies. This implies a conclusion regarding the seeming difference between solving geometric tasks (e.g., mentally tying a knot) and the task of reciting a poem: Like the knot, the meaning of the poem has to be assembled, only that its "syntactic aspects" represent a philological task in themselves (because they belong to the poem's "content"). Nevertheless, it is less intuitive that the quality of a text depends on the coherence of its content (= running environment), because common sense believes to know what the "formal structure" of language is, namely its syntax. Contrariwise, the syntax of a knot would be its formal description as a model not entailed by common sense. In language comprehension, however, syntax facilitates the continuous update of orientation and assembly because language "mirrors" the progression of thought. Language in the narrow sense is itself a formalism existing largely independently of "meaning." Language *use*, however, parallels what the mathematician Jean Dieudonné called the relation of "l'abstraction et l'intuition mathématique" (Dieudonné 1975, cf. Eder 2015).

But how to reconcile the fact that, in introspection, I seem to experience a permanent and unresolvable ambiguity of said verses of Hölderlin's stanza 3, with automata theory implying that state transitions are from one discrete to next discrete state? How to project onto automata theory my experience of suspended (perhaps inhibited) decisions to "give priority" to one or the other schema for the string in question?

In this regard, Wiener, the psychologist of thought, wrote in 2015: "The greatest difficulty of such a projection [...] is the clear-cut symbol concept of automata theory itself. Therefore, we must from the outset define strings as structures and aim at generalization by recurring to the concept of bridges. In my epistemology, either a string is such a bridge between two structures, or a structure is the bridge between two strings" (Wiener 2015a: 2).

Are the verses of stanza 3

Denn, seit Himmlischen gleich Menschen, ein einsam Wild
Und die Himmlischen selbst führet, der Einkehr zu,
Der Gesang und der Fürsten
Chor, nach Arten,

in each and every of my recitation trials really identical strings? Or are they different strings depending on the prosodic and rhythmic-metric segmentation I apply to them, even if the letter sequence trivially remains the same? Is it really the same string fostering and enabling different seeds according to different running environments (as the respective attitude while trying to understand)? And how do structure and strings interrelate in this case? Are they aspects of one another depending on how I view them? Or are they rather two or more schemas/structures/Turing machines „creating" two or more strings by actualizing them?

At this point we have to consider two additional premises, namely

(1) polarization in Wiener's sense: "automata theory in the service of epistemology is based on a categorical distinction between string and Turing machine – [...] introspection, however, does not find any easily interpretable embodiments of Turing machines and/or symbols in conscious processes [...] – how can we construe the other side, let's call it 'psychology of thought,' so that the unequivocal and, in the abstract, undoubtedly correct constructs of an epistemology based on my definition of structure can be located in the facts of introspection?" (Wiener 2015a: 1).

(2) the relation of word and schema in this epistemology: "A word is a 'name' of a schema, i.e., by analogy to computer science a string directly actualizing a schema 'named by it [...].' In contrast to the case of a schema actualized by an 'image,' here assimilation by the schema has not taken place yet. On the contrary, the schema is now waiting to be 'nourished'" (Wiener 1998: 127).

From the perspective of the psychology of thought, however, "we find operands [in introspection] but no strings" (Wiener 2015b: 139). If Werner is skeptical to the notion of strings, but is nevertheless urged to accept strings, then these are only external: "The meaning of a symbol is a model (a cognitive representation, Wiener 2007: 167ff.), which the symbol makes ready to be run ('invoking' it); is the invoking symbol external, then I call it a name of the invoked structure [...] (Wiener 2007: 169). [...] Since meaning is a structure it can only be experienced while operating, that is, as a stepwise temporal sequence. Meaning is never present 'as a whole.' This implies that a name only indirectly invokes a model, namely by way of changing switches in order to unfold ever more specific components of the structure according to their availability and the task at hand. As introspection shows (and parsimony predicts), these developments unfold by way of seeds. Thus, a name at best invokes the seed of a structure. In a narrow sense it *is* the name of the seed in question and its meaning *is* the meaning of the seed" (Wiener 2008: 133f.).

In this longer quote the phrase "these developments unfold by way of seeds" seems crucial to me. Externally identical symbols and strings such as words, sentences, and their syntax may actuate different seeds and their proxy object relations according to the current attunement. So their interpretation depends on the specific orientation in which the organism trying to understand the strings finds itself.

How to relate my tentative introspection of "inhibited decision to 'give priority' to one or the other schema" to the following quote:

"The schema sustains a specific state transition directly depending on its current state and the incoming symbol but not on the effects of its output on other schemas, i.e., the input source as well as the output's further fate are irrelevant for the state transition" (Wiener 1998: 115f.).

Assuming that my introspections and the conclusions drawn from them are valid, this would precisely *not* be the case, because, as I asked above: Do the schemas "create" strings and related structures in the moment of the inhibited, uncompleted state transition? Translated into Wiener's theory this question could be rewritten as: Does the organism assemble meaning by a cascade of seeds in a temporally dynamic process?

Perhaps my experiences are connected to and to be explained by the following:

"My interpretation of relevant introspections suggests that in running environments and construction environments, many schemas are actualized at the same time but there have to be special circumstances in order to achieve the unspecific 'broadcast' of a string (I speculate that this phenomenon of 'general broadcast' together with processes of book-keeping in the respective running environment constitutes what is colloquially meant by 'consciousness;' cf. [...] 'multiple determination')" (Wiener 1998: 121f.).

So, are my attempts at understanding syntactically ambiguous verses instances of such a multiple determination? At the level of acoustically ambiguous (e.g., homophonic) words functioning as names of different schemas, the process seems to me quite well explained in Wiener's aforementioned essay on "cliché:"

"If these words are ambiguous in their acoustic forms, i.e., if they are completely or in part also names of other schemas, they are thus able to call these schemas, and these are able to react by the production of quasi-images, which the original schema cannot assimilate at first. Finally, I am impelled to assume that a large part of these processes is unconscious – at least, but certainly not exclusively, concerning interpolated words (here 'unconscious' does not have to mean more than 'unobserved')" (Wiener 1998: 127f.).

Although this thesis seems plausible in the case of homophonic words, how to transfer it to the level of syntactic construction? How can it help to explain the inhibition to prioritize one specific schema salient in my introspection? Is there perhaps a connection to Sigmund Freud's "work of condensation"?

"To me the truly creative moment seems to be captured in the concept of 'work of condensation' (following Freud). Based on the currently actualized schemas, this work finds strings assimilating all of them, independent of the presets ('task')" (Wiener 1998: 125).

This would obviously correspond to a mechanism enabling several strings to interact with each other.

"Introspection leads me to the assumption that the work of condensation never ceases. It not only elicits quasi-images but implicitly also provides material to be then selected by construction environments. It does so by activating schemas, which in some sense and to some extent have to do with the current requirements. In the fortunate case, one of these schemas can be accommodated to fulfill the 'task.' If such a well-organized construction environment is missing (which would pursue the emerging regularities in the predetermined direction), it 'merely' yields an aesthetic experience. At any rate schemas actualized by undirected work of condensation already are 'contents' of environmental events (strings)" (Wiener 1998: 128f.).

Does understanding a poem, or rather aesthetic understanding in general, result from the mere fact that "schemas actualized by undirected work of condensation already are 'contents' of environmental events (strings)"?

This would imply that the rank and effectivity of verses such as Hölderlin's may be best explained thus:

"Now the mere variation of strings can be viewed as a questioning of the schema. But I *personally* measure the rank of an artwork according to the cost of accommodation I have to pay to be able to coherently assimilate it. This criterion dispenses with the 'direct effect' of the artwork and, hence, will never become popular. By applying it the observer becomes the artist, so that I indeed believe that the 'art of understanding,' which was hitherto deemed a kind of meta-art, should replace all [artistic] canons and methods" (Wiener 1998: 135).

Yet, I hate to confess that in my view, this art of understanding unfolds more likely by means of a poem such as Hölderlin's compared to less intricate poems, even if I naturally could have chosen less intricate ones for my task.

4 Coda

"So what?", asked Wiener, the psychologist of thought, in 2015. Although walking on uncertain ground, let me speculate in the direction of an answer that would need further clarification to which I can only hint at here as a coda:

"– In all cases pertinent to the psychology of thought the bridge [cf. above] will be a structure. If it is a substructure of two (or more) more comprehensive structures, that is, an at least isolable part of each of them (or a prototype of such a structure), then epistemology offers the clue of 'Turing machine–string–Turing machine' as 'association' of two structures via one string. If we conceive of this string as a trivial structure, we can interpret it as a 'suborder' in the sense of traditional logic. But if two structures associate by being produced by a common prototype, then we have to metaphorically interpret the latter as their 'superorder.' So each structure can function as a bridge: a string, viewed as a trivial component of both structures; a more or less prominent, more or less elaborated substructure [...] – the bridge piece in one structure is in some sense functionally equivalent to the respective bridge piece in the other structure, or it is a superordered prototype of both structures 'identified' as being analogue to each other" (Wiener 2015a: 2f.).

If I parrot the third stanza of Hölderlin's ode, I trivially generate a linguistic string serving as a basis for my attempts at understanding. Regarding the discourse on remembering, I reproduce speech events, which I have (largely) learned formally, by triggering and reciting them almost as if I read them in print. This may function on the basis of a sensory memory enabling "internal sound sequences [...] [to] be 'automatically' reproduced over a long time without disturbing conscious thinking about other things." [cf. above] However, it seems inevitable that while reciting, I organize the verses syntactically and begin to disambiguate them. So while I am beginning to understand these speech events as formal linguistic signs, I am in parallel able to smoothly switch to understanding their content.

The consequences of my tendency to keep syntactic attributions open and inhibit disambiguation have yet to be clarified. Crucial remains the question whether thought processes triggered by natural language (poetic language) function serially or in parallel. I suspect the key for answering this question could be referred to as a "super-ordered prototype" conceived of as a structure (cf. Wiener, personal correspondence).

However, it remains open whether I should search for an explanation for my conclusion, that the assumed parallel processing of syntactically ambiguous language material is inhibiting the respective serial decisions, in the direction of this "superordered prototype." For introspectively, I just don't seem to form an analogy between structures, which as such would begin to be formed by a "superordered prototype." Instead, I rather suspend them, perhaps within a cloud of seeds, as which this prototype appears in introspection.[6] If I wanted to conclusively capture and understand what is present in parallel within this cloud of multiply determined seeds I would have to expand it. So, after all, I would have to again revert to serial processing. Translated into the terminology of Wiener, this means that presumably I would have to expand each seed anew. Yet, this would not result in the scaffolded assembly of a reusable model.

References

Afflerbach, Peter, and Michael Pressley, 1995. *Verbal Protocols of Reading: The Nature of Constructively Responsive Reading*. Hillsdale, NJ.

Afflerbach, Peter, 2000. Verbal Reports and Protocol Analysis. In: Kamil, Michael, et al. (eds.), *Handbook of Reading Research*. Hillsdale, NJ, 163–180.

Anderson, John R., 1974. Verbatim and Propositional Representation of Sentences in Immediate and Long-Term Memory. *Journal of Verbal Learning and Verbal Behavior*, 13, 149–162.

Anderson, John R., and Rebecca Paulson, 1977. Representation and Retention of Verbatim Information. *Journal of Verbal Learning and Verbal Behavior*, 16, 439–451.

Asch, Solomon E., John Hay, and Rhea Mendoza Diamond, 1960. Perceptual Organization in Serial Rote Learning. *The American Journal of Psychology*, 73/2, 177–198.

Barclay, J. Richard 1973. The Role of Comprehension in Remembering Sentences. *Cognitive Psychology*, 4, 229–254.

Bartlett, Frederic C., 1932. *Remembering: A Study in Experimental and Social Psychology*, Cambridge.

Bever, Thomas G., 1970. The Cognitive Basis for Linguistic Structures. In: Hayes, John R. (ed.), *Cognition and the Development of Language*. New York, 279–362.

Bühler, Karl, 1909. Über das Sprachverständnis vom Standpunkt der Normalpsychologie aus. In: Schumann, F. (ed.), *Bericht über den III. Kongreß für experimentelle Psychologie in Frankfurt a. Main vom 22. bis 25. April 1908*. Leipzig, 94–130.

Chomsky, Noam, 1965. *Aspects of the Theory of Syntax*. Cambridge, MA.

Christ, Tobias, 2020. *„Nachtgesänge": Hölderlins späte Lyrik und die zeitgenössische Lesekultur*. Paderborn.

Dickson, Lou Ann S., Philipp S. Schrankel, and Raymond W. Kuhlhavy, 1988. Verbal and Spatial Encoding of Text. *Instructional Science*, 17, 145–157.

Dieudonné, Jean, 1975. L'abstraction et l'intuition mathématique. *Dialectica*, 29/1, 39–54.

Ebbinghaus, Hermann, 1885. *Über das Gedächtnis: Untersuchungen zur experimentellen Psychologie*. Leipzig.

Eder, Thomas, 2015. Selbstbeobachtung und Sprachverstehen. Beim Hersagen eines Gedichts von Paul Celan. In: Eder, Thomas, and Thomas Raab (eds.), *Selbstbeobachtung: Oswald Wieners Denkpsychologie*. Berlin, 315–371.

Eder, Thomas, and Thomas Raab (eds.), 2015. *Selbstbeobachtung: Oswald Wieners Denkpsychologie*. Berlin.

Ericsson, Karl A., and Herbert A. Simon, 1980. Verbal Reports as Data. *Psychological Review*, 87, 215–251.

Ericsson, Karl A., and Herbert A. Simon, 1993. *Protocol Analysis: Verbal Reports as Data (rev. ed.)*. Cambridge, MA.

Fuhrhop, Nanna, and Niklas Schreiber, 2019. Hölderlin syntaktisch. *Hölderlin-Jahrbuch*. 41, Vol. 2018–2019. Paderborn, 84–121.

Graesser, Arthur II, and George Mandler, 1975. Recognition Memory for the Meaning and Surface. *Journal of Experimental Psychology: Human Learning and Memory*, 104/3, 238–248.

Groddeck, Wolfram, 2020. Hölderlins Ode „Blödigkeit". In: Reuß, Roland, and Marit Müller (eds.), *Friedrich Hölderlin: Neun Nachtgesänge, Interpretationen*. Göttingen, 157–176.

Hellingrath, Norbert von, 1911. *Pindarübertragungen von Hölderlin: Prolegomena zu einer Erstausgabe*. Jena.

Hickock, Gregory, 1993. Parallel Parsing: Evidence from Reactivation in Garden-Path Sentences. *Journal of Psycholinguistic Research*, 22/2, 239–250.

Hopf, Jens-Max, Markus Bader, Michael Meng, and Josef Bayer, 2003. Is Human Sentence Parsing Serial or Parallel? Evidence from Event-Related Brain Potentials. *Cognitive Brain Research*, 15, 165–177.

Hölderlin, Friedrich, 1984. *Sämtliche Werke. Frankfurter Ausgabe. Historisch-kritische Ausgabe, Vol. 5: Oden II*. Ed. Sattler, Dietrich E., and Michael Knaupp, Frankfurt am Main.

Hurlburt, Russell T., and Eric Schwitzgebel, 2007. *Describing Inner Experience?: Proponent Meets Skeptic*. Cambridge, MA.

Johnson-Laird, Philip N., and Rosemary Stevenson, 1970. Memory for Syntax. *Nature*, 227, 412.

Keenan, Janice M., 1975. *The Role of Episodic Information in the Assessment of Semantic Memory Representations for Sentences*. Unpubl. diss., University of Colarado.

Kintsch, Walter, 1975. Memory Representations of Text. In: Solso, Robert L. (ed.), *Information Processing and Cognition*. Hillsdale, NJ, 269–294.

Kintsch, Walter, 1991. The Role of Knowledge in Discourse Comprehension. In: Denhiere, Guy, and Jean-Pierre Rossi (eds.), *Text and Text Processing*. North Holland, 107–153.

Lashley, Karl S., 1923. The Behavioristic Interpretation of Consciousness II. *Psychological Review*, 30, 329–353.

Leibniz, Gottfried Wilhelm, 1882. Nouveaux essais sur l'entendement par l'auteur du systeme de l'harmonie preestablie. In: Gerhardt, Carl Immanuel (ed.), *Die philosophischen Schriften von Gottfried Wilhelm Leibniz: Band 5: Leibniz und Locke*. Berlin, 39–509.

Leibniz, Gottfried Wilhelm, 1896. *New Essays Concerning Human Understanding*. Translated by Alfred G. Langley. New York.

Lyons, William, 1986. *The Disappearance of Introspection*, Cambridge, MA.

MacDonald, Maryellen C., Marcel Adam Just, and Patricia A. Carpenter, 1992. Working Memory Constraints on the Processing of Syntactic Ambiguity. *Cognitive Psychology*, 24, 56–98.

Marcel, Anthony J., 1980. Conscious and Preconscious Recognition of Polysemous Words: Locating the Selective Effects of Prior Verbal Context. In: Nickerson, Raymond S. (ed.), *Attention and Performance VIII*. Hillsdale, NJ, 435–457.

Marcel, Anthony J., 1983. Conscious and Unconscious Perception: Experiments on Visual Masking and Word Recognition. *Cognitive Psychology*, 15, 197–237.

Massen, Cristina, and Jürgen Bredekamp, 2005. Die Wundt-Bühler-Kontroverse aus der Sicht der heutigen kognitiven Psychologie. *Zeitschrift für Psychologie*, 213/2, 109–114.

Meng, Michael, and Markus Bader, 2000. Ungrammaticality Detection and Garden Path Strength: Evidence for Serial Parsing. *Language and Cognitive Processes*, 15/6, 615–666.

Mergenthaler, May, 2010. The "Paradox" of Poetic Courage: Hölderlin's Ode "Timidity" and Benjamin's Commentary Reconsidered. *The Germanic Review: Literature, Culture, Theory*, 85/3, 224–249.

Meyer-Kalkus, Reinhart, 2018. Voraussetzungen einer Erneuerung der rhythmischen Rezitation von Hölderlins Versen – am Beispiel von *Brot und Wein*. *Hölderlin-Jahrbuch*. 41, Vol. 2018–2019. Paderborn, 147–165.

Moore, Alan Tonnies, and Eric Schwitzgebel, 2018. The Experience of Reading. *Consciousness and Cognition*, 62, 57–68.

Neisser, Ulric, 1978a. Memory: What Are the Important Questions? In: Gruneberg, Michael M., Peter E. Morris, and Robert N. Sykes (eds.), *Practical Aspects of Memory*. London, 1–24.

Neisser, Ulric, 1978b. Perceiving, Anticipating, and Imagining. *Minnesota Studies in the Philosophy of Science*, 9, 89–105.

Neisser, Ulric, 1988. What Is Ordinary Memory the Memory of? In: id., and Eugene Winograd (eds.), *Remembering Reconsidered*. Cambridge, 356–373.

Neisser, Ulric, 1996. Remembering as Doing. *Behavioral and Brain Sciences*, 19/2, 204–205.

Nisbett, Richard E., and Timothy DeCamp Wilson, 1977. Telling More than We Can Know: Verbal Reports on Mental Processes. *Psychological Review*, 84/3, 231–259.

Rubin, David C., 1982 [1977]. Very Long-Term Memory for Prose and Verse. In: Neisser, Ulric (ed.), *Memory Observed: Remembering in Natural Contexts*. San Francisco, 299–310.

Russo, J. Edward, Eric J. Johnson, and Debra L. Stephens, 1989. The Validity of Verbal Protocols. *Memory & Cognition*, 17, 759–769.

Sachs, Jacqueline Strunk, 1967. Recognition Memory for Syntactic and Semantic Aspects of Connected Discourse. *Perception and Psychophysics*, 2, 437–442.

Sanz, Montserrat, Itziar Laka, and Michael K. Tanenhaus (eds.), 2013. *Language Down the Garden Path: The Cognitive and Biological Basis for Linguistic Structures*, Oxford.

Schmidt, Jochen, 2019. Kommentar. In: id. (ed.), *Friedrich Hölderlin: Sämtliche Werke und Briefe in 3 Bänden, Band 1: Sämtliche Gedichte*. Frankfurt am Main, 483–1145.

Watson, John Broadus, 1920. Is Thinking Merely the Action of Language Mechanisms?. *British Journal of Psychology*, 11, 87–104.

Wiener, Oswald, 1996. "Information" und Selbstbeobachtung. In: id., *Schriften zur Erkenntnistheorie*. Vienna, 278–339.

Wiener, Oswald, 1998. „Klischee" als Bedingung intellektueller und ästhetischer Qualität. In: id., *Literarische Aufsätze*, Vienna, 113–140.

Wiener, Oswald, 2007. Über das „Sehen" im Traum: Zweiter Teil. *manuskripte*, 178, 161–172.

Wiener, Oswald, 2008. Über das „Sehen" im Traum: Dritter Teil. *manuskripte*, 181, 132–141.

Wiener, Oswald, 2015a. Diskussionsbeitrag zu „Analogie". Personal correspondence, manuscript in the estate of Oswald Wiener – Kapfenstein, version 5 July.

Wiener, Oswald, 2015b. Glossar: figurativ. In: Eder, Thomas, and Thomas Raab (eds.), *Selbstbeobachtung: Oswald Wieners Denkpsychologie*. Berlin, 99–141.

Wiener, Oswald, 2017. Über das „Sehen" im Traum: Zweiter Teil, *manuskripte*, 178 161–172 (2007), amended manuscript in the estate of Oswald Wiener – Kapfenstein, version 14 February.

1   In the cited essay, Wiener still used a different terminology than both in the later ones and in this volume; cf. Wiener (1996: 300) where he renamed "mental images" to "*quasi*-images" because of their demonstrably non-pictorial character. Apart from quasi-visual images, he also referred to quasi-acoustic images as well as to quasi-movements defined as the perception of innervations of a body part as an imprecise motor impulse.

2   Michael Hamburger's English translation does not adequately reflect the syntactic ambiguity of Hölderlin's original. In an essay, May Mergenthaler (with the help of Amber Suggitt) adapted a translation by Stanley Corngold, which he had produced in the context of translating an essay by Walter Benjamin on Hölderlin's "Blödigkeit," among others. I believe that her version makes clearer the syntactic ambiguity of the German original, which is central to my considerations (Mergenthaler 2010: 230).

3   In English, the more detailed quote reads: "The source of the little application to true goods arises mainly from the fact that in matters and on the occasions where the senses act but little, the greater part of our thoughts are, so to speak, surd (I call them cogitationes caecae in Latin) *i.e.* void of perception and feeling, and consisting in the wholly empty employment of characters, as happens in the case of those who make algebraic calculations without considering from time to time that the geometrical figures in question and the words ordinarily produce the same effect in this regard as the characters of arithmetic or algebra. One often reasons in words without having quite the same object in mind" (Leibniz 1896: 191).

Cf. Leibniz (1882: 172): "Ainsi si nous préferons le pire, c'est que nous sentons le bien qu'il renferme, sans sentir ny le mal qu'il y a, ny le bien qui est dans le parti contraire. Nous supposons et croyons, ou plustost nous recitons seulement sur la foy d'autruy ou tout au plus sur celle de la memoire de nos raisonnemens passés, que le plus grand bien est dans le meilleur parti ou le plus grand mal dans l'autre. Mais quand nous ne les envisageons point, nos pensées et raisonnemens contraires au sentiment sont une espece de *psittacisme*, qui ne fournit rien pour le present à l'esprit [...]" [emphasis TE]. English: "Thus if we prefer the bad it is because we perceive the good which it includes without perceiving either the bad therein or the good in the contrary consideration. We assume and believe, or rather we make the statement merely upon another's belief, or at most upon belief in the memory of our past reasonings, that the greatest good is on the better side, or the greatest evil on the other. But when we do not look at these at all, our thoughts and reasonings contrary to the feeling are a kind of *psittacism [parrot chatter]* which furnishes nothing at present to the mind" (Leibniz 1896: ibid.).

4   In this respect, my introspections partly coincide with, and partly differ from, an observation by Johnson-Laird and Stevenson (1970). They recorded that subjects remembered the specific syntax of a sentence better when previously informed that they would be subjected to a memory test afterwards. It could well be that these subjects memorized sentences by using strategies other than when trying to remember their meaning: "It is plausible that the 'memory' instructions led subjects to retain an acoustic trace of the sentence for longer than usual, perhaps by some form of rehearsal" (ibid.: 412). So far, the Johnson-Laird's and Stevenson's results coincide with my introspections of memorization and recitation. Yet, they continue: "The most striking result, however, was that after a short time (about 50 s) group 1 [those previously informed about being tested afterwards] forgot the deep-structure relations of the test sentence. This result [...] suggests two alternative conclusions: (1) once the meaning of a sentence has been grasped its syntax is usually forgotten completely; or (2) Chomsky's notion of deep structure is a misleading guide to linguistic performance and should be replaced by something much closer to the meaning of the sentence. It would then become impossible to remember meaning without remembering underlying structure" (ibid.: 412). Conclusion (1) is consistent with my experience of memorizing passages that I understand well in terms of their meaning. Nevertheless, my observation that syntactically complex passages that are also difficult to understand or even incomprehensible in terms of their meaning remain memorized and reproducible verba-

tim over long periods seems inconsistent both with Johnson-Laird's and Stevenson's observations and their two conclusions.

5   Using EEG to examine ERPs while processing garden-path sentences versus ungrammatical sentences, Hopf et al. found empirical evidence for serial parsing: "To distinguish empirically between parallel and serial parsing models, we compare ERP responses to garden-path sentences with ERP responses to truly ungrammatical sentences. Garden-path sentences contain a temporary and ultimately curable ungrammaticality, whereas truly ungrammatical sentences remain so permanently – a difference which gives rise to different predictions in the two classes of parsing architectures. At the disambiguating word, ERPs in both sentence types show negative shifts of similar onset latency, amplitude, and scalp distribution in an initial time window between 300 and 500 ms. In a following time window (500–700 ms), the negative shift to garden-path sentences disappears at right central parietal sites, while it continues in permanently ungrammatical sentences" (Hopf et al. 2003: 165). My remarks, however, refer to my attempts at understanding passages of Hölderlin's ode, for which I cannot clearly decide whether I am processing them like garden-path or ungrammatical sentences.

6   Projected on Kintsch's (1991) "*construction-integration* model", this could imply: I stop interpretation before the integration phase, which would reintegrate the many incoherent and potentially contradictory intermediate results of my interpretation produced "according to sloppy inference rules" into a coherent whole. Cf. Walter Kintsch's "construction-integration model": "It combines a construction process in which a text base is constructed from the linguistic input as well as from the comprehender's knowledge base, with an integration phase, in which this text base is integrated into a coherent whole. The knowledge base is conceptualized as an associative network. [...] [I]nstead of precise inference rules, sloppy ones are used, resulting in an incoherent, potentially contradictory output. However, this output structure is itself in the form of an associative net, which can be shaped into a coherent text base via relaxation procedures in the connectionist manner [...]. Thus, the model represents a symbiosis of production systems and connectionist approaches" (ibid.: 110).

Fantasy, Repression, and Motivation in an Ecological Model of Memory

Thomas Raab

Remembering is a kind of doing. – Ulric Neisser (1996)

Introduction

In the course of many years, I slowly came to notice a particular recurring feature: If somebody asks me to remember and report an authentic memory episode, I first notice the energetic effort to pause the behavioral flow. Each biographic episode has to be reconstructed, even if its core, consisting of two or three connected facts, emerges automatically as a short sequence. That is why I – just like anyone, I suppose – always recount almost identical stories with identical points. In sum, these few stories form my available repertoire of memory episodes.

As you can see from this loose self-observation alone, the problem of recollection combines aspects of the psychology of thought, of motivation, of affect, and of personality. Therefore, it should surely be at the center of any general theory of man because feeling, fantasy, and thought are individual experiences, which connect only by memory.

That remembering and memory are *not* at its center, and even fields akin to psychology such as artificial intelligence, linguistics, and neuroscience first treat "executive" problems, i.e., perception and its connection to action, seems to be due to the aspect of personality and the often individually vastly different motives of remembering. The latter obviously feed back on thought and even perception, and that is why, strictly speaking, a truly "general psychology" has always been utopian and will remain so. Conceptually the individual aspects of mind are hard to grasp and methodically (statistically) *not at all*. Furthermore, they are often embarrassingly personal and, of course, always subject to whitewashing in service of the self (Devereux 1967). So better leave it out. May psychology remain a "strict science," although it has never been one.

Nevertheless, remembering and memory remain the kernel of intelligence and thus of psychology. The fact that they are so much ignored leads, I suppose, to the almost total public disinterest in academic psychology and cognitive science.

I believe that our group, which for more than 20 years has been doing introspection studies in psychology of thought with and around Oswald Wiener (Eder and Raab 2015), also often slipped away from the goal of a *comprehensive* psychology of thought because of this "embarrassing" aspect of the personal, which – alas! – makes for the embedding of all thought into one's life path and everyday life. In this respect, our group also fully belongs to mainstream psychology and cognitive science, whose theories of motivation to this day remain either too statistically oriented and / or conceptually too abstract. On that score, it seems characteristic that none of the cognitive science dictionaries I know contains an entry on "motivation."

In contrast, psychoanalysis, seen historically, has put the problem of personal recollection, of the individual, at its core. Based on its "ego psychology" and ideas of the "secondary process," it only later sketched out preliminary theories of thought in general (Rapaport 1950).

Yet, the rare attempts at connecting the psychoanalytical concepts of motivation with general psychology (in the university) by clothing therapeutically effective notions such as "repression," "defense," "condensation," or "fantasy" in terms of cognitive science (Rapaport 1971, Erdelyi 1985, 2006) seem to have failed. They failed, I believe, because neither side managed to convince the other of the sheer *existence* of their respective problems. I further believe that the reason for this is that *both* – cognitive science and psychoanalysis – misconceived the problem of remembering and memory. So here I will try to – anew and hopefully better – reconcile both by using new conceptual means, which Wiener's ideo-motor theory of thought is so far able to supply.

In the following, the italic passages attempt to describe examples of my memory episodes as authentically and soberly as possible. I tried to resist the urge to confabulate and decorate as well as I could and to write them down without poetic decorum or any added nubs. Due to the required brevity of the presentation, these examples are few, and I must hope that they are sufficient to gain empirical support for my theoretical sketch.

"Real-life thought" and "ideal thought"

Even when the thought process is controlled by a defined task, it is ordered only sporadically and at a perceptible affective cost. Each assembly process (intentional orientation in a problem space) requires heightened concentration, i.e., the allocation of almost all cognitive resources to the task to which one has to forcibly return again and again. Intoxication and fatigue instantly lead to lapses into fantasy and the flight of ideas. The same is true for the remembering of situational episodes. Every solution of a task, also of the task of remembering something, results in a structure, that is, a (motorically or socially) applicable regularity. The processes leading to this result may sometimes take months or even years in which the task remains incubated. Potentially, introspection only uncovers the surface of them but it is able to give at least hints towards their functional core and its incidental interaction with the environment.

As long as perception and action aren't interrupted by a task or a biogenetically older and, thus, vitally more urgent reflex, our attention remains controlled by stimuli. A loud sound, for instance, or an error signal during the execution of a sensorimotor schema ("missing an object") may disrupt the behavioral flow. Most of the time the behavioral control by perception is consistent insofar as it leads to gratification or, at least, to no conflict.

But why then do we, despite this consistency of the perceptual world, experience our thinking as being so erratic? Why does it so often consist of fantasies, which seem to have little or nothing to do with either the objective world or the currently conscious task (Varendonck 1921, Stekel 1951, Klingler 2008, among others)?

In Raab (2015), I attributed this restlessness to a heterarchy or (temporally dynamic hierarchy) of incubated complexes of sensorimotor schemas episodically broadcasting tasks or, as their simplest instances, contradictions into consciousness. Sometimes, these are recognizably triggered by stimuli, but more often they are not. Only the habituation of tasks, which "freeze" to an at least medium-term "problem attitude," or challenges from the environment – from internal needs or from bureaucracy – counteracts the rather chaotic nature of the "stream of consciousness." Focused thinking presupposes habituation of this problem attitude. The latter you can observe from the fact that you always have to attune anew to every task once you have deviated from it.

If they are of a mundane kind, these incubated tasks become actualized by somatic changes and environmental cycles (hunger, thirst, fatigue, sexual urge) or are triggered by superficial sensory stimulus constellations (Fisher 1957). They then function as quasi-needs only ceasing when finally resolved (Lewin 1951).

As already mentioned, remembering past life-episodes can be considered tasks too. Usually, you remember only if you are asked, or if the episode, as a "story," is to serve a group as social cohesion or as entertainment (Halbwachs 1925). Special cases of remembering encompass the writing down of memories, as sometimes fostered by professional pressure, or, possibly related to this, spontaneous recollections when losses or shocks necessitate major rearrangements of orientation (Salaman 1970).

On the one hand, the psychology of thought and problem-solving usually deals with concentrated thinking on formally defined tasks with unambiguous solutions. In real life, however, these concentration phases only last for short, often merely second-long periods. In order to be able to devise controlled experiments, psychology thus idealizes the incubated task heterarchy and problem attitude to a single motive, namely solving the artificially prioritized task. In "real-life thought," on the other hand, mundane, professional and psychobiographical tasks and their contradictions intermit unpredictably, because they depend on unpredictable "coincidences" provided by the outer situation.

As an aside, I will try to specify the term contradiction in the psychological and not logical sense below.

Memory episodes caused by unfinished tasks: the fantasies

The peacocks in front of the baroque palace in the west of X majestically crossed the wet (?) meadows, and immediately: my mother, who suddenly ran after one of the male peacocks quite frantically, jumped on his tail feathers and soon happily and proudly presented one tail feather in her hands, probably in order to decorate our apartment or as a gift to someone.

This is one of the few memory episodes from my elementary school years. A memory episode must meet four criteria. First, it must interrupt the current focus of orientation, whether it is directed to the environment or inward; second, it must connect at least two aspects or, in Wiener's terms, "seeds" to a spatiotemporal sequence; third, this sequence must appear automatically and identically and *not* be generated by controlled thinking (i.e., intentionally assembled "stories" do not count, only sequences expanding automatically and, thus, authentically, however embarrassing they may be); and fourth, it must be temporally locatable in one's biography within about five years and geographically in a specific region.

Just like *all* my episodes, the one of the peacock does not carry an overall affective tone but is characterized by always the same *change* of aspect while expanding. In the above episode, the peaceful peacocks in front of the "romantic" palace contrast with the brutal and – to a child – incomprehensible attack by an adult. Generalizing from my entire catalogue of episodes in retrospect, this change of aspect always results from a contradiction, i.e., from a "frozen" everyday attempt at understanding something that remained incubated.

Here are two more examples from my youth.

> *The feeling of suddenly being responsible, as the two construction workers standing in the two-meter-deep trench dug into the ground consisting of river gravel looked up to me from their shovels, because I, barely nineteen years old, had to command them to secure the trench with wooden poles because, as I knew from only a few hours of studying geology, it was critically unstable – and immediately my (political) rage that they, although so much older than me and probably having toiled on construction sites for years, were actually dependent on a high school graduate patrolling the site early in the morning for his vacation job.*

As a newbie, I just had not expected to be forced to instruct somebody on the first workday. The following episode reveals a similar conflict in social hierarchy:

> *The boring view out at the cars and cyclists that I saw passing by as a guard soldier, here and there a single person going from left to right or vice versa, and immediately I see my cartoonish and yet not completely ironic snappishness with which I – my right hand on the automatic rifle – greeted entering officers in order to scare them, just because I felt so renitent and bored.*

The contradictions always result in the identical points when recounting the episodes. Generally, stories without contradictions do not have any points. If I (here as the author) set myself the task of putting an episode in words, I habitually imagine experiencing the episode *pictorially* like a movie clip, probably because the original situation was perceived and not described. Following Wiener (2015a), this pictorial impression is due to *emulation*, i.e., the psychologically naïve qualification of a *structural* experience as a *perceptual* one.

Oswald Wiener's ideo-motor theory of thought is based on the (idealized) distinction between two internalized motor processes not, or only rudimentarily, reaching the musculature. These processes interact, i.e., receive reciprocal impulses from each other. In introspection, this becomes especially apparent during formal tasks (Wiener 2015b). In short, sensorimotor schemas operate on other sensorimotor schemas during an assembly process, which temporarily coagulates a task to allow for spontaneous short-circuits and, thus, simplifications or regularities. Schemas of type 1 provide operands, i.e., surrogate "object features", which schemas of type 2 can operate on. All these processes are, to speak with Freud, "preconscious" and must be kept available to consciousness by concentrating on the task at hand (Kris 1952). The more frequently you turn to a task, the more smoothly both kinds of processes will run. In this sense, productive thinking is a habituation process under motivational pressure yielding structural shortcuts. The mere training of schema sequences gradually coagulates these sequences to a larger structure. *Essentially,* the thought process does not differ from training sensorimotor coordination in sports or instrumental music.

How can we now interpret the history of the psychology of memory from the perspective of this hypothesis? Since the most easily controllable method to carry out memory experiments is the memorization of nonsense phonetic units like syllables or letters, Ebbinghaus (1885) pioneered a whole tradition investigating "short-term memory," as it was to be named later. "Long-term memory" was then believed to simply operate according to the association laws of "similarity," "contrast," and "proximity" of "thing-presentations" and "word-presentations." Of course, in this tradition limiting itself to the "scientific method" of counting and measuring (e.g., of reaction times), introspection is excluded by definition. After all, the syllables were chosen precisely because they carry minimal meaning and, thus, putatively allow for as few associations as possible. On this methodical basis, negative exponential "forgetting curves" could be determined, but not *what* and *how* forgetting functions. Psychologists measured only what is measurable at the behavioral surface, namely the number of memorized syllables or "items" (Bower 2000).

In contrast, introspection shows very clearly that even "meaningless" (i.e., superficially jumbled) letter sequences can only be remembered when the subject "artificially" structures them in order to embed them in meaning. Accordingly, I myself (Raab 2012) was only able to memorize the given letter sequence *bdlhytcyqdnzblvmksqsklkr* by partly constructing the mnemonic support of "bund deutscher luxus hühner you too care-for your queen die neue zone bleibt links vor mksqs klkr" held together by the fictional attunement to a situation – here the situation of a "politician's speech." This mnemonic support by constructing a story was experimentally underpinned by Erdelyi et al. (1976) under the name of "recoding" words into "inner pictures." Yet, the last group of letters I only remembered by way of a superficial analogy, namely to the letter codes attached to UNIX files which are listed in the terminal window behind the file names. "mksqs klkr" I thus memorized "by heart," that is, (almost) purely phonetically. Interestingly, it is just this *structural*, i.e., content-related or – to speak with Erdelyi – "pictorial" support, that is, in longer terms of months and years, *forgotten sooner* than the superficially remembered parts, as Eder (cf., Eder 2023: 245) also observed. As a spontaneous solution of the remembering task, this meaning support does not seem to remain incubated, while the flat parts remain problematic and are therefore retained.

Of course, this constructive character of remembering refers to a book that perhaps has been most often named as a pioneering achievement but nonetheless left surprisingly few traces in the experiments of the following generations of researchers, namely *Remembering* by Frederic Bartlett (1932) who conceived of all remembering as (re-) construction processes. In order to do so, he adapted Kant's notion of schema into the psychology of memory, albeit without being able to define it more precisely. It is clear, however, that he did not mean sensorimotor schemas in Piaget's sense, but schematization in the sense of a "loss of detail," which he undoubtedly verified by his subjects' reproductions of stories or pictures from memory.

Against the backdrop of the association theory of memory, which still either implicitly or explicitly dominates psychology today, stating that "thing-presentations" somehow mirror the relations in the real world, Bartlett thereby basically introduced the notion of a prototype, i.e., a detail-reduced mental representation. Introspection during formal tasks, however, shows that everything, which is imagined in more detail than a seed or a seed sequence of a memory episode must be constructively *assembled*. Hence, mental "entities" such as "thing-presentations" allegedly representing external objects simply do not exist.

In any case, from this perspective short-term memory is nothing but a word denoting the limited capacity of the temporary "scaffold" necessary to assemble several schemas. As long-term memory *(in the broad sense)* I thus postulate – against the empirical background that without assembly nothing at all, not even attunements or seeds are registered (Wiener 2015a) – the stock of all sensorimotor schemas. Long-term memory *(in the narrow sense)* then consists of the afore-mentioned pre-structuring of long-term memory in the broad sense by unfinished tasks, i.e., by contradictions on one ontogenetic level or two ontogenetic levels. If their processing is triggered so that they become conscious, they are experienced as "episodes" or "scenes" functionally representing an unfinished task (Zeigarnik 1927, Lagache 1953, Ietswaart 1995). Additionally, in order to do justice to results of introspection, a larger number of "facts" have to be postulated to form an intermediate layer between schemas and tasks and sharing prop-erties of both. I will try to account for these facts in the next section.

Between 2015 and 2020, I tried to write down *all* my memory epi-sodes satisfying the four criteria mentioned above (hitherto unpub-lished). This attempt forced me to conclude that all of them result from incubated tasks or contradictions in the heterarchy of schemas available. Not only the "lost" affective tone of the episodes but also said automatic change of aspect, which is common to all of them, forced me to this conclusion. Although hitherto unrecorded episodes come to mind ever more rarely, and almost exclusively when traveling to places which I have already visited in the past and which thus scaf-fold memory from the outside, their total number is clearly converg-ing and will definitely remain below 1,000. Furthermore, there are indications that this number does not increase with age (Giambra 1977). That episodes are geographically locatable and are often triggered while traveling to known places obviously relates them to spatial orientation, from which thought, anthropologically speaking, ultimately derives (Neisser 1988: 368ff.). To underscore this conjecture, here is a fourth example:

> *Our vacation apartment was in one of the new buildings designed for more than one family shooting out of the ground everywhere on the coast of Croatia, presumably financed by money earned abroad. Vaguely, I intuit green paint (of the facade probably), and immediately I remember how I dipped one of the landlords' cats by its rear end into a bucket of water polluted by green paint residues, whereupon my brother snitched on me to our parents, and I, although older, got too afraid to confess and so I promptly claimed my brother was the culprit.*

All biographical stories, apart from these maximally 1,000 episodes, are constructions based on my broader orientation in space and time. Therefore, they have to be classified as *abstract*, however "concrete" they appear in terms of their content. They are fiction, and the way they are constructed and narrated is subject to cultural conventions. This seems hardly surprising as their assembly fulfills a task of a different kind. While memory episodes reproduce a contradictory situation without having to impress someone, the biographical story aims at a punch line having a social effect. In contrast to the often boring authentic episode, whose punch line is but a subjective contradiction, the story must be of more *general interest*. In contrast, my memory episodes, as in the following example, are anecdotes that everyone knows in this or a similar way, because their motives are normal, that is, all too human:

> *On entering our Saab in summer it already stank of vomit due to the plastic covers of the seats. More than mine, my brother's stomach instantly reacted – and immediately I remember not only the beige color of the plastic covers shining bright in the glaring sun but also the brooding fug as we went on a trip to southern Styria, on which my brother miraculously discovered a coin while vomiting next to the parked car.*

If I intended to exert a social effect, I would of course be able to *conclude* on the basis of my knowledge that in this year in that place I probably met those people with whom I did this or that simply because I am able to *establish such connections* during an act of assembly. I am inclined to call this potential story repertoire, following Freud, the "ego" because, unlike my authentic episodes, these fictional stories *do not* generate any uneasy contradiction. They just "fit me" – at least in the particular moment. To put it into psychoanalytic terms, they are "ego-syntonic" (Laplanche and Pontalis 1973: 151f.). As such, they only slowly change in accordance with my life circumstances, with changing friends and loves – but also in the course of the psychoanalysis I have been undergoing since 2018.

Let us leave fiction and return to psychological reality. It seems clear that during early childhood all incubated tasks result from *motivational contradictions*. Biological motives contradict socially learned motives and vice versa. The "drive derivatives," which according to Freud emanate from the "primary process," replace the real drive object by "fantasies" (in the psychological, not the romantic sense). Those raw fantasies of wish fulfillment must be assimilated consistently at an epigenetically subsequent, more comprehensive and abstract, insightful level in order to be integrated into long-term memory (in the broad sense). In other words, what you "forget" *as an episode*, sediments to "semantic memory" (Linton 1982: 79), which in turn generates all more refined *fictional* fantasy episodes as the basis of the "ego" (here, "fantasy" in a romantic sense).

What does contradiction mean in the psychological context? In contrast to logic, nature knows no "contradiction" but only processes. Thus, from a psychological perspective every contradiction has to be understood as a failure of accommodation to said structures of the "ego." True memory episodes thus become "ego-syntonic" only over time, because their original experiences have always been "ego-dystonic." That is precisely why they interfere with the sensorimotor flow.

A variant of contradiction is the "negation," which in psychology also has to be understood differently than in logic. In order to negate or deny something, you have to imagine it first, even if only sketchily as a prototype. Clinical psychoanalysis uses this fact by taking just what the patient denounces as "uninteresting" or "inexistent" as a basis for its motivational analyses (Freud 1961). Thereby, it succeeds in bringing forward "ego-dystonic" and, hence, problematic contradictions of the analysand.

In the language of psychoanalysis, contradictions and negations stem from "conflicts." Even in higher mammals, such conflicts arise already during infancy, if two "instincts", that is, two sensorimotor schemas directed at two different objects, become active at the same time. Yet, as the only more urgent one results in behavior, the conflict is resolved *in action*, albeit sometimes after a shorter "behavioral dithering" period. So I was once lucky to test a black sheepdog bred for "group cohesion," who was freewheeling across the fields together with me and his master. As our path arrived at a T-junction we, the two humans, took the opposite path, respectively. Instantly, the dog started to jerk its head alternately to the left and to the right. After a minute or two of such dithering, it finally ran after its master to whom it was more attached.

An inner conflict in the proper psychological sense results from the confrontation of "the pleasure and the reality principles" (Freud 1958). This confrontation requires some epigenetic development well beyond a dog's reach. Internalized and habituated knowledge about the negative consequences of impulsive action inhibits purely stimulus-controlled behavior, because a drive is nothing but a sensorimotor schema primed so as to be satisfied. In psychoanalytical terms, the "ego" (including its "super-ego" as its "social" part habituated in the respective milieu; Freud 1953) inhibits the "id." By this inhibition, instincts are, of course, delayed or transformed to "drive derivatives," which in the simplest case appear as said fantasized drive-objects, produced by schemas of type 1 (Hartmann 1947: 373). In other words, each drive inhibited by more culturally specific structures may also become an unfinished task. As quasi-needs, they then episodically resurface, even if clothed in different fantasies according to the current orientation.

So it is those aspects of a situation that incubate as tasks (thereby becoming pre-conscious), which the current "ego" is unable to assimilate completely. Accordingly, all my memory episodes have one thing in common. In the course of the sequence, the initial aspect of the remembered event changes, revealing that at a more abstract, i.e., a socially more acceptable level, both aspects are evaluated antithetically. In introspection these two aspects express themselves as different attunements. My repertoire of episodes suggests that by this incubation the original affect of the episode is lost. When recollecting experiences of brutality, such as in the peacock episode, I do *not* relive any possible fear but the contradiction that a person, which I firmly deemed as a guardian, suddenly reveals her violence. In the vomiting episode, I don't relive any disgust, but rather the contrast between my brother vomiting and, because of that, happily finding a coin.

In the course of epigenesis, social orientation progressively diversifies. Nevertheless, tasks and contradictions of prior developmental "structural levels" obviously remain and intrude into consciousness as "regressive" fantasies. An important evidence for incubated tasks as the core of long-term memory (in the narrow sense) is the salient but, to my knowledge, never mentioned fact, that – in contrast to external objects or productive thinking – you *never get bored* with your own fantasies. They seem to form the scaffold of your "interests," even if most of them result from passively imposed contradictions.

This topic also extends to observations during Zen meditation, which is, to put it bluntly, designed to learn *not to* expand seeds and to dishabituate the beginning of assembly processes. In short, meditation serves to unlearn the habitual attitude of solving problems by thinking. The sequences of seeds observed in meditation follow each other according to tasks and not according to similarity or temporal proximity. Meditating in the morning usually results in seed cascades beginning with concrete tasks of the coming day, but even if one again succeeds in avoiding further assembly, they easily trigger interpersonal or more professionally or psychologically specific tasks, and so on, until one manages to refocus on breathing. So "association chains" seem rather to be "problem chains" that cascade up and down the task heterarchy.

Seen from this angle, "depth psychology" of all things deals with the *surface* of mental events, namely with the recurring motives for restoring balance with the environment. We just look at mental events with the wrong attitude because the incubated tasks and contradictions have become "ego-syntonic," and we thus perceive them as "parts of us," although they are mostly fantasies. After all, they are the only truly individual aspect of us and thus make up our "personality." It is precisely for this reason that it is only when we collide with our environment that we realize our "neuroses," the internal economy of which only "functions" as long as it does not conflict with the economy of our outer milieu.

Since "ego" development through habituation to and insight learning from experiences with "objects" in the social milieu does not start before toddler age (Piaget 1973), I believe one does not remember any authentic episodes before this time. Any episodes from an earlier age seem to have been suggested by parents, photos, etc. The "ego" just is not an entity and does not appear in introspection as a concrete thing, but only as a "feeling of authenticity," which after all warrants the coherence of all experience. The "ego" is not only transparent but also "embodied," because contradictions are concrete action tendencies opposing each other.

Let's briefly turn from structural considerations to the direct *experience* of fantasy. *What* exactly is it, that introspection allows us to register as a fantasy emanating from an incubated task? I found that it is always some seemingly quasi-pictorial aspects of the task object. They appear yet unordered, that is, in formal geometrical tasks, for instance, as undifferentiated edges or vertices, or, in everyday life, say the impression of holding the hand of the loved one who rejects us. In Wiener's terms, fantasies are "clutter" of yet to be ordered seeds, which always appear in the initial phase of assembly. So even the seemingly uncontrolled daydream is not arbitrary but the effect of an interest (McMillan et al. 2013).

In general, there is no such sharp distinction between the flight of ideas and orderly thinking as psychology suggests, perhaps because of the ideal that every modern human being should always be productive. As with dreams, psychology remains undecided about what function fantasies serve, but their existence alone must be taken as an indication that they are not "purposeless." According to the view presented here, fantasies are first steps of task solutions. Overall, there seems to be no functional difference between memories (of a task in the broad sense) and "free" fantasies. The latter just follow from contradictions between schemas close to the "instinctual object" and reality, and the former can reach up to the level of abstract contradictions of a theoretical kind.

Schemas with residues from everyday tasks: the "facts"

Father's light gray socks in front of me on the floor. Immediately I know: they stink penetratingly.

The snapshot described here pertains to a memory from my childhood, which meets only three of the four criteria I postulated above to define genuine, i.e., non-confabulated episodes. What is missing is its location in space and time, which I can only infer. Nevertheless, both its spontaneously intrusive character and the change of attunement as well as the fixed sequentiality are present. That is why the experience cannot be understood as the activity of a "pure" schema in long-term memory. In other words, because of its biographic connection it isn't a pure intuition. Yet, because its date is too imprecise – I only know that I saw these socks some time during childhood – it cannot be considered a memory episode proper, and thus it's not a part of long-term memory in the narrow, or Zeigarnik's, sense postulated above. All action readinesses necessary for handling this object (it is even unclear whether I remember one or two socks!) are contained in this experience, but yet two, namely the light gray color as well as the smell, are "superfluous." And yet they are not integrated into a truly biographic episode.

To speak with Wiener, facts cannot be assembled into the biographical chronology. In contrast to episodes, they lack the minimal attached context that ultimately makes episodes seem authentic (Wiener and Schwarz, in this volume). This is particularly evident when the context receives support from the *external* situation serving as a stimulus scaffold. Just lately, for instance, I immediately recognized a knitted toy parrot from my childhood when I saw it again in my parents' house. Yet, I would certainly never have *actively* remembered it again, since I am unable to associate any concrete situation with it. To me, the knitted toy parrot is merely an isolated fact.

Further examples of such facts would be city streets, the quasi-image of which I recognize as being from a specific perspective specified by only one additional feature. This feature could be that I know which direction the one-way traffic moves (towards or away from my vantage point) or in which sequence the traffic lights along my sight axis turn red. Also, well-known everyday objects, of which I can give one or two properties like their color or their approximate geometry, fall into this category, which I, following Neisser (1988), prefer to call *facts* instead of "mnemes" as in most literature. The observation that even streetscapes may look completely different depending on the direction in which one walks would suggest the term "sight," but this, again, seems too narrow because of its visual connotation, since many facts are obviously given phonetically or olfactorily.

Most of the pragmatic stories we essentially need to communicate consist of the assembly and, thereby, bundling of such facts. My inner layout of the habitual supermarket near my apartment, for instance, consists of such facts except for only two quite recent authentic episodes representing two social situations I did not fully grasp in terms of my motives. Chiefly, these facts imply the locations of products within the vast supermarket but there are also two slants in the gray tile floor, on which my shopping cart regularly rolls away.

All of this suggests that facts, as stemming from everyday tasks, are of a pragmatic origin and function.

As indicated, introspection shows that these facts contain at least one to a few individualizing features, which are "superfluous" in the sense that they are not necessary for the mere handling of the object remembered and thus add to mere schemas. As such, additional qualities cannot by analyzed further, they amount to "qualia," which make them more apt as nuclei of assemblies as unparameterized schemas, as can be seen in the supermarket example. Hence the term "fact" onto which "clings" a part of its running environment but which is, in contrast to a genuine episode, less specific and, thus, less meaningful. It seems clear that the number of such facts greatly exceeds that maximum of 1,000 memory episodes. Furthermore, I reckon that such a trade-off fits better to the necessary plasticity of memory than an orientation operating on incubated tasks and schemas alone, because ultimately memory too must serve behavior control. So the "layer" of facts would be situated "between" long-term memory in the broader sense and long-term memory in the narrow sense for functional-economic reasons.

From a theoretical perspective, facts could be conceived of as "parameterized schemas." I believe that the supermarket example quite clearly shows that here, too, it is tasks which originally led to the parameterization, because I only remember objects I was intentionally looking for. But to call facts incubated tasks would go too far, even if, just like those, they also seem to be remnants of assembly processes and thus cannot be retained without attention. One might speculate whether the transition from episode to fact is gradual, that is, whether the fact too presupposes a minimal or inchoate assembly. I suspect that only the pragmatic and "meaningless" character of facts and the generality of everyday tasks, which they stem from, prevent a more specific embedding into the web of incubated and, above all, biographically interrelated tasks. Shopping in the supermarket, for example, is normally too ordinary or, psychoanalytically speaking, not "deep" enough to leave any traces. Nonetheless, the supermarket is quite often part of a task environment. Therefore, Neisser (1978: 98) compared schemas to genotypes, which grow into phenotypes depending on the current requirements, which are precisely determined by the actual running environment and external situation. Accordingly, facts seem like fixed phenotypes of genotypic schemas.

Remembering as a task with internal and external scaffolding: repression

After more than three years of psychoanalytic sessions up to several times per week, I must ascertain that to this day that none of the surfacing episodes were new to me, even though some of them I had not remembered for many years. So I am, at least so far, unable to corroborate the psychoanalytic concepts of "screen memory" or the "repression" of "traumas."

In the course of the three marked breaks in my biography, of which the last one forced me to reluctantly seek therapy, I noticed, apart from psychological symptoms, also a sociological one. In the months and years after those breaks, the boldly forced loss of orientation seemed to be connected with an affect storm and the problematization of hitherto unproblematic structures causing the obsessive remembering of tasks having again become unfinished because the newly changing "ego" cannot assimilate them. But additionally, the main general observation was that my respective circle of friends got spontaneously rearranged. Some of them turned away, and I was very prone to find new ones, some of whom even had a socio-structurally similar position or fulfilled a psychological similarly function as their former equivalent (such as protection, inspiration, or identification). Apart from this social reorientation, one has the urge to change flats, buy new clothes, get a new haircut, etc. So obviously a drift into a new, and sociologically measurable, "attitude milieu" takes its course.

This also yields a drift of said "ego" into a new habitual memory "affordance regime," because some episodes tend to be nudged less or more often than before. Sexuality, which also manifests itself by the urge to form new bonds including the respective fantasies, may be the trigger and the catalyst of such phases, but certainly not their cause. The latter rather seems to be the fact that one is forced to re-orient oneself in terms of higher-level goals, which shows at first merely as an uneasy feeling in the present situation. Alfred Adler (1931) subsumed these goals under the heading of "meaning of life."

But *how* are milieu and remembering related? It remains largely unclear how and which stimuli nudge incubated tasks so that we register them as quasi-images. Unfortunately, we seldom manage to identify how a certain thought has been triggered by a specific outer event, although we often know *that* the trigger came from outside (cf. Fisher 1957). If we include somatosensory signals as belonging to the external world, which has been sensibly argued, we could even postulate that no memory, indeed *no thought at all* is ever triggered "from within," i.e. from a "mental need."

What has experimental cognitive science contributed to the issue of the interaction between environment and memory? Since the 1970s, the possibility of measuring eye muscle responses in experiments on perception to control stimulus constellations on computer screens by feedback has not only brought insights into so-called "saccadic suppression" (Bridgeman et al. 1975), i.e., the non-uptake of visual stimuli during saccades, or the "change blindness" to objective stimuli (Simons and Levin 1997). Based on these and other experiments, O'Regan (1992) managed to argue convincingly that – for reasons of parsimony – objects of the external world do not need to be "stored" in memory because they can mostly be "called" by attending toward them any time when needed. So the environment largely serves the sensorimotor system as an "external memory." Perception does not take in information, but rather probes the external world on the basis of the current schema heterarchy, which is in turn recalibrated in order to warrant the flow of action.

The recognition of an object is thus supported by the constellation of the external world, which by its *objective structure* helps to create attunements, which can also be confirmed by introspection. The persuasiveness of these attunements can even lead to so-called *déjà vu* experiences.

This exterior *scaffolding* of perception and memory, however, does not only consist of inanimate things. "Reality" does not only pertain to the environment in the bio-ecological sense, but importantly also to the *proximal milieu* of people with similar interests, whose behavior I must tune my orientation to.

Introspection markedly shows that our friends scaffold our thoughts and our remembering, if only because of similarities in our and their interests. Especially for institutionally independent and, therefore, economically always alert people, repression clearly does not appear as the result of an "inner censor" operating in a "dynamic unconscious" in a Freudian sense but rather positively as adaptation to the current *proximal milieu*.

So crucial parts of the environment comprise – ever since humans exist, but clearly increasingly so in technological societies marked by a growing division of labor – of conspecifics with similar interests. In anthropology, their number has not coincidentally been estimated at a maximum of 150 for each person. This constraint seems to have co-evolved with the capacity of the brain to distinguish individuals as it roughly corresponds to the size of a Stone Age kin (Dunbar 1993, cf. Lindenfors et al. 2021). Moreover, the fragmentation of the population into milieus defined by the division of labor, by attitudes, and, thus, by habits and "tastes" not only supports what I remember, but even more what I do *not* remember. Drift into new circles of friends and acquaintances, but also travel, most of all make me "forget" tasks. So forgetting is not merely a function of the brain, but also a function of the parsimony of behavioral embedding. Strictly speaking, except when physiological reasons pertain, there is no forgetting, but merely non-remembering. In this regard, Ramstead et al. (2016) spoke of "regimes of attention" that may have escaped Freud because in his lifetime social structure was less sharply contoured than it is today.

According to my observations, adaptation to the proximal milieu elegantly explains what is called "repression" in psychoanalysis, where it is conceived of as a defense mechanism of the "dynamic unconscious." Despite repeated attempts of mediation (for instance, by the aforementioned Rapaport and Erdelyi, but also by Jahoda 1977) this term has never been accepted in cognitive psychology, although it has proved useful and effective in therapeutic practice for decades. Yet, a "dynamic unconscious" that actively shields consciousness from unpleasant "thing-presentations" by acting as an internal censor is both physiologically and psychologically implausible (O'Brien and Jureidini 2002, Hutto and Peters 2018). So it has been precisely this putatively active role of the unconscious in remembering and repressing that has received a particularly hostile reception from the cognitive sciences, as one can gather from the numerous commentaries on Erdelyi (2006). The main reason for this is, or so I believe, that it inevitably leads to the infinite regress of a homunculus in the brain controlling the mind.

It can hardly be denied that systematic dishabituation of specific external triggers for orientation serves the economy of cognitive resources. The "internal" economy of mind arguably calibrates itself according to the co-evolved capacity of the brain, which cannot be increased without risk as it is done in the computer industry. However, *what* is "repressed," that is, which incubated tasks and facts are tendentially "forgotten" in the aforementioned sense primarily depends on the *external* economy of prestige in the proximal milieu. Bourdieu (1984), for example, has conceived of this economy as being divided into accounts for cultural, financial, and social capital, which can roughly be estimated in payment equivalents and partly reciprocally exchanged.

To give an example, here is an anecdote illustrating the interaction between internal and external economy. At a work meeting a few years ago, I, as a freelance author, had to ask for the signature of a university dignitary of roughly the same age for a project proposal. During the conversation, the details and background of which are irrelevant here, I noticed again and again the facially expressed astonishment by which he reacted to my half-willful provocations as far as allusions to institution, taste, and sexuality are concerned (the causes of which I will not pursue here). Now the psychoanalyst could justifiably interpret that the dignitary actively "repressed" aspects of his life as regards institution, taste, and sexuality. On the other hand, it occurred to me later, the dignitary too would have to be able to judge from *his* position and *his* proximal milieu that *I am repressing* certain disadvantages of *my* profession largely apart from institutions, such as losses in terms of income, prestige, and authority. So while he behaves more rigidly, i.e., in a more "compulsive manner" within the framework of my milieu, I do the same from his point of view within the framework of his milieu. We simply live in two different proximal milieus, each of which tends to mirror "our" values and egos (Freyd 2006), although our distal milieu, the "educated class," remains the same and although there is even some overlap of friends. Habituation to the milieu, and the "repression" it enacts, seems to be simply necessary for psycho-economic reasons (Horney 1945).

To sum up, passive and ecological repression in the sense described serves to dishabituate those incubated tasks that are useless to the current heterarchy of motives. Of course, these tasks are not completely "forgotten," since they can be triggered again by more unlikely external situations. But certainly the probability for them being triggered decreases. In turn, the proximal milieu makes other situations and episode retrievals more likely. Quite consistent with psychoanalysis, which focuses on contradictions between drive derivatives and social world, repression results from drifting, often for years, into a milieu that no longer supports the unpleasant contradictions from the past. In this milieu, potential "neurosis," which is diagnostically best identifiable by an impoverishment of the behavioral repertoire, can be expressed and acted out unnoticed, i.e., "ego-syntonically." By the definition postulated here, however, it would then no longer count as neurotic because it serves an economic function.

I believe it is likely that this concept of passive repression will not be readily acceptable to traditional psychoanalysts. As a consequence, "neuroses" would not necessarily have to be caused by trauma, but may also result from becoming progressively unable to match needs and quasi-needs within one's proximal milieu. So therapy may, but does not have to "dig up" repressed motives. As a consequence, psychoanalysis would be no depth psychology but rather a kind of micro-sociology because every "neurosis" would, as soon as it becomes noticeable, always be an "adjustment disorder" (Fonagy 1999).

To me, the following seems indisputable: On the basis of the law of parsimony, it is simply more economical to change or distort reality than to repress it internally (Rofé 2008). Accordingly, obsessive fantasies also occur only during those crises in which the proximal milieu becomes "outdated" for somatic or psycho-economic reasons or is suddenly partly eliminated by illness, death, or separation. In mourning, for example, the object that is now missing or cannot be accommodated quickly enough as missing gets "fantasized." Then even perception often becomes temporarily "delusional" (Freud 1957).

The energetic perspective: affect and motivation

Whenever purposeful action is inhibited from within or without, the congestion of the energy already allocated to the action must find a somatic outlet. The nervous system has the property of hysteresis and thus cannot abruptly stop processes already operating.

It is a truism that emotions are registered only when there is an urge to act, but the goal of action is uncertain. Early in childhood, emotions result from the inhibition of instinctive, and later of actions directed at intuited goals. Since those aspects of thinking that we are able to register in introspection also originate from inhibited actions, we probably have to understand the series beginning with purely somatically dominated feelings ("basic emotions") up to the somatically miniscule seeds registered during assembly as a kind of affect continuum.

Contrariwise, the dichotomy of positive and negative emotions commonly postulated in psychology seems arbitrary and too closely related either to the behavioral concept of "flight-or-fight" or to value-guided criteria. In Buddhist psychology, on the contrary, *each and every* affect is neutrally considered a disturbance of equilibrium or equanimity apart from its consensual valence (Jullien 2004). According to this notion, one should thus neither wallow in emotions "for their own sake," nor should one repress them, but rather just let them pass. Frantic thought is thus conceived of as "suffering" just like frantic acting (Kalupahana 1987). Interestingly, Freud (1955) seems to have been guided by a similar idea of homeostasis.

Within the framework of the ecological model sketched above, this definition of affect as focused energy allocation would imply the following: Since all motor impulses becoming conscious originate in a task, and conflicts between instinctual object and reality are also incubated as tasks, all affects could be understood as yes/no control predicates for balancing the trade-off between the inner and outer milieus. In this sense, they are "generic notions" (Raab 2015, Wiener and Schwarz 2023).

The teleological orientation of "motivation theories" such as this has often been criticized as unscientific. To me, too, teleology seems to be rather a necessary premise in which the model has to be embedded in order to contradict neither biological nor psychological theories. On closer examination, Freud's (1955) derivation of motivation from a basic conflict between the "life instinct" and the "death instinct," the interplay of which enables the brain to adapt to reality, seems indeed highly questionable. To me, the most parsimonious and thermodynamically coherent pre-sociological "goal" seems to require the postulate of a "structural drive" enabling the individual to orient in an increasingly differentiated way – either by reducing complexity externally (by action and object manipulation) or by longer-term internal adaptation (structural development by habituation and thought). I speculate that this structural drive is caused by or is a corollary of the production of negentropy in the biosphere (Raab 2006). This view attributes bio-psychological teleology to thermodynamics.

Sticking to this energetic view, "seeds" in the sense of Wiener would psychoanalytically amount to micro-affects (Rapaport 1950). Schemas get energetically "cathexed" and, therefore, consciously registered. Assembly reduces the affective energies ruling the "primary process," by which they produce phantasies, to "small cathexes," which can then be "shifted," i.e., offered as input to a running environment. The necessary "counter-cathexis" breaking sensorimotor flow emanates precisely from the incubated tasks leading to assembly. Moreover, by controlling schemas it is also the assembly process that generates the fiction of free will, which in fact results from the energetically focused coordination of schemas screening off most stimuli.

From this perspective, i.e., of assembly focusing energy, the terms of psychoanalysis would have to be, as it were, reversed. It would be precisely *not* the energies on the instinctual level (of the "primary process") that are "free." In the primary process, several schemas simultaneously strive for their "instinctual objects" uninhibited by cultural influences. I think that the primary process, expressing itself most freely in dreams, would have to be called unfree, so that the question arises as to whether or not one should file instinct-derived fantasies under thought at all, as Suler (1980) did. During thinking proper, which Freud called "secondary process," affects seem to flow more "freely," since attention is, after all, less obsessively bound to an object or one of its features. It's only the task heterarchy that makes our orientation as flexible as it is.

In line with Piaget (1950), who also championed a similar structural view, Freud postulated the function of "fantasies" in the infant as substitutes for the real object to be acted upon. Fantasy replaces the instinctual object with a proxy object, a "mental image," thereby partially satisfying the instinct. Wiener conceived of this process more elegantly. For him, the mental image is the quasi-motor branch of a schema, whose actualization as a procedure of type 1 puts us in a sufficiently similar attunement as if the object were present as the target of action. Affectively, this process consumes part of the energy, which would otherwise be afforded by the action, and is experienced figuratively as a "instinctual derivative" (A. Freud 1993).

In art, these primary fantasies can be utilized. Reinforced by his or her proximal milieu of the "art scene," the artist gradually gets used to playfully allowing even unpleasant, embarrassing, or brutal fantasies. In this milieu, libidinal ideas are allowed as "ego-syntonic," often being expressed "in play." It is the secondary process, however, including artistically formal and milieu-strategic considerations, which further shapes these ideas into a work of art (Hartmann 1951). Accordingly, taboos of others are the artists' quarry, the others' demons their material.

So the interplay between "regressive" individual fantasies and intellectual control, embedding them into an historically informed framework comprehensible at least within the proximal milieu, forms the core of both artistic and scientific creativity (Suler 1980). Yet, while sensorimotor intuitions in art get "trimmed and socially tamed" by being subjugated to historical convention in subsequent processing and educated secondary processes, in science they prove to be either productive or unproductive in the sense of an objectively solvable task.

Summary

By idealizing long-term memory as sensorimotor heterarchy, memory episodes can be conceived of as the outcome of unfinished tasks and contradictions between different onto- and epigenetic structural levels within this heterarchy as well as with reference to the environment. These task situations are "frozen," i.e., incubated, because of the feature of hysteresis of the nervous system, which is not able to spontaneously adapt but must habituate by cascading accommodation episodes. Short-term memory is a name for these episodic attempts, triggered by the interplay of incubated tasks and stimuli, to accommodate schemas, which may be "pure" or specified to represent "facts" bundling two or three seeds, into more comprehensive structures (internal models). Fantasies are "broadcasts" intermittently issued by these tasks, with the help of which the latter can be solved not by action, but by such structural adaptation.

For reasons of parsimony, however, in dynamic environments still a good part of this adaptation takes place *in action* through social drift, whereby repression in the sense of Freud can be seen as adaptation to a specific and specifiable proximal milieu. The motive underlying this entire orienting behavior does not originate from sexual or death instincts, but ultimately follows a structural trend controlled by thermodynamics (towards "negentropy"). Depending on genetic predisposition as well as reinforcement within the milieu, this trend expresses itself, according to temporary circumstances and individual, as either a tendency towards manipulation of the environment or towards internal structural adaptation. Individual orientation and, thus, homeostasis develop either through complexity reduction of the outer world by action or complexity increase of the inner world of orientation by thought.

References

Adler, Alfred, 1931. The Meaning of Life. *The Lancet*, 217, 225–228.
Bartlett, Frederic C., 1932. *Remembering: A Study in Experimental and Social Psychology*. Cambridge 1967.
Bourdieu, Pierre, 1984. *Distinction*. Trans. Richard Nice. Cambridge, MA.
Bower, Gordon H., 2000. A Brief History of Memory Research. In: Tulving, Endel, and Fergus I.M. Craik (eds.), *The Oxford Handbook of Memory*. Oxford, 3–32.
Bridgeman, Bruce, Derek Hendry, and Lawrence Stark, 1975. Failure to Detect Displacement of the Visual World during Saccadic Eye Movements. *Vision Research*, 15/6, 719–722.
Devereux, Georges 1967. *Anxiety and Method in the Behavioral Sciences*. Paris, The Hague.
Dunbar, Robin I.M., 1993. Coevolution of Neocortical Size, Group Size and Language in Humans. *Behavioral and Brain Sciences*, 16, 681–735.
Eder, Thomas, 2023. Reciting "Timidity": Remarks on the Memorization of Speech Events Using the Example of an Ode by Friedrich Hölderlin. In this volume, 237–271.
Eder, Thomas, and Thomas Raab (eds.), 2015. *Selbstbeobachtung: Oswald Wieners Denkpsychologie*. Berlin.
Erdelyi, Matthew H., 1985. *Psychoanalysis: Freud's Cognitive Psychology*. New York.
Erdelyi, Matthew H., 2006. The Unified Theory of Repression. *Behavioral and Brain Sciences*, 29/5, 499–551.

Erdelyi, Matthew H., Shira Finkelstein, Nadeanne Herrell, Bruce Miller, and Jane Thomas, 1976. Coding Modality vs. Input Modality in Hypermnesia. *Cognition*, 4, 311–319.

Fisher, Charles, 1957. A Study of the Preliminary Stages of the Construction of Dreams and Images. *Journal of the American Psychoanalytic Association*, 5, 5–60.

Fonagy, Peter, 1999. Memory and Therapeutic Action. *International Journal of Psycho-Analysis*, 80/2, 215–223.

Freud, Anna, 1993 [1937]. *The Ego and the Mechanics of Defence*. London.

Freud, Sigmund, 1953 [1900]. *The Interpretation of Dreams*. In: Strachey, James (ed.), *The Standard Edition of the Complete Psychological Works of Sigmund Freud*, Vols. 4 and 5. London.

Freud, Sigmund, 1955 [1920]. Beyond the Pleasure Principle. In: Strachey, James (ed.), *The Standard Edition of the Complete Psychological Works of Sigmund Freud*, Vol. 18, London, 7–64.

Freud, Sigmund, 1957 [1917]. Mourning and Melancholia. In: Strachey, James (ed.), *The Standard Edition of the Complete Psychological Works of Sigmund Freud*, Vol. 14, London, 243–258.

Freud, Sigmund, 1958 [1911]. Formulations on the Two Principles of Mental Functioning. In: Strachey, James (ed.), *The Standard Edition of the Complete Psychological Works of Sigmund Freud*, Vol. 12. London, 214–226.

Freud, Sigmund, 1961 [1925]. Negation. In: Strachey, James (ed.), *The Standard Edition of the Complete Psychological Works of Sigmund Freud*, Vol. 19, London, 233–239.

Freyd, Jennifer J., 2006. The Social Psychology of Cognitive Repression. *Behavioral and Brain Sciences*, 29/5, 518–519.

Giambra, Leonard M., 1977. Daydreaming about the Past: The Time Setting of Spontaneous Thought Intrusions. *Gerontologist*, 17/1, 35–38.

Halbwachs, Maurice, 1925. *On Collective Memory*. Trans. Lewis A. Coser. Chicago 1992.

Hartmann, Heinz, 1951. Ego Psychology and the Problem of Adaptation. In: Rapaport, David (ed.), *Organization and Pathology of Thought*. New York, 362–396.

Hartmann, Heinz, 1948. Comments on the Psychoanalytic Theory of Instinctual Drives. *Psychoanalytic Quarterly*, 17/3, 368–388.

Horney, Karen, 1945. *Our Inner Conflicts*. New York.

Hutto, Daniel D., and Anco Peters, 2018. The Roots of Remembering: Radically Enactive Recollecting. In: Michaelian, Kourken (ed.), *New Directions in the Philosophy of Memory*. Oxford, New York, 97–118.

Ietswaart, Willem I., 1995. Die unbewußte Phantasie in der Übertragung. *Psyche*, 49, 141–158.

Jahoda, Marie, 1977. *Freud and the Dilemmas of Psychology*. London.

Jullien, François, 2004. *In Praise of Blandness*. New York.

Kalupahana, David J., 1987. *The Principles of Buddhist Psychology*. Albany.

Klingler, Eric, 2008. Daydreaming and Fantasizing: Thought Flow and Motivation. In: Markman, Keith D., William M.P. Klein, and Julie A. Suhr (eds.), *Handbook of Imagination and Mental Simulation*. London, 225–239.

Kris, Ernst, 1952. On Preconscious Mental Processes. In: id., *Psychoanalytic Explorations in Art*. New York, 303–318.

Lagache, Daniel, 1953. Some Aspects of Transference. *International Journal of Psychoanalysis*, 34, 1–10.

Laplanche, Jean, and Jean-Bertrand Pontalis, 1973 [1967]. *The Language of Psycho-Analysis*. Trans. Donald Nicholson-Smith. London.

Lewin, Kurt, 1951 [1926]. Intention, Will and Need. In: Rapaport, David (ed.), *Organization and Pathology of Thought*. New York, 95–153.

Lindenfors, Patric, Andreas Wartel, and Johan Lind, 2021. Dunbar's number' Deconstructed. *Biology Letters*, 17, 0210158.

Linton, Marigold, 1982. Transformations of Memory in Everyday Life. In: Neisser, Ulric (ed.), *Memory Observed*. New York, 77–91.

McMillan, Rebecca L., Scott Barry Kaufman, and Jerome L. Singer, 2013. Ode to Positive Constructive Daydreaming. *Frontiers in Psychology*, 4, Article 626.

Neisser, Ulric, 1978. Perceiving, Anticipating, and Imagining. *Minnesota Studies in the Philosophy of Science*, 9, 89–105.

Neisser, Ulric, 1988. What is Ordinary Memory the Memory of? In: id., and Eugene Winograd (eds.), *Remembering Reconsidered*. Cambridge, 356–373.

Neisser, Ulric, 1996. Remembering as Doing. *Behavioral and Brain Sciences*, 19/2, 204–205.

O'Brien, Gerard, and Jon Jureidini, 2002. Dispensing with the Dynamic Unconscious. *Philosophy, Psychiatry, and Psychology*, 9/2, 141–153.

O'Regan, J. Kevin, 1992. Solving the "Real" Mysteries of Visual Perception: The World as an Outside Memory. *Canadian Journal of Psychology*, 46/3, 461–488.

Piaget, Jean, 1950 [1947]. *Psychology of Intelligence*. London.

Piaget, Jean, 1973. The Affective Unconscious and the Cognitive Unconscious. *Journal of the American Psychoanalytic Association*, 21/2, 249–261.

Raab, Thomas, 2006. *Nachbrenner: Zur Evolution und Funktion des Spektakels*. Frankfurt.

Raab, Thomas, 2012. Selbstbeobachtung Mnemotechnik. Unpublished manuscript, 5 pages.

Raab, Thomas, 2015. Zur Affekttheorie. In: Eder, Thomas, and Thomas Raab (eds.), *Selbstbeobachtung: Oswald Wieners Denkpsychologie*. Berlin, 143–161.

Ramstead, Maxwell J.D., Samuel P.L. Veissière, and Laurence J. Kirmayer, 2016. Cultural Affordances: Scaffolding Local Worlds Through Shared Intentionality and Regimes of Attention. *Frontiers in Psychology*, 7, Article 1090, 1–21.

Rapaport, David, 1950. On the Psychoanalytic Theory of Thinking. *International Journal of Psychoanalysis*, 31, 161–170.

Rapaport, David, 1971. *Emotions and Memory*. New York.

Rofé, Yacov, 2008. Does Repression Exist? Memory, Pathogenic, Unconscious and Clinical Evidence. *Review of General Psychology*, 12/1, 63–85.

Salaman, Esther, 1970. *A Collection of Moments: A Study of Involuntary Memories*. Harlow.

Simons, Daniel J., and Daniel T. Levin, 1997. Change Blindness. *Trends in Cognitive Sciences*, 1/7, 261–267.

Stekel, Wilhelm, 1951 [1925]. The Polyphony of Thought. In: Rapaport, David (ed.), *Organization and Pathology of Thought*. New York, London, 311–314.

Suler, John R., 1980. Primary Process Thinking and Creativity. *Psychological Bulletin*, 88/1, 144–165.

Varendonck, Julian, 1921. *The Psychology of Day-dreams*. London.

Wiener, Oswald, 2015a. Glossar: Weiser. In: Eder, Thomas, and Thomas Raab (eds.), *Selbstbeobachtung: Oswald Wieners Denkpsychologie*. Berlin, 59–98.

Wiener, Oswald, 2015b. Glossar: figurativ. In: Eder, Thomas, and Thomas Raab (eds.), *Selbstbeobachtung: Oswald Wieners Denkpsychologie*. Berlin, 99–141.

Wiener, Oswald, and Michael Schwarz, 2023. Pleomorphism in Thought and the Computational Metaphor. In this volume, 101–163.

Zeigarnik, Bluma, 1938 [1927]. On Finished and Unfinished Tasks. In: Ellis, Willis D. (ed.), *A Source Book of Gestalt Psychology*. New York, 300–314.

Editors

Thomas Eder
Thomas Raab
Michael Schwarz

With the financial support of

RD Foundation Vienna Gemeinnützige Privatstiftung

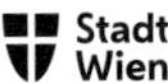

RD Foundation Vienna
Research | Development | Human Rights
Gemeinnützige Privatstiftung

Austrian Federal Ministry for Arts, Culture, Civil Service and Sport

Bundesministerium
Kunst, Kultur,
öffentlicher Dienst und Sport

Cultural Department of the City of Vienna

Stadt
Wien

Acquisitions Editor: David Marold, Birkhäuser Verlag, Vienna, Austria
Content and Production Editor: Bettina R. Algieri, Birkhäuser Verlag, Vienna, Austria
Translation from German into English (including quotations unless stated otherwise):
    Thomas Raab, Vienna, Austria
Proofreading: Sue Pickett, Cologne, Germany
Layout, cover design, and typography: Fuhrer visuelle Gestaltung OG, Vienna, Austria
Printing: Beltz Grafische Betriebe GmbH, Bad Langensalza, Germany
Paper: Salzer EOS blauweiß 90 g/m²
Typeface: Publico Headline, Publico Banner und Px Grotesk

Library of Congress Control Number: 2019947317

Bibliographic information published by the German National Library
The German National Library lists this publication in the Deutsche Nationalbibliografie; detailed
bibliographic data are available on the Internet at http://dnb.dnb.de.

ISBN 978-3-11-065961-0
e-ISBN (PDF) 978-3-11-066289-4
German print 978-3-11-065960-3

© 2023 Walter de Gruyter GmbH, Berlin/Boston

www.degruyter.com

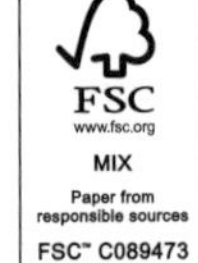